P9-DIG-280

America's

Child Care

Problem

America's
Child Care
Problem

~

THE WAY OUT

Suzanne W. Helburn and Barbara R. Bergmann

palgrave

for St. Martin's Press

First published 2002 by
PALGRAVE™
175 Fifth Avenue, New York, N.Y. 10010.
Companies and representatives throughout the world.

PALGRAVE™ is the new global publishing imprint of St. Martin's Press LLC
Scholarly and Reference Division and Palgrave Publishers Ltd (formerly Mac-
millan Press Ltd).

ISBN 0-312-21149-X hardback

Library of Congress Cataloging-in-Publication Data
can be found at the Library of Congress.

Design by planettheo.com

First Palgrave edition: January, 2002

10 9 8 7 6 5 4 3 2 1

Printed in the United States of America.

Strand M.-02220 3-5-02 #32⁵⁵

CONTENTS

ACKNOWLEDGMENTS

We all build upon the work, advice, and inspiration of others. We have drawn heavily on the experience and findings of the Cost, Quality, and Child Outcomes in Child Care Centers project. In particular, we are indebted to Mary Culkin and John Morris, close associates of Suzanne Helburn's during that project and major contributors to the thinking that has gone into this volume.

On specific topics, we want to thank a number of people who gave us valuable feedback and suggestions: Myra Strober on the economics of the child care industry; Mark Greenberg on child care public policy; Louise Stoney on financing child care; Marcy Whitebook on the child care workforce; Denise Dowell on unionization efforts among child care workers; Yasmina DeVinci, Gail Wilson, and Sandy Skolnick on the resource and referral system; and Harold Gazan and Pauline Koch on state regulation of the child care industry. Joseph McCluskey and Preston Sowell helped with the research and Mary George helped with prose. We contacted countless people at state licensing agencies, resource and referral agencies, child care unions, child care accrediting agencies, and professional associations. We learned from observing many child care centers and from the dedicated directors and staff who shared their knowledge and concerns. Nick Helburn has helped with literature reviews and many critical reviews of chapters.

We are very grateful for the financial support of the Foundation for Child Development and for the ongoing intellectual contributions of the foundation's president, Ruby Takanishi, and the many people with whom she has put us into contact. Gwen Morgan, to whom we dedicate this book, has been a loyal critic and guide and a major inspiration, helping us develop a broader and more realistic view of the issues. We are also grateful to the Rockefeller Foundation for awarding us a residency at the foundation's Bellagio Study and Conference Center in Italy, which provided a month of close collaboration in a beautiful and stimulating setting.

None of the above carry any responsibility for errors or omissions. The views and conclusions are those of the authors. Barbara Bergmann was primarily responsible for chapters 1-3 and chapter 9, and Suzanne Helburn for chapters 4-8. Each had input into all of the chapters.

LIST OF TABLES

To Gwen Morgan, mentor and friend

CHAPTER ONE

The Problem: What's Wrong with Child Care in America?

"I'm a single mom with a one-year-old and a three-year-old and a job with a not-so-hot wage. I went down to the local child care center and was quoted a price of $13,500 per year for the two kids. That would take half my pay and leave me without money for rent. So I looked around for care that's cheaper. I found a lady who already cares for three kids in her home. Really, I have no way of knowing how nice she is to the children when she is alone with them or how many hours the kids will be propped up in front of a TV set or even left to themselves. I also don't know how often her boyfriend comes around while the kids are there and how nice *he* is to them. She has never bothered to get a license. But her price is half the center's—still a huge part of my budget, but just barely manageable. That's what I ended up "choosing."

A friend next door works in the child care center I can't afford. Her wage doesn't make it into the not-so-hot category—it's $8.50 an hour. She says the center has some good workers on the staff, but because of the pay, the center has to fill some of its slots with people pretty much off the street who have no training at all. Turnover is

this is hard on the center's operations and on the kids, who keep
_āg attached to caregivers, only to lose them. She is thinking of
_.g out soon herself."

—Bank loan officer

      ~•   ~•   ~•

Looking back over the twentieth century, historians may well decide that the most important transformation it brought to America was the change in the role of women and the resulting change in the way our society finances and arranges for the care and rearing of young children. Yet as we enter the twenty-first century, we haven't yet faced up to the child care needs created by women's large-scale entry into the labor market.

The American child care system, in which parents, largely unassisted, must buy the care they need in the marketplace, has not worked well. It is in the public's interest that the services children receive be of good quality, but millions of parents are unable to pay what standard-quality services currently cost, much less what they would cost if quality were improved. Parents need assistance in two ways. They need more help in meeting the cost of child care. And they need more help in assuring the safety and quality of the care their children get.

As, in the twentieth century, fertility declined, as women's educational achievement and aspirations grew, as wages and jobs available to women increased, and as single parenthood grew through the rise in divorce and out-of-wedlock births, the two-parent family with one parent at home became less and less common. Now only about a third of preschool children are cared for that way.[1] Mothers' paychecks are an important source of support for millions of families, and, in a growing proportion of cases, are an indispensable source of support. Yet the high cost of child care makes severe inroads on those paychecks, and therefore on the standard of living of families. Child care costs can take away 25 percent or more of the incomes of low-wage families who have to pay for it.[2] And millions of children are not getting the quality of care that provides the safety, nurturing, and help with development that they need.

The kind of care children get, and the effect of the cost of that care on their family's standard of living are problems that deserve national attention. Fortunately, the country is starting to turn to this issue. The high cost of child care is a major cause of low living standards in families with children and of the social pathology that such conditions often cause. Obviously, that is—or should be—a public concern. The low quality of care that many young children are

receiving should also be of public concern. It affects the kind of adult populat
we will have in the future–it helps determine how psychologically secure, how
socially mature, how economically productive the future citizens of this country
will be. Equally important, the care they are getting affects the quality of the
life our children are leading right now—their feelings of happiness, security,
and self worth. The care children get affects parents' ability to get to work
reliably, as well as the level of security they feel while at work that their children
are in good hands. This in turn affects worker productivity, labor turnover, and
employers' costs of production.

Though there is general agreement that the American child care problem
is serious, there is little agreement on what to do about it. Conservatives say
mothers (with the exception of single mothers, perhaps) should stay home with
their children, and they attribute many of today's societal ills to mothers' job-
holding. Libertarians would rely totally on the free market to evolve a supply of
care that would be appropriate to the country's needs in terms of quality and
cost, and would favor withdrawing what government subsidies and regulations
are now in place. Some argue that government and employer help to families
with children discriminates against the childless, while others argue that parents
are aiding society by raising children and deserve society's help in doing so.
Many advocates of increased help from society look to community action—by
business, charities and foundations—to mobilize the resources to improve the
quality and availability of care in each locality. Others hope that state and local
governments will contribute more than they now do to help parents with child
care, and look to solve at least part of the problem through the increased
provision of free prekindergartens. Finally, there are those, the present authors
among them, who believe that only a large, active, and expensive federal
program, providing both finance and a national framework for quality improvement, will serve the nation's purposes adequately.

Government assistance in child care is likely to come in the form of financial
help to parents and to child care providers and in an improved regulatory system,
rather than in a takeover by government of what has developed as a private industry.
Nevertheless, the need for help is extensive, and its cost would run in the tens of
billions of dollars of additional spending each year.

Government already provides expensive help to parents with the cost of
children's upbringing. It pays the full cost of primary and secondary education.
Government provides and pays for a major part of college education as well.
Some government help has been extended for care and education in the
preschool years, but that help is grossly underfunded. Many parents of young

great financial stress, are eligible for help under the current
eceive nothing because government funds appropriated for this
fficient or because they do not know of the program. A major
rnment funding for early care and education and a far better
outreach to inform parents of the programs that exist are necessary if we are to
relieve parents' financial stress, improve the quality of care, and make progress
in reducing child poverty.

THE AFFORDABILITY PROBLEM

Child care is a "big-ticket" item for families. Care in a center for one preschool
child averages more than $5,000 a year, and in some parts of the country, it is not
unusual for center care to cost more than $10,000. Noncenter care can be had for
10 percent less, and care from providers who are not registered and may evade
taxes comes somewhat cheaper. Even so, for most families who have to buy care,
child care costs take a big chunk of the family's budget. The problem of costs is
particularly acute for families with below-average wage incomes, many of which
are single-mother families. The pay from a minimum-wage job would just about
cover the average fees for two preschool children in a child care center, with
nothing left over for food, clothing, and shelter. But the problem of affordability
is by no means restricted to poor or near-poor families. Good quality child care
is expensive even relative to the income of many two-earner families.

Child care is different from most other industries, in which labor can be saved
by using machinery to do much of the work. In mechanized industries, improved
machines are invented and put on line. As a result, productivity rises and even less
labor is needed. This kind of labor-saving is, of course, not achievable in child care.
In fact, we can confidently predict that with the passage of time child care costs will
steadily rise relative to the cost of most other things that families buy, as productivity
rises in most industries but remains static in child care.

Child care's requirement for large amounts of labor is what makes it so
expensive relative to parents' resources. Yet child care is performed by people who
get low pay. (Lots of labor hired at low pay still costs a lot.) Some child care workers
are college graduates, but many of them have poor education and minimal or no
training. Turnover is high. Reforming the industry's hiring and pay practices would
contribute to better quality care but would raise costs still further.

The high cost of child care raises questions about government help to
pay for it. Should our society, through government programs, help parents with

the cost of child care, as it helps them with the costs of elementary school, high school, and college? Should government support child care for all families, regardless of their income, as some countries do, or should government help be restricted to the lower-income families? Should government subsidize care by nannies, or by grandmas? Should government money subsidize child care by mothers who stay home with their children?

THE QUALITY PROBLEM

The quality issue is present wherever children are cared for—whether by their mothers or by others. Children need care that keeps them safe and happy. But they can be held back if care fails to address their developmental needs. Most experts—people whose profession is the study of child care—argue that care that fails to provide stimulus to development should not be considered good quality care. For children to develop properly they need to grow mentally, physically, morally, and emotionally. Moreover, they need to be socialized to interact amicably with others.

Quality and affordability are, of course, connected problems. Child care's high cost tempts some parents to go to off-the-books providers who may save them some money but who may provide care of lower quality or doubtful safety. Most of the low-income parents who get no government help feel they have no alternative to the cheapest care they can find. More affluent parents do have more leeway, but many don't spend the extra amount it takes to provide good quality. But price is not the only problem. Parents claim to want the kind of quality that experts specify, but many parents are not able to detect mediocre child care or even bad care when they see it.

As a result, many poor-to-mediocre child care facilities flourish in America, and indeed are in the majority. A high proportion of children are cared for by solo providers—friends, relatives, nannies, and family child care providers, who are women who take children into their homes. In such care, there is virtually no oversight—by supervisors, by colleagues, by regulators, even by the parents. Some of this solo care is of good quality. But given the lack of oversight, it is difficult to find out what is going on, much less to tell good from bad care. In the absence of evidence, parents have to resort to hearsay and intuition, which do not always give accurate assessments.

Child care provision has been changing from a mostly do-it-yourself basis into an industry with providers who charge for their services. A major problem for the industry is lower-cost competition, often from untaxed and unregulated suppliers, which limits what can be charged. To keep their prices in line with their unlicensed and underground competitors, the above-board providers scrimp in ways that lower quality. The situation is paradoxical: A product that is viewed as too expensive, as "not affordable," still has too low a price to support good quality. The quality problems of the child care industry cannot be solved without a rise in costs, principally needed to hire better qualified staff and pay them appropriately. The money to pay these extra costs is unlikely to come from parents or from business or charitable sources.

As necessary as money is, however, that alone would not solve the quality problem. Effective government oversight of child care providers is lacking in many states, and research shows that in such states quality is particularly low.

The child care quality problem raises questions concerning possible government action to improve it. Should government take actions that would raise quality or leave the matter to the free market? If government were to make a major commitment to subsidizing child care, what standard of quality should it insist on? What changes would have to be made in the ways child care facilities are regulated? How could child care markets operate more effectively?

GOVERNMENT INVOLVEMENT WITH CHILD CARE: A SHORT HISTORY

Even in the days when women were expected to quit paid work on the occasion of their marriage and remain at home for the rest of their lives, the care that children needed couldn't always be performed or financed within the family. There have always been single mothers who needed to work and whose children hence needed care from others. There have always been married mothers who had to work because their husbands couldn't earn much or couldn't earn anything. Typically the pay those mothers earned was not enough to feed and house their families adequately, much less pay for child care.

In the nineteenth century and the beginning of the twentieth century, these mothers' need for help with child care was viewed as something private charities should address. Some of these charities took children from their parents' homes and put them into orphanages, and some provided "day care." The charity day care was run and financed by socially prominent, wealthy women. The facilities tended to be gloomy and ill-staffed, and the children's behavior tightly controlled. The mothers who had to rely on such care were made to feel that they and their children were objects of charity. Mothers found the use of such care disagreeable and demeaning and used it only if they lacked relatives or friends who would charge little or nothing.[3]

Starting in the New Deal era, government took a more active role in helping mothers who were lacking male support. But nonparental child care was not a prominent feature of the U.S. program, as it became in France, Sweden, northern Italy, Canada, and the countries of eastern Europe. On the contrary, the help that the government gave took the form of support for the mother herself to stay home and take care of her own children. Widows who stayed home with children became entitled to survivors' benefits paid by the Social Security system. In 1935, divorced or never-married mothers who could not claim such benefits were given an entitlement to far less generous cash payments through a program that later became notorious as "welfare" under the name Aid to Families With Dependent Children (AFDC).[4] AFDC remained the centerpiece of government help to single parents for six decades. Although not commonly thought of as a "child care program," AFDC was in effect a major government effort devoted to securing children's needs for care.

A major, although temporary, exception to the emphasis by government on mother-care for children came during the years of World War II, when the government needed women to take jobs to produce goods needed for the war and the home front. Extensive government-run facilities for the care of children of women workers were provided. However, at the war's end, the aim of government policy shifted to reestablishing the sex-role pattern of the prewar era—reserving jobs for men and sending women back to the home. The government abruptly closed its child care facilities; women factory workers were fired and their jobs turned over to men.

Despite the heavy postwar opposition to government involvement with nonmaternal child care, a modest federal tax break for working parents with child care expenses was enacted in 1954. Programs that were viewed as purely developmental also gained political support. Public kindergartens spread, and the 1960s saw the establishment of Head Start, a program aimed at giving children from deprived backgrounds an early socialization and educational experience–at getting them ready for school. However, even today, many kindergartens and Head Start programs offer only half-day sessions during the school year, thus giving minimal help with child care to job-holding parents.

While the government continued in the postwar period to direct most of its child care subsidies to home-based maternal care under AFDC, there was a massive movement of mothers, both single and married, into jobs. The participation in the workforce of married mothers with children under six years old grew from 11 percent to 64 percent between 1949 and 2001. Each year, more families needed to buy and pay for child care, and the child care industry expanded to meet the demand.

The rise in single parenthood, as well as the movement of married mothers into the labor force, eroded support for the AFDC program, which allowed single mothers to stay home and care for their own children. In the 1960s, conservatives' complaints that AFDC was encouraging family breakup, male irresponsibility, dependency on government handouts, and out-of-wedlock births became louder. The result was a steep drop in the real value of welfare grants and a series of "welfare reform" initiatives in both Republican and Democratic administrations that tried to get mothers off welfare and into jobs. The bills authorizing these reform efforts included some provision of child care for mothers participating in training programs and some time-limited help with child care for mothers leaving welfare for jobs. But child care was never put on an "entitlement" basis—which would have provided a place for every child whose family situation met the specified eligibility criteria. On the contrary, limited appropriations were provided, the number of children for whom funds were available was far below the number of children eligible, and long waiting lists for government-subsidized child care places were the norm. The meagerness of the child care provision these welfare-to-work programs offered is one of the major reasons that all of them—one after another—failed to produce the desired fall in the numbers of mothers on welfare.

In the decades when support for at-home child care under AFDC was dropping, efforts to fund child care for children of job-holding mothers had meager results. The U.S. Congress passed a federal child care bill in 1971, but it was vetoed by President Nixon; another was vetoed by President Ford in 1974.[5] Title XX of the Social Security Act, passed in 1975, provided the states with funds for social services for the low-income population and included a requirement that some of the money be spent for child care. When that requirement was later removed, during the Reagan administration, a third of the states stopped using any of the Title XX funds for child care. Sonia Michel, in her history of American child care policy, calls the overall impact of Reagan-era cuts in federal child care funding "devastating" for low-income mothers.[6] Given this history, the creation of the Child Care and Development Block Grant of 1990 was a hard-won turnaround, although the scope of the bill that enacted it had been significantly reduced in the course of the legislative battle and its funding had been brought down to less than $1 billion a year.

The welfare reform that occurred in 1996 was designed to be more rigorous than its failed predecessors. It abolished the AFDC entitlement to support for stay-at-home mothers caring for their own children and replaced it with a time-limited program controlled by the states called Temporary Assistance to Needy Families (TANF). Whatever else it accomplished, the welfare reform forced a recognition of the fact that working mothers were here to stay and that many of them needed and deserved help in obtaining care of decent quality for their children. Larger appropriations for child care were embodied in the reform package. However, they were far below the level needed to fund care for all families who, by existing regulations, are eligible for benefits, to say nothing of those who are not now eligible but arguably should be. This situation persists today.

THE WAY OUT OF AMERICA'S CHILD CARE PROBLEM

In this book, we recommend an aggressive assault on the country's child care problem, led by and mostly financed by the federal government but with most of the administration performed by state and local governments and most services given by private-sector providers. Our proposal would solve the affordability problem and would allow us to make progress on the quality problem. (Appendix A gives a complete listing of all policy proposals recommended in this book.)

We argue that care for children of families with incomes at or below the poverty line should be subsidized completely out of public funds. Such families cannot afford to spend any of their income for child care; they need all of it for food, clothing, shelter. For families with incomes above the poverty line, we propose the following standard of "affordability": No family should have to lay out for child care more than 20 percent of its income *in excess of* the poverty line. If parents and the public were to share the costs of child care on such a basis, millions of middle-class families would be helped, along with millions of lower-income families. (For example, a married couple with one three-year-old would receive substantial help if their income was less than $40,000 under such a program). Funding should suffice to cover all families eligible for services who apply for them.

There is currently little direct provision by government of child care for children under five, and therefore a large privately-run industry has come into existence. We do not envision the possibility that a substantial move away from private sector provision is likely or necessarily desirable. Whatever the merits and demerits in the use of vouchers for children in the K-12 grades (and we consider the demerits substantial), we do consider vouchers useful in administering a subsidy program for the early care and education of children under five years of age and for before- and after-school programs. They would give parents flexibility in choosing their child care provider.

The providers of care reimbursed under the program we advocate could be for-profit or nonprofit, public or private, religious or secular, home based or center based. We recommend that only licensed providers be eligible to receive reimbursement with public funds. Some caregiving for four-year-olds would take place in the prekindergarten programs that states are currently advancing, and in Head Starts. The move to full-day kindergarten for five-year-olds would provide some additional hours of care, as well as additional hours of activities aimed at getting children ready for the first grade. Children under 13 would have access to before- and after-school programs and summer programs subsidized on the same basis.

We use the rubric "affordable care of improved quality" rather than "affordable quality care" because we believe a rapid and drastic improvement in child care quality, while eminently desirable, is not a realistic goal given the current state and organization of child care. Affordability can be provided in relatively short order if the will to spend the necessary funds is there. Quality is a more difficult matter. Improving the financial help to parents will allow many to switch their children out of low-cost informal care into licensed care, where the current quality is likely to be better. But raising the quality of existing providers will not be rapid or easy. Slow and gradual progress, under policies designed to encourage such progress is, we believe, the best that can be hoped for in the near term. Making progress on the quality problem would require that the 20 or so states with low standards in the ratio of staff to children amend their requirements. States should also set training requirements for center staff members and for those running family child care homes, where children are cared for in the caretaker's home. We advocate an improved regime of inspection of licensees and less delay in the suspension of those found to be delivering service of less than minimum adequacy. An increase in the number of providers who seek and are granted accreditation and an expansion of resource and referral services would be helpful. Setting up standards that providers must meet in order to receive federal funds would also be desirable.

Efforts to improve quality could not succeed without a flow of funds to pay for the costs to providers of meeting the higher standards. We recommend that reimbursement of providers be at a level that would allow them to deliver

services of a quality that is average in the United States
reimbursement rates for those who demonstrate significa
(Providing funds to pay the cost of currently average q
providers delivering quality below the current average en
their quality. If such an improvement by the bottom half c
occur, the quality average would, of course, rise accordingly.) The additional
funds many providers would receive would enable them to pay higher wages,
which would, over time, be expected to increase the supply of trained workers
and reduce turnover among them.

The total expenditure such a program would require is, we estimate,
about $50 billion a year. The federal government now spends about $15 billion
on child care, and the states together spend about $4 billion. So our proposed
program would require about $30 billion of new money a year. It would be
unrealistic to hope that employers and voluntary philanthropic efforts in each
community would suffice to fill the funding gap. Nor can we expect state and
local governments, with their limited taxing power, to be able to come forth with
the needed resources. Only the federal government would be able to finance a
program of this magnitude and insure that children in every community in the
country get the care they need.

We recognize that an expensive public program of this magnitude does
not accord with the common assumption that "the era of big government is over"
and with the seeming widespread acceptance of the idea that the closing of that
era was a good thing. Nevertheless, certain large expenditures do from time to
time get added to the federal budget. Prescription drug coverage for the elderly
was advocated by both candidates in the presidential election of 2000. Additions
to the military budget of funds that would be sufficient to pay for much if not
all of the child care program we propose is in prospect at this writing. A much-
expanded program of subsidies for child care would not be politically possible
without considerable agitation for it, even in an era of budget surplus. Yet polling
data indicate that there is already a basis in public opinion for considerably
expanded government help with child care, particularly for lower-income
working parents; in one recent poll 63 percent of respondents gave support to
increased federal spending to provide child care assistance to working parents.[7]

Powerful opposition will come from those who regard the movement of
mothers out of the home and into jobs as a terrible mistake. Yet most people
understand that for better or worse the mothers of small children will continue
to hold jobs and need child care. Whether mothers "need" to work, want to work,
or find that working is the best of all the alternatives open to them, they do and

work. The practical question that faces the country is how to deal with the child care needs that result.

A system built around the principle that parents should have to pay no more than 20 percent of their income above the poverty line for child care of approved quality, if enacted and funded so that all eligibles who sought places in the system could have them, would effectively solve the "affordability" problem. The trend that is evident toward free public provision of full-day kindergarten and prekindergarten, which could provide care and education for children of age four and five, and the increases that have been recently made in appropriations for child care subsidies show that these are popular and politically viable programs.

A program like the one we have outlined should garner support from the public school teachers' unions and the more organized parts of the private child care industry—the for-profit companies and the religious groups that run child care centers. There is a third group, far more powerful than the first two, from which support might also be enlisted: employers. Employers stand to gain in two ways. First, a more reliable child care system would reduce absenteeism and tardiness. Second, employers would be relieved of pressure to provide subsidized child care as a fringe benefit. There is, of course, a fourth group: Parents, many of whom would be relieved of a good portion of the heavy financial pressure that paying for child care involves, and who would be relieved of the anxieties that attend sending one's child to "informal" care of doubtful reliability, quality, and safety.

The remainder of this volume is an extended justification for the program we have outlined: Chapter 2 discusses our understanding of the meaning of and justification for the call by child care advocates for a better supply of affordable high-quality child care. It argues that the problem is not in most cases on the supply side but is caused by a lack of funds to finance an appropriate level of demand. It suggests a practical definition of the term "affordable" and shows what this definition implies concerning proper benefit levels. It demonstrates that families considerably above the poverty level require child care subsidies if they are to live above a poverty-line standard and use reasonably good quality child care. Chapter 3 takes up some of the important issues that need to be resolved if the country is to have a coherent and adequate child care policy—the possible provision of child care as an employee benefit, the use of tax breaks as a form of child care subsidy, the use of vouchers, the extent of direct public provision, and whether we should subsidize care given by a child's own parent.

In chapter 4, we examine what the designation "good quality" has been taken to mean, the methods used to measure quality in child care, why good quality is important, and what level of quality we should strive for. Chapter 5 reviews what recent research has revealed about the quality of the various forms of child care in America; that it generally does not come up to the standard the experts would call "good" and that a lot, particularly for infants, may be dangerous to children. The regulation of child care providers is discussed in chapter 6, which shows that states vary considerably in what they require and who they subject to regulation. It suggests the necessity of doing a better job of regulation if we are to raise quality significantly and eliminate unsafe providers, and provides estimates of the cost of an adequate regulatory program. The chapter describes professional enforcement of quality control through accreditation, how accreditation can be used as a funding standard for higher subsidies, it's importance in promoting quality, and potential problems associated with it.

Chapter 7 concerns the peculiarities of the child care industry and their effect on quality. The problems that purchasers of care have in judging and valuing quality are discussed. The competition between the home-based and center-based sectors, which constrains the latter in financing quality services, is also described, as is the competition among nonprofit and for-profit centers that also compromises quality. The part that resource and referral agencies might play in improving industry performance is discussed, as well as the cost of creating an effective national network of these agencies.

Chapter 8 discusses the workers in the child care industry—their pay, how much education and training they have and should have, and the desirability of upgrading their qualifications and pay. It reviews some means that might, if they could be implemented, work to that end, and other ideas that have been suggested but would be unlikely to work. It suggests that we give priority to solving the affordability problem while supporting increased training opportunities and monetary incentives to good quality providers, which would permit them to raise wages.

In chapter 9 we present our estimates of the cost of three possible programs: (1) a modest interim plan that would provide help for all those eligible for the state-run programs currently in force, (2) the program outlined above that would make many more families eligible for subsidies and would provide funding at a level that could improve quality, and (3) a still more ambitious plan for universal free care.

NOTE ON NOMENCLATURE

Many writers in this field speak of "early care and education" (abbreviated to ECE) rather than "child care." In doing so, they convey the useful message that all arrangements for young children should be appropriately designed to further their development. However, we have resisted dropping the term "child care" in most contexts for several reasons. First, we believe the country needs a new policy to help the children of job-holding parents get the enriched care they need at a price that leaves the family with enough resources to live decently. To most of the people we hope to address with this message, "early care and education" would sound like jargon. Second, we believe it important to keep attention directed to arrangements that do facilitate parents' job holding. At present, there are in existence many "early education" programs—half-day kindergartens and prekindergartens and half-day Head Start programs—that fail to provide, along with their educational content, child care arrangements that working parents can use without hassle. Speaking of "child care"—albeit child care with an adequate educational component— keeps the focus on the national need for arrangements, including full-day educational programs, that do help working parents.

CHAPTER TWO

The Question: How Could We Make Child Care Affordable to All?

"My husband and I spend more on daycare every month than we do on our house payment. Now, true, we get a tax break on both, but still, daycare is by far our biggest expense—$1,500 a month, or about $18,000 a year. Next year it'll be even more. I'm not saying that it shouldn't be that way; making sure your kids are well cared for while you're both at work is at least as important as having a roof over your head. And we made the choice to have three children, knowing that the first few years were going to be lean. But it means that, at least until our kids are in public school, most of what one of us makes is going to pay for daycare, and we are living on a shoestring. I clip coupons, my kids wear hand-me-downs and if a friend agrees to watch the kids for an hour on a Saturday night, we might go out for coffee—that's it. We won't be going on vacation to Disneyland, we won't be buying bedroom furniture, and we won't be saving for their

college educations or our retirements until we're done with the
daycare years."

—30-year-old pregnant Denver-area mother of two,
ages 18 months and 3 years. She works as a
human resources representative for a
high-tech company. Her husband works
as a bank loan officer. In 2000, their combined
gross income was $70,000.

~&   ~&   ~&

When people say, "There is a shortage of affordable quality child care," they
mean that large numbers of parents can't find care of a quality they are happy
with at a price they feel comfortable paying. The implication of that statement is
that we, as a society, should do something about the child care situation. What
the exact nature of the problem is, and what, if anything, should be done about
it are central issues in child care policy.

The prices parents have to pay to buy care are a crucial aspect of the
"affordability" problem. For a large proportion of families, paying these prices
means parting with a painfully large portion of their incomes. If the cost to the family
of buying care for a child were as low as the cost of keeping that child in diapers,
we would not be hearing of the lack of affordable care. The price of child care keeps
some parents from working. Other parents, because of those prices, put their children
into care that they know or suspect is poor and that might even be harmful or
dangerous. Still other parents feel themselves forced to use so much of their income
for child care that their ability to buy the basic goods and services they need to live
decently is severely compromised.

There is an urgent problem with the affordability of child care that the
country needs to remedy. Obviously, it is a problem that troubles low-income
working people most acutely; however, it is also troubling to families whose
income exceeds the official poverty level by a large margin. Solving the
affordability problem would help millions of children gain safer, better care and
would allow their families to attain a higher standard of living, bringing many
out of poverty-level living conditions. In doing so, some of the acute social
problems that mar our general prosperity would be significantly relieved.

While there is a great deal of concern about the lack of affordable child
care, reasonably precise definitions of what might be considered "affordable
care" and suggestions as to how it might be provided to all children in the country

are quite rare. We propose this definition for the term "affordability": Parents should not have to devote more than 20 percent of their income *in excess of the poverty line* to paying for child care. Using this definition, we can estimate the cost of a government program that would make care affordable to all families.

The existence of a set of programs paid for by federal and state governments that do provide some help to some parents in paying for child care demonstrates that most of the public and many of the politicians recognize that employed parents of young children have a difficult burden and that government help with that burden is desirable public policy. However, as we shall see, these programs have not come close to solving the "affordability" problem, whether one uses the definition of affordability that we propose or anybody else's. They give no help at all to many families in acute need. We need to consider how we might change and augment these programs.

To say that the high price of care creates big problems for families is not to say that the price the market has set is abnormally high. As we shall see, current prices are fully justified by costs that have to be met if minimally decent care is to be provided. If costs were cut, quality would go down; costs would be higher than they are now if the child care industry were to deliver a higher level of quality than it currently provides. (In later chapters we will explain why it should be encouraged and enabled to do so.) The question we face is not how to reduce or avoid those costs but who is to pay for them and how.

Help in relieving parents of some or all child care expenses could (and does) take many forms. One example is the free full-day kindergarten that some, but by no means all, school districts provide. Another is the free provision of full-day prekindergarten classes that a number of states are moving toward. Government payments to designated private child care providers, which allow providers to enroll children at a reduced or zero price to the parents, is still another. Subsidies can also take the form of government-issued vouchers or certificates given to parents, which promise government payments to approved child care providers, chosen by the parents, and which cover all or part of the providers' fees. Government can provide child care services in public institutions, charging the parents no fees, or alternatively charging the parents for part of the cost, as is done with public higher education. Government can reimburse parents for fees they pay to private providers by allowing them tax deductions or tax credits for part or all of their child care expenses. The government is not, of course, the only possible source of child care subsidies. Employers or philanthropies can set up and run child care facilities and charge parents fees that are below cost, or zero. In this chapter, we will explore the extent to which parents at various income levels might reasonably be relieved of some or all of their child care costs, whatever the form of the subsidy.

IS THERE A SUPPLY PROBLEM?

The commonly used phrase "shortage of affordable child care" conveys the suggestion that the problem is not just with price—that there is a problem of insufficient supply that should be remedied. There are several reasons that people talk of shortage in this context.

In family child care, vacancies may exist but be hard for parents to find, giving the illusion that there are fewer places than there are children needing them. For example, if each provider wants to take care of three children, and one in four providers has a vacancy, it would not be unusual for a parent to have to contact five or more providers before finding a vacancy. Yet the vacancy rate in that case would be more than eight percent. Though in that case there is no shortage, there is a problem, which could be cured by better provision of information about the location of vacancies.

Through government subsidy programs, some child care slots are available to low-income parents at prices that are below cost or free. The number of government-subsidized slots in programs like these is far fewer than the number of children eligible to use them, as a result of political decisions to keep appropriations at a low level. So the demand for them is bound to be greater than the supply, and waiting lists develop. In this sense there is a "shortage" of such government-subsidized slots. Opponents of government subsidies, such as Darcy Olsen of the libertarian Cato Institute, which opposes virtually all government programs, argue that the subsidies cause this kind of shortage and so should be abolished.[1] Indeed, without a doubt, less would be heard about the shortage of government-subsidized child care slots if we abolished the program entirely and forgot about it. But doing that would obviously not get rid of the need for such help. The way to get rid of the shortage of subsidized slots would be to increase the appropriation for subsidies.

Many children are receiving care in unlicensed settings, and this is sometimes interpreted as a shortage of licensed care. However, children are not in unlicensed care because the market fails to supply the amount of licensed care that parents demand. Rather, they are there because parents are unwilling or unable to pay what it costs to put their children in licensed care, are oblivious to the existence of licensing and the general superiority of licensed care, or find unlicensed forms of care more appealing or more convenient.

Many of the parents with children in unlicensed care have incomes so low as to allow them no real alternative. But there are parents who have ample resources out of which they could purchase licensed care for their children but who choose not to. Some have found an unlicensed provider whom they think superior to the licensed alternatives available. Some parents put their children into the care of relatives whom the parents trust and who are free or relatively cheap. Some parents use nannies or housekeepers, who are relatively expensive but allow the parents to follow a flexible time schedule. Some parents think their children will be better off in family day care, cared for by a woman in her own home with just a few other children, than they would be in a center. Most of these family day care homes are unlicensed; the parents who use them may not consider the lack of a license particularly important. Other parents in this income bracket may suspect that their children would be better off in licensed care but hope that no great harm will be done if they buy a lower-price alternative. They make the choice to take some of the money that might be spent on higher quality licensed care and use it instead to finance better living conditions for the family.

If an expansion of subsidies designed to be used only in licensed care created more willing and able customers for licensed care, we would expect the supply to expand accordingly. For-profit operators, faced with increased demand at a price that would provide a standard profit, would expand their operations and create new slots, and probably nonprofit operators and family day care providers would do so as well. In particular, we would anticipate that increased subsidies would have the effect of increasing the provision of child care in lower-income neighborhoods by creating the demand for paid care currently lacking there.[2] There might be a lag before supply caught up with increased demand. But this would be temporary and would not alter the fact that the basic problem to be dealt with by public policy is a shortage of money on the demand side rather than a persistent shortage of facilities on the supply side.

We would expect persistent supply-side problems only in situations where the demand for the product is thin and enterprises find it unprofitable to set up shop. Some would-be users of child care are thwarted in finding it because they are in thinly populated rural areas. Others need service of a type that few others need or that may have high costs that are unaffordable for most would-be customers. An example would be the care of sick or disabled children. Still others need service during hours or days when few others do, when most providers are not willing to work at anything like standard pay. These kinds of problems can be solved by enhanced subsidies that attract supply into thin markets or by direct provision on the part of government.

Some opponents of government subsidies to child care are glad to have an alleged lack of availability of child care as an easily attacked straw man. They correctly point out that the market seldom allows or creates a shortage of any good. But they then declare that this means there is no child care problem. We agree that, in most cases, it is not supply-side shortages that are the problem. Rather, the problem is the prices that are charged and what parents choose to do or are forced to do in reaction to those prices. For the most part, we cannot cure the availability problem by supply-side remedies, nor, as we shall see in the next section, can we hope to solve the problem through cost reduction or by actions that cut the profits of for-profit suppliers.

COSTS AND PRICES

Full-time care for a child under five for a year is expensive; in many states it is about twice as expensive as paying a child's tuition for a year at a four-year public college.[3] A survey by the Children's Defense Fund suggest that parents with a one-year old who worked full-time paid an average of $6,651 for licensed care in a center in the year 2000. Those who used family day care meeting the licensing requirements of their states paid $5,242 on average. The care of a four-year-old cost $5,219 in a center and $4,738 in family care.[4] Some families had a relative who provided child care at no charge, but about a third of relatives (other than fathers) charged for care. Even a middle-income family with two preschool children in licensed care has a large financial burden.

If the heart of the affordability problem is the price of child care, then we need to ask how that price is determined and whether there is anything about that determination that could or should be changed. One possibility is that suppliers of child care are charging too much, given their costs, and are thus making excessive profits. Another possibility is that there are inefficiencies that could be eliminated. If either or both are true, then it might be possible for prices to come down. If neither of these situations exist, then we are faced with the fact that the price of child care is unavoidably high. That would mean that if we want to solve the affordability problem we must search for ways to give at least some parents substantial relief from the heavy financial burden that such high prices impose.

Child care prices have to cover costs, and they barely do that. In industries where competition is weak, prices can rise far above costs, but that is not true in child care. The child care industry is marked by vigorous competition and relative ease of entry for new competitors, and so we would not expect to see—

and in fact do not see—prices unreasonably elevate
centers run with a margin of 3 percent above costs.
a profit margin of 5 percent above costs.[5] All cente
fees to cover their costs and could not survive if

Could costs be reduced? The cost of labu.
cost of providing child care—79 percent of cost in nu.
percent of cost in the for-profit centers.[6] Child care inevitably ta.
time; providers cannot hope for the steady evolution of ever more lau.
machinery, which raises productivity and cuts cost through time in most ou.
modern industries. (The main labor-saving machine available for this industry
is television, whose extensive use degrades the quality of care.) If they try to
economize on labor by giving caregivers larger groups of children to supervise,
quality will suffer. This is not to say that every child care center is optimally
managed; undoubtedly some providers could achieve cost-savings through
better management. However, the opportunities for lowering costs appear minor
compared to the forces that are leading to higher costs per child.

Prices for child care have been on an upward trend. Between 1990 and
2000, while the overall consumer price index was rising by 29 percent, fees
charged by child care centers and nursery schools were rising at a far faster
rate—by 56 percent.[7] We can expect this upward trend in child care prices,
relative to prices charged for other goods and services, to continue. As most
other industries experience rising labor productivity over time, we can expect a
resumption of the economy-wide upward trend in real wages which, until
relatively recently, has been a long-run feature of Western economies. Rising
wages will have an especially heavy impact on costs and prices in a labor-
intensive industry like child care. Upward changes in the legal minimum wage
will also raise costs in child care relative to costs in other industries. Moreover,
a successful campaign to improve child care quality would require better-trained
and better-paid workers, raising costs still further.

Thus, when we talk about making child care affordable we are not talking
about getting costs down. Quite on the contrary, they are rising, and we can expect
them to continue to rise over time relative to the cost of most other goods and
services. Whatever the inflation rate we have in the general level of prices, the rise
in child care costs and prices is likely to exceed it by a considerable amount.

So reducing child care costs is not something we can realistically hope
to achieve through any sort of government policy. The only way to make child
care affordable to families with children is to transfer the burden of some or all
of those unavoidably high costs from parents to some other set of persons. Many

d that employers could be persuaded or forced to subsidize the child
sts of their workers as a fringe benefit. We believe a major move in this
ion is unlikely and probably undesirable. The only realistic way of shifting
burden would be to place it with the taxpayers at large, using tax revenues
fund government subsidies of child care costs.

GOVERNMENT SUBSIDIES

The federal and state money for subsidies for early care and education that we
already spend, which in 2000 was on the order of $20 billion, can be thought of
as a "down payment" on a more extensive national program. About $7 billion
went to part-time "early education" programs—many Head Starts and prekindergartens—which would have to be converted to all-day programs if they were
to make a significant contribution to helping working parents with their need for
child care. About three-quarters of the government funds that pay for child care
originate with the federal government. States vary considerably in how much of
their own revenues and how much of federal block grant money they devote to
child care. In a recent year, West Virginia covered 25 percent of its eligible
children while Nevada covered 6 percent.[8]

Government funds finance two types of programs for subsidizing child
care—one for families well-off enough to pay income tax and another for lower-
income families. The two programs differ considerably in the size of the benefits
they offer and in the extent to which those benefits are actually available to
families who are eligible to receive them.

The Americans whose incomes are middle class and above receive child
care benefits from the federal government through a "dependent care tax credit,"
or alternatively through the "flexible account" system. This kind of tax break
cost the U.S. Treasury $2.2 billion in 2000. It is not "refundable" and so can
only be used to offset whatever federal taxes the family owes. Thus it does not
give any benefits at all to those who owe no federal taxes and only a partial
benefit to those whose tax amounts to less than the credit. So the credit gives no
help at all to lower-income families. A single mother with two children under
five would get little or no benefit from it unless she had a wage income of about
$21,000 or above, a wage earned by only a minority of such mothers.

The amount of help that the current tax-based dependent care credit gives
is modest. Center care of average quality for two preschool children can cost
$20,000 or more in some localities, but few families get a credit as high as

$1,000, and most families claiming the credit get less. Some states also give child care benefits through credits on the state income tax.

The tax breaks for child care expenses are not limited by yearly appropriations. Whoever is eligible can claim them, to the appropriate amount. All anyone has to do is fill in the appropriate form when filing a federal income tax return. These "funds" never run out, and there are no waiting lists for benefits.

Lower-income families can receive child care subsidies paid for out of the federal Child Care and Development Fund (CCDF), or from funds appropriated by state governments. In 2000, these funds approached $10 billion.[9] The advent of welfare reform has brought an increase in spending for these programs, but there has been a greater emphasis on using these funds to help families leaving welfare and less on helping other lower-income families. Programs under the CCDF are run by the state governments and differ considerably from state to state in the size of the child care fees they will pay and in their other details. In most states, families whose income is below or close to the poverty line and who get accepted into the program would get child care costs fully paid for. Families with somewhat more substantial incomes are required to pay part of the cost by making a copayment.

Unlike the dependent care tax credit, help under the CCDF is not an entitlement that any eligible family can receive merely by applying for it. The number of families who can actually get benefits depends on the amounts appropriated for these programs by the federal Congress and the state legislatures.[10] Although the amounts appropriated have grown considerably recently, a large majority of eligible families still receive nothing at all. Of the 15 million children eligible under federal rules to receive benefits in 1999, only 1.8 million actually received them.[11] This means that while some few families receive quite sizeable benefits, other families in the same kinds of circumstances receive nothing. The shortage of places can lead localities to encourage families to rely on informal arrangements. Administrators must choose which families among those eligible actually get help and which are excluded, opening the door to arbitrary and unfair selection.

One simple way to expand child care subsidies would be to increase the funding for all the existing state programs financed by the CCDF, sufficient to enable them to enroll all eligible families who applied. That would in effect make the program into an entitlement, and in that way put it on a par with the tax credit benefiting the middle class.

While the $5.3 billion expenditures for Head Start in 2000 are conventionally listed with other child care subsidies, the program in its traditional format—half day only during the school year—has contributed little to parents' ability to work at jobs. In this respect Head Start resembles the half-day kindergartens and the half-day preschools that some states fund. Advocates for these types of programs typically emphasize their purely educational mission, and attempts to fund all-day sessions for these kinds of activities are sometimes opposed by conservatives as merely providing "baby sitting."

The most glaring weakness of the current set of U.S. federal and state programs for subsidizing child care is that most families at the lower end of the income scale get nothing at all. Other weaknesses include the low limitations on fees that some states will reimburse, which makes beneficiaries of the programs unable to purchase care of reasonable quality, and the limited help given the middle class through the tax credit. A program to provide "affordability" must repair these weaknesses.

CHILD CARE FOR THE NEEDIEST FAMILIES

We now take a closer look at the question of "affordability." The issue is how high a payment can be considered "affordable" given a family's size and financial circumstances and how much of the cost of child care for each family should be borne by public subsidies. By looking at particular cases it is possible to zero in on an idea of "affordability" that, if not meeting everybody's exact standard, would be considered reasonably close to the mark by most people.

We could bypass this discussion entirely if we were willing to assume that the only public program worthy of consideration would be one that offered care and early education entirely free of charge for all children below five. When the children enter public school a few years later, there are no fees. Some other countries subsidize considerable amounts of child care to the same extent they subsidize elementary and secondary schooling.[12] While there is much to be said for such a child care program with zero fees, it would, of course, be the most expensive in terms of the expenditure of public funds. Therefore it is worthwhile giving consideration to programs in which parents would be expected to make some payments.

Our discussion of affordability starts with the simplest and most obvious case, that of a single mother working full time at a minimum wage job who, we will assume, has two children, ages 1 and 4. She may recently have moved off welfare or may never have been on welfare. In the latter case, she is likely to be getting no help at all in paying for child care from any current government program. The case of the low-wage single mother is not one that politicians find the most politically compelling. People like her don't vote in large numbers, and single mothers who need help are not popular with large segments of the American public. Her plight may be the result of a broken marriage. It may have been the result of having children out of wedlock. Nevertheless, hers is a good case to start with because her need is so stark, obvious, and understandable. And whatever her history, by holding a job she is now "playing by the rules."

Obviously, she needs someone to care for her children while she works. Some people assume that the typical single mother has a relative who will take good enough care of her children for free. But the truth is that not all low-income mothers have relatives who are capable of giving—and willing to give—care at no cost to the parent.[13] About half of the currently working single mothers do get free care, mostly from relatives. But we are concerned here with the half who must pay.

What child care fees should be designated as "affordable" for such a family? One obvious way to think about the family's ability to pay for child care is to see how much money the family takes in during a year and how much it would cost to buy the goods and services (other than child care) that would provide a poverty-line standard of living. Out of her income the mother needs to pay taxes, buy adequate food, keep a roof over her head, get transportation to work, get clothes washed, and buy many other items, such as shoes, children's clothing, toothpaste, and, perhaps, diapers. (We have left medical expenses out of the list because she is eligible for Medicaid.) After accounting for the cost of buying a minimally necessary list of these things, we can see how much money is left over to cover the cost of providing care for the family's children. If the amount left over is insufficient to buy care of an acceptable quality, then keeping this family from falling below a poverty-line standard of living would require some form of government help. Only with that help would it make sense to say that she had access to "affordable" child care.

The financial situation of the family of our working single mother in the year 2000 is summarized in table 2.1. Working full time at the minimum wage would bring in $10,712 a year. To see how much money she will have available to spend—her "disposable income"—we need to subtract from her wage income the taxes the family owes and add in any benefits to which she will be entitled. This mother has income too low to owe any federal or state income taxes, but she does need to pay Social Security taxes. She is eligible to receive an Earned Income Tax Credit (EITC) and food stamp benefits. If she does apply for and receive such benefits, which is far from always being the case, she has a "disposable income" of $15,736.

ñcial poverty-line budget for this family is $13,898. The method of
: official poverty line was established in the early 1960s, when most
ı preschool children had a stay-at-home mother and there was no
ıy need for purchased child care. Health care needs were also not taken
account of, since at that time low-income people would typically receive care on a
charity basis. It is therefore reasonable to take the official poverty line as a
specification of a family's minimal needs exclusive of health care and child care.[14]

It is obvious that this mother can bear little of the burden of paying for
child care. If she uses $13,898 out of her disposable income of $15,736 to buy
the goods and services that would constitute a poverty-line standard of living,
she would have $1,838 left. This is clearly not nearly enough to pay the market-
level fee for licensed care for her two children in an average state, given in table
2.1 as $9,980-11,870. If this mother is required to divert anything but a small
portion of her disposable income to pay child care fees, she and her children
will be forced into a standard of living way below the poverty line. It seems
reasonable, then, to say that an affordable price for child care for this mother is
$1,838 or less. To arrange an affordable price for her, the government would
have to pay all or almost all of the market-level fees for her child care.

What is the rationale for government action to make child care
"affordable" for this family? It is clearly needed if we want to adhere to the
principle that when people work and "play by the rules" in America, one of the
richest of all countries, they and their children will have a standard of living that
comes up to some basic minimum and their children will have care of a decent
quality. Of course, while most people would be willing to subscribe to the
proposition that such a family ought to be helped with child care costs, some
might disagree. They would argue that people whose income doesn't allow them
to support children decently and pay for good quality care out of their own
resources simply shouldn't have children. In this view, if such people do have
children, it is best if they (and the children) suffer the consequences; government
help to them would merely encourage irresponsible behavior and dependency.

Families like the one in our illustration are currently eligible to get free
or almost free care under most states' CCDF program. But, as we have seen,
most such families in actuality do not receive that help. The additional cost to
the taxpayers of covering all such families would be substantial. In thinking
about whether the CCDF should be abolished, expanded, or replaced with
something more or less generous, the reader should remember that we are talking
about a mother who works full time all year round at an unskilled job, perhaps
cleaning offices or hotel rooms, who has nobody with whom to share family

TABLE 2.1

Financial situation of two families, each having two preschool children, year 2000.

		SINGLE MOTHER EARNING THE MINIMUM WAGE	MARRIED COUPLE, BOTH WORKING
1.	WAGES	$10,712[1]	$30,000
2.	DISPOSABLE INCOME (AFTER TAXES AND GOVERNMENT BENE-FITS)[2]	15,736	27,962
3.	REQUIRED EXPENDITURE FOR POVERTY-LINE LIVING EXPENSES[3]	13,898	17,493
4.	AMOUNT LEFT OVER THAT COULD BE USED TO PAY FOR CHILD CARE [LINE (2) MINUS LINE (3)]	1,838	10,469
5A.	COST OF LICENSED CENTER CARE FOR BOTH CHILDREN[4]	11,870	11,870
5B.	COST OF FAMILY CHILD CARE CONFORMING TO LICENSING REGULATIONS FOR BOTH CHILDREN[4]	9,980	9,980

1. Pay for 52 40-hour weeks at the minimum wage in the year 2000 of $5.15 per hour.
2. Calculated using federal and Colorado state income tax schedules.
3. Official U.S. poverty lines, year 2000.
4. Weighted national average of state-level fees given in Karen Schulman, *The High Cost of Child Care Puts Quality Care Out of Reach For Many Families* (Washington, D.C.: Children's Defense Fund, 2000).

chores, and who is bringing up children who will be future citizens, future earners, and future taxpayers. A quarter of the nation's children live in families in a similar situation or close to it. The question at issue is whether we as a nation want to insure that such children and their parents do not have a lower-than-poverty-line standard of life.

AFFORDABILITY FOR BETTER PAID PEOPLE

We now consider the situation of families with more than minimum-wage earnings and ask about the cogency of increased government help with child care costs for them. As an illustration, we can use the situation of a married couple with two preschool children, also shown in table 2.1. This family's wage income is almost three times that of the single mother in our previous example.

Are child care costs a strain for this family? The family has a disposable income of $27,962.[15] They might or might not be provided with health insurance by their employers. A poverty-line standard of living for such a family, including no allowance for the costs of health care or child care, would cost $17,493 a year. If the family restricted itself to that level of living, they would have $10,469 left with which to buy child care.

Suppose this family wanted their children in licensed care. They could buy center care, and be $1,400 short of the money needed to have a standard of living at the poverty line. Or they might buy family child care and live at a standard just above the poverty line. Either way, they would have to lead a bare-bones existence, with no recreation, no vacation expenses, no new clothing. Any out-of-pocket medical expenses would be at the expense of other needed expenditure. With two people working, the parents could be excused if they thought that their efforts entitled them to an existence above a bare minimum. They would certainly be inclined to look for care that could be obtained cheaply, which would most likely be care that was unlicensed. If there were any uncertainties as to quality, many families in this situation would resolve them in favor of cheapness.

This family currently can get only a little help from government in meeting the cost of care. They can get a dependent care credit on their federal income tax of $717.[16] Although they would qualify for some child care aid under some states' CCDF regulations, they would be unlikely to receive any under current budgetary conditions.

Should this family have to spend all of its above-poverty-line income, or even more, on child care? Should it have to choose between bare necessities and licensed care? Should it be in a position where it is tempted to look for cheap care? We would argue that an American family that earns wages above the poverty level should not have to be pushed into a poverty-level living standard—or even below it—by child care costs. Rather, the cost of child care to this family should be low enough so that, after paying it, the family would retain some of its above-poverty-line income and be able to use it to provide itself with a standard of living that includes some amenities. If such families are given little or no help with child care expenses, they are likely to choose to enjoy some of those amenities anyway, at the expense of the quality of their children's care.

These considerations suggest that "affordable child care" is costs to the parents would take away only a fraction of their incom poverty-line. How large a fraction is the subject of the next section.

A REASONABLE DEFINITION OF "AFFORDABLE" CHILD CARE

The argument so far has demonstrated some simple principles: If we wish working families with children to have a living standard that at least comes up to the poverty-line, then families with incomes below or at the poverty line should pay nothing for child care. And families with incomes above the poverty line should be required to spend for child care *only some fraction of the amount by which their income exceeds the poverty line.* That would guarantee that working families with children would not have to endure a below-the-poverty-line standard of living because of what they have to pay for child care. We believe these principles to be at the core of any reasonable definition of "affordability." A program in accordance with them will provide child care subsidies to families with incomes considerably above the poverty line.

What copayment rate—the percentage of their income over the poverty line that parents would pay for care—should we aim for? The lower the copayment rate, the higher the cost of the program to the taxpayers. While there is no "scientific" answer to the question of what copayment rate constitutes the best policy, there are some considerations pointing to a rate toward the low end of the spectrum. The copayment rate determines how high into the income distribution the aid for child care will go. A 50 percent copayment rate on income over the poverty line restricts aid for couples with two preschool children to those earning $41,234 or less, while a 20 percent rate extends aid to such couples with incomes up to $76,845.

A second consideration in choosing the copayment rate relates to quality of care. The higher the copayment rate, and hence the less help given to parents, the greater the number of parents who will ignore the subsidy program and instead seek bargain-basement care from unlicensed providers. So the higher the copayment rate, the lower the quality of care that children receive on average. It would be good public policy to give parents an adequate incentive to use licensed care. Subsidies that pay part of the cost of care that is of better-than-minimally-acceptable quality do provide an incentive, especially if their use is restricted to providers that come up to such quality standards. But subsidies that pay only a low share of the cost give only a weak incentive, especially for parents

TABLE 2.2.

Illustrative payments by parents and government under a plan

FAMILY COMPOSITION	SINGLE MOTHER WITH ONE CHILD		SINGLE MOTHER WITH TWO CHILDREN	
CHILDREN'S AGES	1		1 AND 4	
COST OF CARE	$6,651		$11,870	
POVERTY LINE	$11,889		$13,898	
FAMILY INCOME	GOV PAYS	PARENT PAYS	GOV PAYS	PARENT PAYS
$10,000	$6,651	$0	$11,870	$0
15,000	6,029	622	11,650	220
20,000	5,029	1,622	10,650	1,220
30,000	3,029	3,622	8,650	3,220
40,000	1,029	5,622	6,650	5,220
50,000	0	6,651	4,650	7,220
60,000	0	6,651	2,650	9,220
70,000	0	6,651	650	11,220
80,000	0	6,651	0	11,870

with low-to-middling incomes. How large the subsidy would have to be in order to induce most families to use it to improve their children's care would be a fruitful topic for further research.

A third consideration is the "phase-out rate" for benefits. We don't want to construct a system where a rise in wage income causes the family to lose benefits and pay additional taxes that add up to almost as much (or in extreme cases, even more) than their gain in income. That would make hopeless any attempt by the family to increase its standard of living. A 50 percent copayment

to provide "affordable care of improved quality."[1]

COUPLE WITH ONE CHILD		COUPLE WITH ONE CHILD		COUPLE WITH TWO CHILDREN	
1		10		1 AND 4	
$6,651		$3,470		$11,870	
$13,885		$13,885		$17,493	
GOV PAYS	PARENT PAYS	GOV PAYS	PARENT PAYS	GOV PAYS	PARENT PAYS
$6,651	$0	$3,470	$0	$11,870	$0
6,428	223	3,247	223	11,870	0
5,428	1,223	2,247	1,223	11,369	501
3,428	3,223	247	3,223	9,369	2,501
1,428	5,223	0	3,470	7,369	4,501
0	6,651	0	3,470	5,369	6,501
0	6,651	0	3,470	3,369	8,501
0	6,651	0	3,470	1,369	10,501
0	6,651	0	3,470	0	11,870

Source: Constructed by the authors.

1. Poverty line and cost of care in a center, as of year 2000. Parents' copayments are figured as 20 percent of family income over the poverty line. Government payments are equal to the cost of care, less parents' copayment.

rate means a drop in the child care subsidy of 50 cents for each additional dollar earned. But as the family earns more, and for that reason is losing dollars off its child care subsidy, it is at the same time losing benefits from the EITC and from food stamps. It is also having to pay more income tax and payroll tax. Under a 50 percent copayment rate, every extra dollar the family earned would cause a loss of benefits and an increase in taxes that would add up to about 90 cents. For that reason, such a rate is much too high. A 20 percent copayment rate lowers the loss rate to around 65 cents. We believe that if copayments are charged, the

things considered, would be a rate no higher than 20 percent of
e poverty line. Table 2.2 illustrates the benefits to five families
mposition and the copayments they would have to make under a
ayment rate, depending on the family's income. This plan would
provide substantial benefits to many middle-class families.

Obviously, there are other designs that might be considered. The
Canadian province of Quebec has a publicly subsidized system that provides
care for $5 a day per child whatever the parents' income.[17] Another commonly
cited proposal would have families pay no more than 10 percent of their *total*
income for child care. Its main drawback is that, if applied consistently, it would
extract substantial copayments from families below the poverty line. It would
also make families with incomes less than twice the poverty line pay more than
does the design we suggest, while those with income more than twice the poverty
line would pay less.[18] If a scheme of subsidies and copayments were established
that helped a majority of families, the benefit given through the dependent care
tax credit might be abolished or replaced by a minimum child care subsidy,
which would provide help equivalent to that given by the tax credit for upper-
income families.

A decision to make quality child care affordable to all American families
would go far to solve the problem of child poverty in the United States. Much
of the money families now pay for child care could go instead to raise their living
standard. If administered well, a program of affordable child care for all
featuring low copayment rates would also be likely to get children out of care
that is low quality and dangerous and into care that will help them to develop
and prosper. Such a program would require an annual flow of considerably larger
amounts of public money than we are now providing.

CHAPTER THREE

The Design: What Should a New Child Care System Look Like?

"About a year ago I testified in front of a U.S. Congressional committee working on welfare reform. Following me was a Catholic priest who ran a home for unwed mothers. In his testimony he urged the committee to cancel all their programs and leave social assistance to the churches and the private sector. I chatted with him briefly afterwards, partly because I had never talked with anyone who truly believed there was no role for government in assisting the poor. . . . He claimed that private assistance could easily replace all types of government aid; even when I pushed him about the disparities between the level of charitable assistance and the level of government assistance, he argued that at best there may be a role for a little bit of state or local funding, but no role at all for federal money."

—Professor Rebecca Blank[1]

~ ~ ~

We now turn to the question of where the resources to finance a program of affordable care of improved quality might best come from, in what form they should be delivered, and what kind of child care providers should be eligible to receive them. A program that would address the country's major child care problems could take many possible shapes. It could provide help to parents with their child care expenses while giving them maximal freedom to choose caregivers for their children. Or it could restrict subsidies to parents who choose licensed or trained providers that have been accredited as providing good quality services. It could subsidize parents who care for their own children as well as those who obtain nonparental care. Or it could restrict subsidies to job-holding parents who pay for out-of-home care. The physical and financial arrangements could take many forms: provision in public facilities, contracted slots in nonpublic facilities, vouchers to parents, or tax breaks to reimburse parents' child care outlays. The program could depend entirely on federal funding or recruit additional funds from states, localities, employers, and charities.

Many of the design issues have political aspects to them, in the sense that one design would be likely to provoke a high degree of opposition while another would rally support. These political aspects need to be addressed if we are to have some hope that a substantial program might become a reality. Of course, the most difficult political hurdle would be overcoming the current conventional wisdom that a new large, expensive government program would be out of the question. However, it would be a mistake to assume that the present state of public opinion will persist into the future, and that what currently lacks support and is not achievable now can never come into favor.

A "UNIVERSAL" CHILD CARE PROGRAM?

Child care advocates frequently speak of the desirability of a "universal" system. The United States is, at the time of this writing, far from any system, publicly provided or not, that might be called universal. We are advocating a move toward a new system of subsidies for child care, which, together with tighter regulation, would provide "affordable care at improved quality." Would it be fair to describe this system as "universal"?

If by "universal" we mean a child care delivery and finance system modeled on the public schools, then the system we are proposing—which requires that parents above the poverty line pay part of the cost of care—would not meet that definition. It would, however, be broadly inclusive. It would end the current system of one mode of financing for lower-income families and an entirely different one for the middle and upper classes. It would be provided with enough funds to maintain services for all who wished to participate. It could accommodate some components that are free to all, such as free prekindergarten.

The advantage of fees or copayments that vary with family income is, of course, that public funds are economized by letting the better-off families carry more of the burden of the cost of the program than the poorest-off, who may carry little or none. That makes funds available to finance other public programs deemed to have higher priority than the free provision of services to higher-income families—those for whom the full charges are deemed "affordable." The example of public higher education shows that a system that charges fees can still be broadly inclusive, in the sense that its clientele includes people from all income groups. The child care system we are advocating would also serve children from all income groups. It surely deserves to be called broadly inclusive and universally affordable.

WHICH PROVIDERS SHOULD RECEIVE PUBLIC MONEY?

A massive new government child care program should raise the quality of care that American children are getting as well as help parents with financing. "Quality" is a term that encompasses safety, practices that lead to good health and avoid illness, activities that help the child develop, and the child's experience of the care as pleasant and comfortable. It would seem natural, then, to insist that taxpayers' funds be used only for services whose quality measures up to some predetermined standard.

The identification and improvement or termination of providers who give a quality of care that is less than minimally adequate is the job of the licensing authorities. Many parents use unlicensed family child care and care by unlicensed relatives, nannies, au pairs, and "baby sitters." These caregivers, who are subject to no oversight (even from the parents, who cannot effectively monitor what goes on in their absence), are not checked for a history of criminal activity or child abuse. Should the payments parents make for this kind of care be reimbursed with public money? One possibility would be to require that only licensed providers be eligible to receive government funds. In this case, parents would remain free to put their children into informal care, but would not get the benefit of the subsidies if they did.

Requiring licensing without exception as a condition for reimburse-ment with government funds (as a "funding standard") is no doubt the safest course and would do the best job of protecting children from risk. This is particularly the case if all states required licensees to have background checks for criminality and child abuse, required meaningful preservice training, did some on-site inspection for safety hazards, enforced reasonable limitations on the caregiver/child ratio, and made periodic unannounced inspections. In this case, a program restricted to supporting only licensed care could have the effect of switching millions of children to better quality providers. In particular, we would expect some shift of children into child care centers and away from solo providers.

We would expect that restricting funding to licensed providers would reduce tax evasion and kickbacks by providers. More children would be cared for in centers, where such practices are relatively rare. And those of the solo providers who were motivated to get a license and come under regulatory scrutiny might be the most professionally oriented and the least likely to engage in such practices.

As welfare reform has progressed, officials in some states have encouraged single mothers who are receiving public help with child care fees to use unlicensed care as a way of keeping state costs low. Many of the children of these mothers are in particular need of care that helps them to develop, and the kind of care to which they are being relegated is less likely to provide that than is care in a licensed setting. A federal program that was restricted to licensed care would prevent states from economizing on the backs of young children.

One argument against adopting a funding standard that requires licensing without exception would be the decrease in the range of choice that parents would have as a result. To the extent that current providers might decide not to apply for a license, the supply of care convenient for parents might for a time be reduced. Those who felt that a nanny or a relative would do best for them would have the choice of foregoing the subsidy from the program or making do with a form of child care they found less suitable to their and their children's needs. However, in a program that seeks to improve the quality of care, it may be necessary to declare some providers off-limits and eliminate the freedom of parents who receive the subsidy to choose them.

A funding standard requiring licensing would cause many family child care providers who are now unlicensed to apply for a license. Some nannies and relatives might also apply. This would probably be felt, especially by the latter, to be quite burdensome and might detract from the program's popularity and political viability. One compromise would be to make obtaining a license easy for those caring for no more than one or two children, requiring them only to undergo background checks for criminality and child abuse and to attend training sessions lasting a day or two. If it were to turn out for some reason that requiring licensing would work a special hardship on parents in poorer neighborhoods, special assistance might be given to help would-be providers in such neighborhoods get licensed.

The administrative burden on the licensing agencies would grow considerably if no exceptions to a licensing requirement were made. However, ten states currently require that all persons engaging in family day care (defined as care given in the caretaker's home) be licensed. Presumably these states have not found the administrative burden unbearable.

While recognizing there are arguments to be made for allowing some informal care to be eligible, we would argue that the safety and quality considerations should have the greatest weight. Accordingly, we believe it is best to require that all caregivers eligible to receive government funding be licensed.

ALTERNATIVE SOURCES OF FINANCE

The child care policy we have outlined would involve a considerable increase in the help that parents get in paying for child care, on the order of tens of billions of dollars annually. Is federal government spending the only way such a program could be financed? Are there other sources of financing that might make major contributions? The attacks by conservatives on "big government" and on policies of "tax and spend" that have gone on since the 1970s have been very successful in conveying the idea to the public that new high-cost federal programs should never be considered and that some of the ones we already have (particularly Social Security and public schools, although not defense) are ripe for dismantlement. The statement by a Democratic president that "The era of big government is over" appeared to put beyond the pale any ambitions for a public program of the type and magnitude we are advocating.[2]

Those who press the view that large new programs are unthinkable, or at least politically infeasible, and those who acquiesce, albeit unhappily, in that view have, while continuing to press for increased government appropriations, tended to look in other places for financial resources to expand the supply of high quality affordable care. They have looked to charities and to employers.

Much of the activity of advocacy organizations has aimed to encourage employers, local voluntary agencies, and public/private partnerships to set up and finance new high-quality child care centers.

The Role of Charity

Charities, particularly those associated with religious groups, have offered relief to needy families and individuals for centuries. However, private charities have limited resources and generally fail to cover a high proportion of those needing help. It has always been understood that when large numbers are deemed to be in need of aid, governments have far superior resources and organizing abilities than do charities and provide help on a more rationalized basis. The Poor Laws enacted in Elizabethan England, the establishment of welfare state programs in Western Europe in the twentieth century, and the programs introduced in the United States in the administrations of presidents Franklin Roosevelt and Lyndon Johnson all reflect that understanding.

Conservatives, in trying to limit or abolish the welfare state, have claimed that private charities are to be preferred to government action. They assert that we do not need expensive government programs because people whose unmet needs are truly worthy of being met could be detected and helped by the many foundations, civic associations, and charities that dot the American landscape.

Currently, charities in the United States do help parents with some child care expenses. In their survey of child care finance sources in the first half of the 1990s, Louise Stoney and Mark Greenberg, in their tally of charitable contributions to child care programs, refer to $193 million from United Way contributions, $18 million from private foundations, and an unspecified sum of contributions by religious organizations in cash and services to the child care centers established on their premises.[3] They estimate that this amounted to less than 1 percent of the cost of child care and early childhood education. While charitable contributions may have grown since their survey, there is little realistic possibility that charitable contributions to child care could grow enough to make up a major share of the tens of billions of dollars needed each year to provide families access to affordable care, as we have defined it. Even if charitable contributions expanded ten-fold, they would not begin to provide a major share of the funds needed. The large infusion of resources for child care that would be necessary to achieve the "affordability" and quality goals cannot be raised through the initiatives of charitable enterprises.

President George Bush, in promoting the superiority of the work of charitable and civic organizations to government activities, admiringly called them "a thousand points of light."[4] However, a more realistic nickname for their activities is "a thousand bake sales." It does not denigrate the people who organize and run them to remember that such activities take enormous amounts of energy, and to suggest that the same energy devoted to mobilizing the political will for government action might be expected to give more help to more people on a more systematic basis.

The Role of Employers

Some of those despairing of a significant increase in government provision or subsidy of child care are attracted to the idea that employers might take a prominent part in providing resources and organizing programs. America has a tradition of leaving social needs like health insurance, sick leave, and vacations to be provided by employers as "fringe benefits" rather than by government programs, as is done in Europe. Child care centers located in workplaces offer important advantages such as convenience and contact during the work day between parents and children. And child care is a work-related need for many workers. Some unions have bargained for child care benefits financed by the employer.[5] The child care package proposed to Congress by President Clinton in 1998 contained tax incentives for employers to set up new centers, and employer-supported child care was a prominent theme in the White House conference on child care in that year.

Child care centers set up under the auspices of employers tend to be of high quality.[6] And every additional high-quality child care center helps raise the standard of care in the country. However, we need to ask whether it is realistic to expect employers to contribute much to solving the country's child care problems. There is no reason to believe that employers are voluntarily going to provide an appreciable share of the additional billions of dollars needed every year to finance good quality child care, or that they could be forced to do so by legislation, cajoled into it by tax incentives, or bargained into it by unions. On the contrary, employers are currently making big efforts to reduce the funds they pay out in fringe benefits, largely by increasing the share of their employees in a part-time or temporary status, statuses that traditionally make the worker ineligible for benefits. Many employers are reducing their share of health insurance costs for those workers still getting benefits.

Care for one child is more expensive than health insurance for an entire family. Everybody needs health insurance, so an employer offering it is giving something that all employees will use. But many employees have no children requiring care, so an employer providing a high share of the costs of child care would be giving highly favored treatment to some employees.[7] Some employees without children are starting to make this argument and are mobilizing resentment on this basis.[8]

Large and progressive employers may organize child care centers on the premises of some of their larger work sites, but the subsidies they offer usually cover a minor share of the centers' costs, so fees to parents remain high and only highly paid employees can use them. Smaller businesses are particularly unlikely to provide room on their premises for child care. Of all workers, only 13 percent work for employers with 1,000 or more workers, and 55 percent work for employers with 100 or fewer.[9] Employers are not going to provide us with a solution to the resource problem faced by parents with children needing care. They may currently provide a somewhat bigger share of the cost of child care than the 1 percent that was tallied a decade ago, but it would be unrealistic to hope that they would ever make a major contribution.[10]

Some remarkably frank testimony concerning the possibilities of major corporate contributions to solving the child care problem was given to the Senate Finance Committee in 1998 by Donna Klein, director of programs for Marriott International that help employees to harmonize their work lives and family lives.[11] She said that it makes sense for a company to use child care benefits to cater to the needs of high-skill workers, who are difficult to replace, so as to reduce the chance they will leave. But many of Marriott's workers are of low skill and are easily replaced. It is not cost effective for the company to make major expenditures on child care subsidies for such employees in the hope of reducing turnover.

If a company subsidizes child care for the highly-paid skilled employees that the company is afraid of losing, but feels that it cannot make unprofitable provision for the lower-paid employees, it is increasing the gap between the haves and the have-nots. Klein noted that providing child care for the upper-level employees may get the company lionized as "a good corporate citizen and a responsible employer" (and invited to White House conferences on child care) but that such behavior might sensibly be viewed as impairing the social fabric by further increasing inequality among workers.

Even in the unlikely event that employer help with child care expenses became as common as employer help with health insurance is now, there would still be a lot of people without coverage. We would be left with the same spotty picture we have today in health insurance. In health insurance, the coverage of a high proportion of the American people through their workplace makes transforming the system into one that covers everybody more difficult and complicated. It is not too much to say that in child care we are lucky that employers do as little as they in fact do.

In her statement to the Senate Finance Committee, Donna Klein of the Marriott Corporation said that what is needed to support female workers and dual-income families is "minimum standards of child care that are available to all workers, regardless of employer affiliation."[12] That sounds remarkably like support for a large public program of child care subsidies. Such a program would be in the interest of employers like the Marriott Corporation because it would increase the supply of unskilled labor to the corporation and reduce absenteeism. Activists in promoting child care should certainly explore the possibility of mobilizing major employers to back and lobby for government subsidies for child care.

A HIGHER EDUCATION MODEL FOR CHILD CARE FINANCE?

A group of foundations has supported the development and discussion of a plan for a system of finance for child care modeled after the financing of higher education.[13] On average, college students and their families pay in tuition only 28 percent of what their education costs, and they are assisted in paying that by grants and by loans on easy terms. Even those relatively well-off families that pay college tuition in full are in most cases covering only a fraction of what the education costs. By contrast, fees paid by parents cover on average 60 percent of the cost of child care. Most parents, including those of very modest incomes, pay the full cost of the child care services their children get.[14] Government pays a similar fraction of college and child care costs—36 and 39 percent respectively. Colleges can charge parents a smaller proportion of the cost of the services than do child care providers because they get more revenue from gifts, and earn income on endowments (due to past gifts) and from auxiliary sales and services. Those advocating the "higher education model" envision that child care might also draw in substantial additional financing from these same sources—loans to parents, philanthropy, auxiliary sales, and that government's share of child care costs would expand as well.

"Financial aid community hubs" would receive financial aid applications from parents similar to those used in the request for college aid and disburse aid according to need. The hubs would "become the locus for contributions to scholarship funds, savings plans, and an endowment fund, as well as government subsidies,"[15] all of which would serve as sources for the aid money. As in higher education, accreditation would be the primary method of identifying providers eligible to receive subsidized children.

Like ours, the suggested program contains a scheme of subsidies to parents on a sliding scale, with lower-income parents getting more help and upper-income parents getting less. And it envisions a considerable expansion in the government contribution to the financing of the services. It differs from ours in its suggestion that government contributions and parental fees, now the only important sources of child care funding, could be appreciably augmented by some of the other kinds of funding available to institutions of higher education.

As we have noted, even a doubling or tripling of charitable contributions to child care, unlikely as that would be, would not begin to meet the need for the funds needed to achieve affordability and better quality. College endowments are accumulated over decades, mainly from contributions by alumni. We cannot expect the alumni of child care centers to be similarly generous. We also have to view with considerable skepticism the idea that even middle-income parents would be willing and able to take out loans to pay for child care fees. College students can repay loans out of the extra income their education enables them to earn; parents have no such financial gain from child care. As for auxiliary sales, colleges make profits on bookstores, clothing, short courses to special students, conferences, research contracts, and the like. For child care providers, the prospect of substantial additional financing through such means cannot be considered a realistic prospect.

DIRECT PUBLIC PROVISION OF CHILD CARE

One possibility for organizing early care and education would be the broad expansion of direct public provision. The system used in France provides a possible model.[16] Under the auspices of the national Ministry of Education, the French have set up a publicly run and funded nursery school system—the *écoles maternelles*—that enrolls almost all preschool children two-and-a-half years old through five, including those whose mothers do not hold jobs. The parents pay no fees, regardless of their income. The buildings and classrooms are pleasant and well maintained, and the quality of the care and instruction appears to be good. Children may be enrolled as soon as they are toilet-trained and attend until they enter first grade at age six. There are enough places to accommodate all children presented for enrollment. Before- and after-school care is well organized and inexpensive, so the system serves the needs of working parents. Some publicly-supported and administered centers for the care of infants and toddlers (*crèches*) are also provided. The *crèches* charge fees that are graduated according to family income.

Professor Edward Zigler of Yale University, one of the originators of the Head Start program and a long-term and influential advocate for better care and education for young children, proposes making the public schools the principal locus of early care and education activities in the United States. He entitles his program "The School of the 21st Century."[17] He calls for all-day, year-round, high-quality child care for children aged three, four, and five, operating from 6:00 A.M. to 6:00 P.M., with some facilities possibly open later. The program would be administered within the public school system and, where possible, located in public schools. He proposes before- and after-school and vacation care for school-aged children to the age of 12, with summer programs as well. In Zigler's plan, schools would not care for children under three, who would presumably be served by the present types of providers.

Zigler envisions each school becoming a "family resource center." In addition to formal schooling and child care, such a school would provide many other services that families with children need, such as home visitation programs, health referrals, and nutrition education. The school would provide support services and training for family child care providers, who would care for the younger children in the area, and run a referral service to help parents locate the associated providers. Funding for the program would come from parent fees on a sliding scale, from existing public funding streams, and from private philanthropy. The public support would come from the same sources as current public school funding and in roughly the same proportions—most from the locality, some from the state, and relatively little from the federal government.

Zigler plans on some increased financial help from philanthropy but sees the budgets of localities as the major source of funding, as it is with the public schools. He calls for minimal additional help from state and federal government. Again, we question the view that philanthropy could become a major contributor and that the tens of billions of dollars needed to make the care reasonably affordable to parents could come from anywhere but the federal treasury.

There would be, of course, some important benefits in extending the public school model of provision and financing down into the preschool years.

The qualifications of the teachers and aides, and the wages and benefits they would get, would likely be considerably higher than is currently the case in the U.S. child care industry. If parents paid little or nothing, they would not have to divert large portions of their income to paying for care. However, some child care experts question the wisdom of housing child care in public schools; they see a danger that there would be drift toward a much more regimented, "scholarly" curriculum than they consider appropriate for this age group.

The quality school-based care Zigler envisions would certainly be a valuable component of the supply of child care under the federally funded program we are advocating. The movement to establish free prekindergarten for three- and four-year-olds would also fit in with his plans. Presumably, public schools could compete with private child care providers, as they do in the prekindergarten program that some states fund. However, any plan based exclusively or even mainly in public schools would cause a considerable diversion of customers away from the private part of the child care industry. Private providers might be an ally in achieving expanded public funding of child care, but would turn into a deadly enemy of public funding if they were threatened with extinction. Moreover, while the existing child care industry leaves much to be desired in the way of quality, a transition to a totally different system is unlikely to offer the improvements needed and might well cause some deterioration.

FOOTING THE BILL:
TAX BREAKS VERSUS PROVIDER PAYMENTS

A rationalized system of child care finance would concentrate on just one of the two modes of help we now have for parents who face child care fees—either the block grants to the states, which finance payments to child care providers, or the tax breaks that reimburse parent expenses. A one-mode system would be more efficient to operate and would clarify the extent of the system's generosity and equity. Even if we were to keep two modes, we would have to decide which to expand.

If one of the existing systems is to be expanded, which should it be? One possibility would be to expand the tax break mode we now use to finance child care help for the middle class and use it as the basis of a larger and more inclusive system of help to parents with child care expenses. That would mean increasing considerably the tax benefits available to lower-income families and making the tax credits refundable.

It seems politically easier in the United States to provide social programs in the form of tax breaks than to get Congress to finance such programs by appropriations. Conservatives say that expenditures "spend the people's money" while tax breaks "give the money back to the people who earned it." However, this distinction is misleading. Tax breaks take money out of the treasury just as expenditures do; for this reason economists call them "tax expenditures." A dollar given to a provider to help a parent with child care fees benefits the parent and costs the government treasury no more or less than a dollar rebated to the parent by the tax authority, provided the restrictions on the parent's use of the dollar are the same in both cases.

The Earned Income Tax Credit (EITC), which provides money benefits to low-wage working parents, is the leading example of a social program dressed up as a tax break. The benefit has the effect of lowering the amount owed on the family's federal income tax. It is "refundable," meaning that any part of it not offset by the income tax is provided to the family as a cash benefit. The same effect could have been achieved with appropriated funds in the form of a cash benefit unconnected to the income tax. But such a program would surely have been maligned as a "government handout."

As we have noted, tax breaks are not limited by yearly appropriations. As a result, no one is turned away or put on a waiting list (as happens frequently to applicants for child care subsidies financed by the child care block grants or to applicants for housing benefits) because the amount that has been appropriated is insufficient to provide the benefit for all those entitled to it. The entitlement aspect to benefits distributed through the tax system is certainly an advantage from the point of view of those who would like to see more expenditures on behalf of child care and more equity in the distribution of those expenditures.

Sending social subsidies via tax credits may be less stigmatizing than cash benefits. On the other hand, benefits that go to families well up into the middle class are unlikely to be stigmatizing no matter what form they take. The cash benefits that most European countries provide to families with children, which go to families up and down the income scale, are not considered stigmatizing in the slightest degree.

There are some important disadvantages to using the tax system to fund child care subsidies. First, the size of the subsidies that are needed for low-income families are large. A poor family with three preschool children might require $20,000 a year or more in child care subsidies, and subsidies of this magnitude, so out of proportion to any taxes owed, would be awkward to distribute as a refundable tax break. Child care subsidies, especially those that cover a high proportion of the cost, need to be paid or reimbursed at least on a monthly basis, something the tax authorities are not in a good position to do. The administration of the EITC by the Internal Revenue Service has been troubled by a considerable number of fraudulent claims; the much larger amounts to be handed out in child care subsidies would make an even more tempting target for false claims.

Perhaps the most telling argument against using tax breaks as child care subsidies relates to quality assurance. The modest amounts that are currently given out via tax breaks have no quality conditions whatever attached to them. A fee paid by a working parent to anyone at all for the care of a child can serve as a basis for a tax credit, provided the fee is paid to someone with a Social Security number or other identifier that can be reported to Internal Revenue. The caregiver can be licensed or unlicensed, trained or untrained, have guns in the house or not, can be a criminal, a drug addict, a known child abuser, even a child. Internal Revenue, as the program is now set up, is not equipped to pay attention to such things. A major purpose of the child care program we are proposing, which would fund the considerable fees that licensed caregivers charge, is to provide our children with care of decent quality and safety. That purpose would be nullified in a system that reimbursed fees to anybody with a Social Security number.

A child care program of the magnitude we are suggesting would need to be overseen by state agencies devoted to child care administration and coordinated by a federal administrative agency especially devoted to handling it. These agencies already exist in the Department of Health and Human Services (HHS), and in each of the states. They would audit the enrollment of child care providers eligible to receive reimbursement under the program and determine which met the licensing and/or registration requirements. They could arrange for higher reimbursements to higher quality providers. These kinds of functions are not well suited to an agency whose major function is the collection of income tax.

We would argue, then, that financing any significant expansion of child care subsidies through tax breaks would be a major mistake. Rather, we consider it preferable to rely entirely on federal and state appropriations administered by states.

THE VOUCHERS CONTROVERSY

American children, even those benefiting from government subsidies, currently receive most of their early care and education from nonpublic providers. So, barring an unlikely shift of child care provision to the public sector, a considerable share of public funds for child care will be used to pay fees to such caregivers.

If we rule out the possibility that large flows of funds could take the form of refundable tax breaks to parents, then they must take the form of payments from federal and state treasuries to providers. This is now the case with the state programs financed by the Child Care and Development Fund (CCDF) program, with some of the prekindergarten programs being set up by the states, and with much of the Head Start program.

How should such payments be managed? Currently, there are two common arrangements. In one, the public child care authority signs contracts for child care services with private providers, presumably attending to their licensing and quality. Eligible families choose among vacant contracted-for slots or are assigned to one by the authority. Contracts are particularly useful in building up supply in places it is deficient, in making provisions for services during nights and weekends, and in providing for the care of infants and sick children. In the second type of arrangement, parents are told to shop around for the provider that suits them best (but perhaps only among licensed providers willing to provide services in return for a fee specified by the authority) and then given a voucher covering all or part of that fee, depending on the family income. The provider then bills the state agency for the value of the voucher.

A bitter controversy rages about proposals to use public money to give tuition vouchers to parents with children in the K-12 grades that could be used to pay part of their tuition in private schools. Those in favor argue that the public schools have failed many children and that parents should have the freedom to take their children out of bad public schools and send them to presumably better private schools. Those against voucher schemes argue that the loss of funds such schemes entail would gravely weaken still further the public school system, a system that, for all its faults, has proved immensely valuable, and that in any case will continue to serve most of the least advantaged students. They view it as the foot in the door for the public financing of religious education. Opponents of vouchers argue that other ways can be found to improve badly functioning schools.

The K-12 voucher controversy has infected the discussion of the way to finance care for the under-five-year-olds. Vouchers for child care are vigorously opposed by teachers' unions because they are considered to strengthen the likelihood of vouchers for public schools. Yet there is a major difference between the two sets of services: There is currently very little provision for children under five in public facilities, so vouchers for child care do not represent a diversion of funds from the public to the private sphere.

The question of vouchers versus contracted spaces for children under five and the best mix of these two financing methods should clearly be debated on the merits. Under current legislation, vouchers are the preferred method. We should not allow the allergy or attraction to the word "voucher" on the part of the combatants in the K-12 controversy to influence a debate about the best way to administer arrangements for younger children. Many of the state agencies that have been running the block grant programs have experience in running both kinds of financing modes, and their experience with each should be allowed to inform us as to the direction to go.

Those who operate nonprofit child care centers serving subsidized low income children strongly prefer contracts to vouchers because contracts bring them customers and provide a stable source of funding. But a voucher system can offer parents greater flexibility and freedom of choice. It leaves more room for family child care providers, who are dotted around residential neighborhoods. This greater flexibility means that parents who can't find contracted spaces that are convenient for them can still receive a subsidy.

Vouchers might make it easier to keep public money away from unsatisfactory providers, assuming that parents can recognize and avoid them. Douglas J. Besharov and Nazanin Samari, of the right-leaning American Enterprise Institute, strongly favor vouchers over contracts. They argue that contracts tend to be arranged with those providers serving a large number of disadvantaged families, and thus promote economic and racial segregation.[18] Unfortunately, residential segregation will in many cases produce segregation in child care facilities, whichever finance method is used. Vouchers are more likely to be subject to kickbacks from providers to parents of fees paid with government money, especially if informal providers and relatives are eligible to receive them. However, Besharov and Samari do not consider kickbacks a bad thing; in fact they favor allowing and encouraging them. They claim kickbacks would spur parents to look for low-cost care, saving money for both the parents and the government. On the contrary, parents seeking kickbacks will look for care whose price is high relative to its quality. Kickbacks waste government money and degrade quality.

We would suggest that a judicious mix of vouchers and contracted spaces might be the best solution. Contracts could assure a stable supply of services in locations that might otherwise not be able to support them. Whether vouchers or contracts are used, the size of the payments the government makes to providers will be a crucial determinant of the quality of the services that will be delivered to children. Currently, states are supposed to give reimbursements for care that are high enough to allow parents benefiting from the CCDF program to have the same range of choice of care that middle-class parents have. HHS requires states to collect information on market prices, and considers reimbursement payments from the state up to the 75th percentile price to provide parents with adequate choice. States, however, are not required to pay up to the 75th percentile. Unfortunately, many states allow long intervals between price surveys, and their reimbursement rates may slip below what is necessary to procure even minimally adequate services.

The methods that should be used to set such payments deserve considerable thought and research. Ideally, reimbursement rates should be set by taking account of the costs that have to be incurred in providing good quality. Many states are starting to experiment with a differential reimbursement schedule that pays higher rates to centers and family child care providers that give higher quality services. This should provide a way to contain costs on lower quality services while rewarding higher cost, higher quality providers.

UNEARMARKED CASH BENEFITS

Conservatives who wish to encourage maternal care and discourage nonmaternal care tend to resist providing subsidies to paid care and advocate instead cash benefits "for helping parents with child care" that are not conditional on or earmarked for child care expenses. The standard argument for them is that they give parents freedom to choose how they wish to care for their children. These unearmarked benefits are helpful to family budgets and therefore useful in providing a better living standard for children. However, if they are set up as a total replacement for subsidies earmarked for nonmaternal child care, they are harmful, because they lack a major characteristic of earmarked subsidies: The latter encourage parents to upgrade the quality of the care their children get. A family getting an extra cash payment worth several thousand dollars, labeled "for child care" but which they can spend any way they want, may spend some of it to improve their child's care. But they are unlikely to spend all of it, or even most of it, in this way. This is particularly true if the family has a low income and is lacking many of the goods and services commonly thought necessary to a decent lifestyle. By contrast, a voucher worth several thousand dollars that can only be used to purchase licensed care may succeed in shifting a child from unlicensed to licensed care.

To drive the point home, we can draw the analogy to methods of giving health care benefits. If we wish certain children to be covered by health insurance, the only sure way to bring that about is to have their families signed up for health insurance, with the government payment going to the providers. Nobody would imagine that a $3,000 unearmarked payment "to help families buy their children health insurance" would have as much impact on the number of children covered, or of the quality of the coverage, as would the presentation of a noncashable voucher for the health insurance itself. Similarly, a $3,000 cash benefit that was sent in an envelope marked "To help the family pay its child care bills" would have much less impact on the quality or type of care that was bought by the family for the child than a voucher worth $3,000 that could only be used to pay part of child care bills.

SHOULD AT-HOME PARENTS RECEIVE CHILD CARE SUBSIDIES?

When a government subsidizes child care by providing places in child care facilities or by reimbursing parents for their child care expenditures, the question arises as to whether parents caring for their own children at home should also receive subsidies. They could take the form of cash payments equivalent to the subsidies that working parents get from vouchers or they could take the form of paid parental leave. We believe that there are substantial reasons for giving child care subsidies (although certainly not other kinds of subsidies) only to families that pay for child care.

Consider two families that have equal income from wages, each with a preschool child. In one, both parents work and each makes $15,000. In the other family, only the father, who makes $30,000, holds a job. Although both families have $30,000 coming in, they are by no means equally well off. The first uses nonparental care that must be paid for, while the second has a mother at home full time caring for the child. So the single-earner family, which has no expenditure on child care, has a greater amount of cash to buy other goods.

Even if the working couple gets entirely free child care, the one-earner couple would be better off. Both families would have the same amount of cash to spend on items other than child care. But the at-home mother usually performs more household services (other than child care) than the members of the two-earner couple do, and those extra services enhance the standard of living of the one-earner couple. These services can produce extra amenities, such as a neater house, and home cooking, which can replace more expensive restaurant meals or takeout food. This allows cash to be freed up and devoted to other expenditures.

So the one-earner couple already has a higher standard of living than the subsidized two-earner couple, without any stipend being sent to the mother at home. Sending a stipend to the one-earner couple with the mother at home would increase their advantage over the two-earner couple. For similar reasons, one-earner couples are far better off than single working parents getting free care from the government, even if they have same income. Families with a parent at home full time may need and deserve government help. But if help is given to them, equity considerations suggest that the same help (*in addition* to help with child care fees) should go to the more hard-pressed families with nobody at home full time.

A large majority of the American public apparently favors the idea that single mothers should help to support themselves by taking jobs. So a program of subsidies to at-home parents would most likely be designed so as to be accessible to married couples, but not to single women. Allowing mothers with husbands to stay home at government expense, but denying that right to mothers without husbands seems grossly inequitable.

The 1993 Family and Medical Leave Act requires larger employers to provide up to 12 weeks of leave to employees at a child's birth or adoption. Currently, the law does not require that the leave be paid; however there is some advocacy for allowing the states to use unemployment insurance funds to provide stipends. That would be the first step toward providing paid parental leave in the United States. Paid parental leave, with a stipend equal to or close to the wage, is the most expensive form of subsidy for child care, because most parents earn more than child care workers do, and child care workers take care of more children than parents do on average. A child care worker can give good care to three infants. By contrast, three mothers, each taking care of one infant, expend triple the labor and might cost four times as much.[19]

Long paid parental leaves (say of longer than two or three months) have another disadvantage. They would undercut the labor market gains women have made in recent decades. Much of the improvement in job opportunities for women workers derives from the increase in recent decades in the willingness of most new mothers to return to work soon after the birth of a child. Employers no longer assume that all women workers under 40 are in essence temporary workers, and the better employers have stopped treating them as though they were. In the current state of the culture, the provision of paid parental leave, even on a gender-neutral basis, will put social pressure on mothers, but not fathers, to stay home. Anything that increases the social pressure for having children cared for full time by their own mothers is a step back in the direction of different roles for women and men. If the day were ever to arrive when fathers would take paid parental leave for as long and as often as mothers would, long paid parental leave would no longer damage gender equality. But that day is not here.

The Swedes provide long parental leaves, mostly taken by mothers. This appears to have reinforced a highly gender-segregated occupational structure, with a very limited penetration of women workers into the more prestigious professions. The Swedes have attempted to encourage fathers to share the parental leaves, but with limited success; Swedish fathers take less than 10 percent of the parental leave days.

Because paid parental leave is popular, more help with child care costs to employed parents may pass only on the condition that we also provide benefits to nonemployed parents caring for children at home. In that case, we believe it would be counterproductive to resist also subsidizing the latter, despite the inequities, inefficiencies, and loss of gender equality it would entail.

ARE SUBSIDIES AN UNWISE INTERFERENCE WITH THE MARKET?

All subsidies, those to child care included, "interfere" with what the market ordains and tend to be opposed for that reason by those who believe that interference with the market is almost always bad policy. Some subsidies do have the potential to promote excessive usage and therefore waste. When the government subsidizes a good, the price that consumers have to pay for it is usually reduced. That, in turn, usually causes consumers to buy more and to buy a better quality of the good. If, for example, the government subsidized clothing, and all varieties were free or much reduced in price, people would keep much larger wardrobes. They would wear some clothes only once, or never, and be careless about acquiring unsuitable clothing. They would throw clothing away instead of having it cleaned. People would obtain fancier clothing than they otherwise would, clothing that required more labor to produce, without worrying about the cost. As a result of the increase in the quantity and quality of the clothing obtained by the population, the subsidies would cause a lot of extra productive effort to go into making clothing. The extra labor and other resources used in producing carelessly acquired clothing would be withdrawn from the production of nonsubsidized goods and services that would be of greater value to consumers. In these kinds of cases, economists tend to oppose subsidies.

These kinds of considerations have prompted the economist Sumner Rosen to attack child care subsidies.[20] Taking the case of Sweden, which provides extensive subsidies to child care, he claims that such subsidies result in the production of too much child care and also foster the use of a quality of care that is wastefully high. We believe that Rosen is mistaken, because subsidies given to child care would not induce the same kind of wasteful behavior as would be induced by subsidizing a commodity like clothing. The argument that shows that subsidies to clothing are a bad idea does not apply to subsidies to child care.

Small children require care every hour of the day and night. They generally do get that amount of care, whether from their parents, from relatives, or from nonrelatives who are paid to provide it. If they don't get continual care, they should. So although a subsidy to clothing would increase the amount of clothing consumed, a subsidy to paid child care cannot have the effect of unduly increasing the amount of child care produced, because the right amount of child care (paid plus unpaid) is the maximum amount, at least for the youngest children. On the matter of quality, there is no public interest in improving the quality of clothing beyond that supplied by an unsubsidized marketplace, but there certainly can be a legitimate public interest in improving the quality of the care that is being provided to children through the market.

A subsidy to paid child care will most likely decrease the amount of caregiving by family members and increase the amount of caregiving by nonfamily people. In Sweden, the subsidy induces some mothers to stop caring for their own children at home, put their children in out-of-home care, and take jobs. Some of them will end up in jobs caring for other people's children in government-subsidized child care centers. So Rosen complains about "cross hauling": a woman taking care of other women's children in publicly provided centers, while the latter takes care of hers. Cross hauling is usually exemplified by a truck carrying products from New York to California while a truck carrying identical products is being sent in the opposite direction. That is inefficient, without question. But removing production from the home and siting that production in commercial enterprises or government institutions is not cross hauling; it has nothing in common with the cross-hauling trucks. In fact, the movement of production out of the home usually improves efficiency and is the very basis of the improvement in our standard of living since the days when almost all goods were manufactured at home. In the case of child care, its movement out of the home can improve the efficiency with which caregiving labor is employed, although regulations against too high a child/ staff ratio are, of course, needed.[21]

AN IMPORTANT NATIONAL TASK

Designing a program for the public support of child care that would be broadly inclusive and would avoid important pitfalls is no easy task. Well-intended suggestions have been made that such a system could be financed to a significant degree by funds from employers, charitable contributions, loans to parents, through tax breaks to parents, or as part of local school budgets. But such suggestions appear to us to be wide of the mark. They drain energy from a vital national task: designing, campaigning for, and eventually enacting an adequate program, financed with federal government money, that would provide quality affordable care, available to all of America's children, in Mississippi as well as Massachusetts.

The Yardstick: What Child Care Deserves to Be Called "Good"?

Camille Sparn, an insurance adjuster, and her husband, Peter, a bookstore manager, were in a quandary over new child care for their two-year-old son, Jackson. They decided to go with a day care center, because centers seemed to better accommodate their full-time work schedules. Now they were down to two possibilities, both located on their routes to work.

The Arbor Heights Children's Learning Center operated in a large new building designed as a child care "village." The center hallway was decorated as "Main Street," and each room was a "neighborhood" painted with beautiful murals and neatly filled with new and colorful learning materials. There were well-equipped playgrounds for each "neighborhood," a music room and a computer lab with the latest software for preschool children. For discipline, staff were instructed to use distraction on younger kids, talking through problems with older ones, and, as a last resort, timeouts, starting with two-year-olds. The director candidly told the Sparns that only she and the education director had bachelor's degrees, and that staff turnover was a problem in the tight job market. But, she added, by having standard routines and policies in place, it was relatively easy to orient new staff members.

The Sparns also liked the smaller Sand Valley Preschool and Child Care, which was located in a four-room converted VFW hall. The building was somewhat shabby, with a large outdoor play area that included old shade trees and a huge sand dune, along with access to hoses for water play. The rooms were filled with children's artwork and projects. In the space where Jackson would spend most of his time, children had made collages of leaves that they'd collected on a recent walk. One corner was set up with mirrors and a basket of old clothes for playing dress-up; another area had an aquarium, an ant farm, and seedlings in "caterpillar" decorated egg cartons. The director explained that groups of same-aged children were assigned to a teacher, and then the teacher moved along with the group as they progressed from being toddlers to preschoolers and so forth. Out of the core staff of eight, four had college degrees and three had worked at Sand Valley for more than four years.

The directors at both centers were welcoming and informative. Both seemed genuinely interested in helping Camille and Peter choose the care for Jackson. But which child care center would provide the best care for their son?

We can't talk about public policy on child care without taking account of the issues surrounding the quality of care. The subject is a difficult one, because ideas on quality vary widely. Some think that any care is bad if it isn't given by the child's mother. Others deem adequate any care that the parents have chosen. For still others, any care that fails to help the child develop his or her cognitive and social skills is sub-par, even if it keeps the child safe and happy. The characteristics of the care we decide to subsidize out of the public purse, if any, will determine how much additional public money we will have to spend to get it, how much and what kind of regulatory regime we should set up, and what types of providers (centers, family day care, nannies, relatives) should be eligible for public subsidies and what types, if any, should not.

One way to approach the quality issue is to examine the systems the experts have set up to measure quality and to look at the descriptions of the care they label as "inadequate," "minimally adequate," "good," and "excellent." The reader can then form his or her own view of the appropriateness of these labels and will be able to come to a judgement as to whether the standards that the experts are advocating are too high or too low.

Higher quality care comes, of course, at higher cost. As we consider expanding the public support for child care, we cannot avoid paying attention to the relationship between cost and quality. The quality of the care a child receives, as measured by these quality evaluation systems, affects that child's later life. The benefits that come from higher quality care have to be considered in thinking about public policy.

IS A MOTHER'S CARE INDISPENSABLE?

According to one school of thought, the only good care for a child below school age is care given by its own mother. Some adherents of this view are motivated, for religious or other reasons, by their devotion to the patriarchal form of the family. They believe the father should be the head of the family and that to be the head he needs to be the family's sole earner. For others, the belief that children should get mother-only care rests on the idea that nature commands a mother to love her child and that the care given by a loving mother will be attentive, affectionate, instinctively wise, and considerate, way above and beyond what might be expected from anybody else who might care for the child. Care by someone lacking mother love must, according to this point of view, be far less beneficial than mother care to the child, perhaps downright harmful.

The early editions of Dr. Spock's baby manual took the view that mothers should be dedicated to full-time care of their children, presumably because the care they provided was so much better than any other care that might be procured. Through 1975, Spock called good mother care "vital to a small child." Dr. Spock relented in his later editions and granted mothers the right to choose to take jobs.[1] However, others took up the representation of mother care as not merely the best care but the only good care. The most prominent exponent of this point of view in recent times has been child development psychologist Penelope Leach, who argues that every baby needs "one special person to attach herself to," most probably her mother, and that the vital, continuous one-to-one attention a baby or a toddler needs can rarely be achieved in group care. She argues that children are not ready for day care until they are well into their third year.[2]

Of particular concern has been the wisdom of placing newborns in nonmaternal care. Putting an infant into care has been suspected of interfering

ent" of the mother and child, something considered indispens-
's security and development. The most prominent advocate of
has been child development psychologist Jay Belsky.[3] In the
cal studies that have been done, cause and effect have been difficult
wn, and the meanings of the results have been hotly debated.

To provide better information on these and other questions, in 1991 the National Institute of Child Health and Human Development (NICHD) started tracking over 1,300 babies, looking at the kind of care they have had and how that has affected them.[4] They found that, except in certain special cases, the mother/child attachment was not affected by either the quantity or quality of child care and concluded that child care during preschool years does not appear to affect the emotional security of children.[5] At 54 months (4 and one-half years old), with one exception, children's social development were unaffected by nonmaternal care. About 17 percent of those who had been in nonmaternal care for more than 30 hours a week were rated by teachers (although not by parents) as being aggressive toward other children, as compared with 6 percent of children in care less than 10 hours per week. Behavior labeled "aggressive" includes such things as grabbing toys from another child and defying the teacher, things that children in exclusively mother care may have had little or no occasion to learn and practice in the years before their entry to nursery school or kindergarten. From five on, almost all children do attend classes of some sort and get a chance to practice aggressive behavior. Future results of the NICHD study will reveal whether such behavior differences persist into the later years.

With regard to cognitive development, the NICHD researchers and most other recent studies suggest no harm from nonmaternal care and the possibility of gain if the care is of good quality.[6] One study did report a negative relation between a mother's employment during her child's second and third years and the child's reading and math achievement at age 5 and 6, but the effect was largely offset if children attended a child care center.[7] To summarize, the bulk of the research suggests that children are not disadvantaged by nonmaternal child care.

Whatever the research on children experiencing nonmaternal care has shown, there has been a readiness in the press to run sensational articles the purpose of which seems to have been to scare mothers into remaining home. In the 1960s, when the baby boom was ending and mothers of young children were beginning to enter the labor market in very large numbers, the press gave extensive publicity to experiments on monkey infants. In those experiments, a baby monkey's mother was totally replaced by a heated, terry-cloth-covered post with a milk bottle attached. As might be expected, a baby monkey brought up by a terry-cloth post exhibited neurotic behavior. That research was widely quoted as showing that American children in care might suffer as those baby monkeys had and that nonmother care could severely damage human children.[8] The fright created by the baby monkey experiments soon died down; the public was able to see that the experiences of the monkeys and the human babies were hardly comparable.

Nevertheless, almost 40 years later, in 1998, the *New York Times Sunday Magazine* featured an article describing the gross neglect of the young children in Russian and Romanian orphanages, and the devastating results of that bad care on their psychological state and their behavior. The article gives voice to a dreadful suspicion: that American children whose mothers are employed might well be suffering from similar problems. The article cited no research and provided no facts that would justify equating Romanian children living in orphanages with American children living with working parents and going to care during the day. In fact, toward the end of the article there is a brief mention of the NICHD study that found that outside care of decent quality does not, in fact, harm children. That study provides solid evidence that the main point of the article was quite wrong, but the *Times* editors printed it anyway.[9] The Romanian orphans had replaced the baby monkeys in the attempt to scare mothers.

The report from the NICHD study that came out in 2001 on four- and five-year-old children suggested that on most measures, children who had experienced lengthy nonmaternal care showed no more problems than those who had not, and those in high-quality care showed some benefits. However, with Jay Belsky (a member of the NICHD research team) as the presenter of the results, reporters ignored most of the presentation, and the finding of a greater incidence of aggressive behavior on the part of such children made front page news and was much talked about by right-wing broadcasters. A skit on "A Prairie Home Companion" satirized the excessive reaction. In it a mother laments: "I come home from work, exhausted, I open up the paper, and there's an article that says that any child who spends more than 30 hours a week in child care, away from its mother, turns into a psychopath. . . . [N]ow I find out I was condemning my kids to becoming aggressive monsters who will never get along with anybody and wind up living alone barricaded in mobile homes with their Rottweilers. . . . It's Mom's fault that the kids grow up to become vicious skinheads with poor social skills and a collection of automatic weapons. It's all because Mom put them in day care."[10]

IS ANY CARE GOOD ENOUGH?

The opposite of the view that only a mother's care is good (or good enough) for a child is that any care, or any care the parents choose, perhaps with rare exceptions, is good enough. While most people would deny that they believe such a thing, many act as if they did believe it. In many cases very little care or investigation is put into the decision about what provider to use. In one study of mothers using a relative, partner, sibling, or leaving the child by itself, only 30 percent reported considering an alternative.[11] For parents using centers, studies indicate that surprisingly few parents visit more than one center program before enrolling their child, although they may do a lot of sleuthing beforehand by getting advice from friends, relatives, and coworkers. One study of families using for-profit centers indicated that 9 percent of families did not even visit the center where they enrolled their child.[12] Many parents consider that a nanny, a relative, a family day care operator, or the employees of a center need nothing besides common sense and a big heart. Lack of training is generally not considered a problem by parents.

This point of view gains strength from the uncritical attitude we take toward mothers' care. Our social arrangements are based on the assumption that, in the absence of strong evidence to the contrary, any particular mother will give care that is at least good enough. Any other assumption would require unbearable intrusion by government authorities into family life. However, the assumption that any mother, regardless of her education, intelligence, personality, disposition, age, mental health, or experience with children, will give good care is a short step away from the assumption that any woman can and will give good care to children placed in her charge. A center hiring untrained people who are available at close to the minimum wage is assuming that such persons will be good enough.

A leading expositor of the notion that any care chosen for a child by its parents is good enough is the Cato Institute, which advocates a libertarian point of view in all policy questions, including matters of environmental protection, financial regulation, health care, and workplace safety.[13] Whatever the issue they are addressing, Cato analysts argue for minimal or no regulation, little or no government help to individuals or groups, and very low government spending. The Cato point of view is based on the idea that the consumer, whether buying broccoli or child care, should be as free as possible to choose among the alternatives provided by the freest possible market, without help or hindrance by government. Cato's economists tend to downplay the possibility that the free market might contain sellers whose products might be low quality or even downright dangerous, and that consumers, especially those with low incomes, might be under pressure to settle for such products. They also downplay the possibility that consumers do not have the knowledge to avoid a product that is of low quality and that avoiding a low-quality product might be more important in the case of child care than in the case of broccoli.

WHAT CONSTITUTES QUALITY CHILD CARE?

In the report "Eager to Learn: Educating Our Preschoolers," a distinguished group of experts writing for the National Academy of Sciences emphasizes the importance of early education in determining the pace of children's development in their first five years of life. The authors stress that, for the very young, education is an inseparable part of care and vice versa:

> A central premise of this report, one that grows directly from the research literature, is that *care and education cannot be thought of as separate entities in dealing with young children.* Adequate care involves providing quality cognitive stimulation, rich language environments, and the facilitation of social, emotional and motor development. Likewise, adequate education for young children can occur only in the context of good physical care and of warm affective relationships. Indeed, research suggests that secure attachment improves social and intellectual competence and the ability to exploit learning opportunities. Neither loving children nor teaching them are in and of themselves sufficient for optimal development; thinking and feeling work in tandem.[14] (Emphasis in original.)

The report argues that caregivers of young children are educators who have an obligation to help children to "develop a receptivity to learning" that will prepare them for continued active engagement in learning throughout their lives.

This viewpoint underlies recommendations about good-quality child care made by the National Association for the Education of Young Children (NAEYC), the largest and most influential of the early childhood professional organizations. NAEYC emphasizes the importance of the educational aspects of child care, even for infants, so that a program is not considered good quality unless it promotes children's growth and development.

NAEYC stresses that good quality care involves "developmentally appropriate practice" that organizes children's activities around what is known about how they develop and learn.[15] Child care providers need to engage children in activities that are safe, healthy, interesting, achievable, and challenging. Creating caring, responsive relationships between providers and children is the foundation for all aspects of the children's development, including cognitive development. Children need emotional support as a precondition for normal development. In addition, caregivers must be able to tune into the needs, abilities, and cultural background of each child.

Good quality child care, according to the experts, also involves encouraging child-initiated activities. Programs for preschoolers should not mimic schools—impose skill development, strict schedules, discipline that suppresses spontaneity, testing, and the like. While good quality care certainly prepares children to succeed in school, that is not the same thing as starting school-like programs several years early.[16] In child care children mainly learn through play that offers opportunities to explore, develops skills, gives them a sense of control, feeds their curiosity and imagination, and helps them learn to get along with other children. The teacher's job is to create the opportunities, provide encouragement, help children explore, and extend their knowledge. Finding and watching earthworms in the garden or damming up a little river to make a lake in the playground may be more appropriate settings than a formal classroom.

The experts in early care and education who have devised methods of evaluating child care have developed checklists, to be used in classroom observations, that identify what should be looked at when child care is observed and judgements are made about quality. Whether the methods the ECE profession have created really do measure "quality" and whether the standards they propose should be adopted are questions we will reserve until after we have looked at one of the widely accepted assessment methods in some detail.

The ECERS System

The Early Childhood Environment Rating Scale, or ECERS,[17] has been developed as a tool for measuring quality of programs for preschool children (aged three to five) in centers. It translates research and professional judgements about best practice into a structure for assessing the quality of child care services. The system has been used in most recent major evaluations of center quality.

ECERS identifies seven different dimensions of services and evaluates a program (more accurately, a classroom) on each of the 43 subcategories shown in table 4.1. These subcategories provide a quick inventory of the program characteristics professionals consider important, whether provided in a center,

TABLE 4.1.

Aspects of child care center operations evaluated in the ECERS methodology.

PERSONAL CARE
- Greeting and departing
- Meals and snacks
- Nap and rest
- Diapering and toileting
- Health practices

FURNISHINGS AND DISPLAY
- Indoor space
- Furniture for routine care, playing, and learning
- Furnishings for relaxation and comfort
- Room arrangement for play
- Space for privacy
- Child-related display
- Space for gross motor play
- Gross motor equipment

LANGUAGE AND REASONING
- Books and pictures
- Encouraging children to communicate
- Using language to develop reasoning skills
- Informal use of language

ACTIVITIES
- Fine motor materials
- Art
- Music and movement
- Blocks

Sand and water play
Dramatic play
Nature/science
Math/numbers
Use of TV, video, and computers
Promoting acceptance of diversity

INTERACTION
- Supervision of gross motor activities
- General supervision
- Discipline
- Staff-child interactions
- Interactions among children

PROGRAM STRUCTURE
- Schedule
- Space to be alone
- Free play
- Group time
- Provisions for children with disabilities

PARENTS AND STAFF NEEDS
- Provision for personal needs of staff
- Provision for professional needs of staff
- Staff interaction and cooperation
- Supervision and evaluation of staff
- Opportunities for professional growth
- Provisions for parents

Source: Thelma Harms, Richard M. Clifford and Debby Cryer, *Early Childhood Environment Rating Scale, Revised Edition* (New York: Teachers College Press, Columbia University, 1998).

in a family child care home, or in the child's home. The list shows the scope and complexity of child care services.

In an ECERS evaluation a trained observer assesses a particular room in a center on each of the 43 items. The observer spends at least two hours observing a room at the center and awards ratings that range from 1 to 7 for each item, based on several written indicators for each item. The authors of the ECERS manual have attached the characterizations "inadequate," "minimal," "good," and "excellent" to grades 1, 3, 5, and 7, respectively. To get a measure of overall quality in the room, ordinarily an unweighted average of the ratings on all characteristics is used. Table 4.2 illustrates assessment criteria by summarizing the indicators observers use in rating the level of quality in a preschool room for 8 of the 43 ECERS items. We describe the criteria for three of these items in detail.

For diapering and toileting a score of 1 is assigned if any of the following are observed: inaccessible toilets or hot water; failure to use sanitary practices, like washing hands between changing children and cleaning toilet facilities after each use; or unpleasant interactions with children. A score of 3, or minimally adequate, requires *all* of the following: observance of hygiene standards and basic provision of facilities for children's use. What distinguishes a score of 3 from that of 5 is the nature of the interaction between caregiver and child. When a provider is changing a baby's diaper or helping a youngster use the toilet she has a perfect opportunity to be affectionate, talk to the child, and give the child her undivided attention. In understaffed settings where an undertrained aide changes the diapers, she may be too stressed or alienated from an admittedly messy job to do much talking at all. The other quality characteristic that discriminates between a "minimally adequate" and a "good quality" center is convenience of the toilet facilities, how easy it is for children to use the toilet and sink, and how much work it is for the child care worker to keep the area clean and help children. If children can't reach the water faucets it is harder for them to learn to wash their own hands; they can miss out on the hygiene and the fun of water play. A room gets a 7 or "excellent" rating, if, in addition to the indicators found in 5, child-sized sinks and toilets are provided adjacent to the classroom, and the staff help children learn self-help skills when they are ready.

Children in child care need to develop their language and reasoning skills through informal conversation throughout the day and need to use language to develop reasoning skills. They should be learning about similarities and differences, classifications, spatial relationships, temporal relations, and cause and effect by using these concepts to solve problems of interest to them. In a poor quality center, staff usually ignore children's questions about how and why and do not give them an opportunity to explore or question. Instead they subject children to a routine schedule that stifles their natural curiosity. Activities involving concept formation are often either too elementary or too advanced for some of the children. In minimally adequate settings staff pay some attention to helping children learn concepts, for instance, getting children to classify kinds of animals or shapes, or helping them count objects or order them by size. There are some games available to teach these concepts, but often they are not used with adult guidance or not generally available for children to use. In a room rated "good" there are lots of games and materials available that help children learn concepts, and children are encouraged and shown how to use them to explore how they "work." Staff talk to children while they are so engaged, naming the processes of matching, ordering, classifying, numbering, sequencing, etc., encouraging children to explain what they are doing and why. In excellent settings, staff continually encourage children's reasoning, using actual events and experiences as a basis for concept development. For instance, they teach the concept of growth by having children plant seeds and tend them as they grow, care for baby animals, or observe insects as they go through their life cycle. Staff members, sensitive to each child's interests and level of development, encourage each child's development.

The criteria used to evaluate center disciplinary practice illustrates the profession's preference for discipline styles that help children develop self control and encourage them to learn valuable social skills. In a room rated poor, either discipline is practically nonexistent, so that chaos reigns, or adults use punitive methods for keeping children in line, such as shouting, spanking, isolating misbehaving children for long periods, or denying them a snack or lunch. In rooms with a minimally adequate rating, staff maintain enough control to prevent children from hurting one another, do not use abusive punishment, and do not expect more self control than children can muster for their age level. To get a "good" rating of 5, staff must use positive discipline methods to help children learn appropriate behavior. They set up the program to avoid conflict by having enough materials and equipment so children do not need to share, or they help children learn rules of sharing. They react consistently to children's behavior so the children learn the rules. In an excellent setting, staff use strategies and learning activities to help children learn to solve their own conflicts and understand the reasons behind accepted social norms of behavior. In addition, staff know enough to know when they need to call in help from other professionals to solve particularly difficult discipline problems.

We saw a good example of positive discipline in a toddler room where a frustrated eighteen-month-old was about to burst into tears. The teacher kneeled down to ask what was going wrong, and when the child didn't respond, she said gently, "Joanie, tell me what you want, use your words!" On went the light bulb in Joanie's head and she triumphantly asked for the toy she wanted. In a "good enough" center Joanie could have been ignored long enough to start screaming uncontrollably and then faced a reprimand. She could have turned into a problem child requiring disciplining. In Joanie's center discipline problems rarely arose, because children's needs were met. Children were not expected to perform beyond their capabilities, but teachers had confidence in children's abilities and

TABLE 4.2.

Examples of quality evaluation under the ECERS system

1 = Inadequate	3 = Minimal	5 = Good (in addition to 3)	7 = Excellent (in addition to 5)
DIAPERING AND TOILETING			
Lack of provisions interferes with care of children (e.g., no hot water in area, inaccessible toilets). Sanitary conditions not maintained by staff (e.g., facilities not clean, adults do not wash hands between children). Unpleasant supervision of children.	Sanitary conditions maintained, basic provisions exist but may not be convenient (e.g., water must be carried to diapering area). Staff and children wash hands after toileting *most of the time*. Adequate supervision by staff.	Provisions convenient and accessible (steps near toilet or sink if needed), sanitary conditions easy to maintain (warm running water near toilets, easy to clean surfaces). Pleasant adult-child interactions.	Child-sized toilets and low sinks to promote self-help. Self-help skills promoted as child is ready. Toileting used as time for conversation and to relate warmly to child.
INFORMAL USE OF LANGUAGE			
Staff talk to children mainly to control their behavior and manage routines. They rarely respond to children's talk and children's talk is discouraged much of the day.	Sometimes staff talk with children in conversation, but children are asked primarily "yes/no" or short answer questions, and staff give short answers to children's questions. Children allowed to talk much of the day.	Frequent adult-child conversations. Language is used primarily to exchange information with children and for social interaction. Staff add information to expand on the children's ideas. They encourage communication between children (e.g., remind children to listen to one another).	Staff have an informal conversation with each child everyday. Adult verbally expands on ideas presented by children and encourages them to give longer and more complex answers, by asking questions: "What?" "Where?" "Why?" "How?"
USING LANGUAGE TO DEVELOP REASONING SKILLS:			
Staff ignore children's questions & curiosity about why things happen, do not call attention to sequences in their daily routine, similarities and differences. Concepts--same/different, classifying, sequencing, spatial relationships, cause & effect--introduced inappropriately.	Staff sometimes talk about logical relations (differences in sizes of blocks), introduce some concepts at appropriate age levels, help children figure out why, for instance, ice melts. Some games and materials focus on concept development, but developing reasoning skills is not a major focus.	Many materials to stimulate reasoning, staff talk about logical relationships while children play with them. They encourage children to explain their reasoning in carrying out a particular task (e.g., why they sort objects into different groups, similarities and differences in a group of pictures).	Staff encourage children to reason throughout the day, using actual experiences to help children build reasoning skills and concepts. Staff introduce concepts in response to children's interests & needs (e.g., the notion of balance in constructing a building from blocks, or of sequence in the steps in making cookies).

TABLE 4.2 (CONTINUED)

1 = Inadequate	3 = Minimal	5 = Good (in addition to 3)	7 = Excellent (in addition to 5)
DISCIPLINE			
Children are controlled with severe methods (spanking, shouting, confining children for long periods). Or discipline is so lax that there is little order or control. Expectations for behavior are largely inappropriate for age and development level of the child (requiring children to be quiet at meals, wait quietly for long periods).	Staff do not use severe methods of punishment, they maintain enough control to prevent children from hurting one another. Expectations for behavior are largely age appropriate.	Staff use nonpunitive discipline methods effectively (redirecting children's activities, positive reinforcement for positive behaviors). Program organized to avoid conflict and promote age-appropriate interaction (duplicate toys, child with favorite toy given protective place to play with it). Staff react consistently to children's behavior.	Staff actively involve children in solving their conflicts and problems (help children talk out problems and find solutions, sensitize children to feelings of others). Staff use activities to help children understand and practice social skills. Staff seek help from other professionals concerning behavior problems.
INTERACTIONS AMONG CHILDREN			
Interaction among children discouraged (e.g., talking, choosing own playmate). Little staff guidance for positive peer interaction. Little positive peer interaction (teasing, bickering, fighting are common).	Peer interactions encouraged (e.g., children allowed to move around freely). Staff stop negative and hurtful child interactions. Some positive peer interaction occurs.	Staff model good social skills (e.g., are kind to others, listen, empathize, cooperate). Staff help children develop appropriate social behavior (help them talk through conflicts, encourage shy children to find friends, help children understand feelings of others).	Children's interactions are usually positive (children usually play well together, older children often cooperate and share). Staff provide some opportunities for children to work together on a task (painting a mural, cooking, hunting for insects, or moving furniture).
ART			
Art activities are rarely available to the children. No individual expression in activities (children cannot select subject matter or medium, instead use of coloring work sheets, teacher-directed projects where children copy an example).	Some materials, primarily drawing and painting, available for at least 1 hour daily. Some individual expression permitted (children decorate precut shapes in their own way) but major emphasis on copying something created by the teacher.	Many and varied art materials accessible a substantial portion of the day. Individual expression and free choice encouraged with art materials. Very few projects that involve copying an object created by the teacher.	Three-dimensional art materials included (clay, art dough, wood gluing, carpentry). Art projects are related to other classroom experiences. Older children engage in extended projects over several days.

TABLE 4.2 (CONTINUED)

1 = Inadequate	3 = Minimal	5 = Good (in addition to 3)	7 = Excellent (in addition to 5)
FREE PLAY (AND CHOICE)			
Either little opportunity for free play or much of the day spent unsupervised. Inadequate toys, games, and equipment for children to use in free play.	Some opportunity for free play, with casual supervision as a safety precaution. Free play not seen as an educational opportunity (e.g., adult misses chance to help children think through solutions to conflicts with others, to encourage children to talk about what they are doing, or to introduce concepts relating to their play).	Ample and varied toys, games, and equipment provided for free play. Adult supervision provided on a regular basis (e.g., staff help children get materials they need; help them use materials that are hard to manage). Free play for a substantial portion of the day both indoors and outdoors.	Supervision used as an educational interaction (e.g., staff help children think through solutions to conflicts, encourage talk about activities, introduce concepts related to their play). New materials and experiences for free play added periodically.
SPACE FOR PRIVACY			
Children are not allowed to play alone or with a friend, protected from intrusion by others.	Although space is not specially set aside, children are allowed to find or create space for privacy (e.g., behind furniture, in the play ground). Space for privacy can be easily supervised by staff.	Space set aside for one or two children to play, protected from intrusion by others (e.g., no interruption rule, space out of sight). These spaces are accessible for use a substantial portion of the day	More than one space available. Staff set up activities for one or two children to use away from general group activities. Play alone activities are part of the curriculum for development of concentration, independence, and relaxation.

Source: Thelma Harms, Richard M. Clifford and Debby Cryer, *Early Childhood Environment Rating Scale, Revised Edition* (New York: Teachers College Press, Columbia University, 1998).

did expect, therefore got, children to use what they knew. In this way children gradually learned self control.

Centers that rate minimally adequate on most characteristics generally maintain a relatively safe and healthy facility and treat children kindly most of the time. However, these centers don't provide what children need and would enjoy. They do not provide a stimulating environment, a curriculum that encourages children's development, or a lively place where children want to spend their time. Children do not develop caring relations with individual staff members on whom they can depend and who take pleasure in encouraging their development. In a facility that receives a rating of 5, staff members relate warmly and effectively with each child, they engage in developmentally appropriate practices, and they are sensitive to individual children's needs, making appropriate accommodations to them. They create a place where children want to be. Center staff are sensitive to cultural differences among children and able to successfully integrate children with special needs into the community of children.

A room with mostly ratings of 5 on ECERS provides good, developmentally appropriate care, but by no means the best possible. Centers rating a 7 or "excellent" on most characteristics combine first rate facilities, furnishings, and materials that are specially designed for children's use with a lot of individualized attention, and more complex learning activities or projects that extend over a number of days, including activities that explore nature and scientific subjects. Staff are highly skilled in encouraging the development of mutual respect between children and adults, successfully teaching children self control. The result is an atmosphere that is usually tension-free, with children cooperating and sharing. To receive a grade of 7, a center needs a superlative, highly talented staff. Realistically we can't expect to see that very often.

The ECERS procedure does not provide a scheme that ranks the 43 categories by their importance. But taking an unweighted average of the grades given in each of the categories, as is sometimes done when an overall evaluation of a center classroom is being prepared, allows grades on the ten items listed in table 4.1 under "Activities" (art, blocks, sand, etc.) to outweigh the grades on the five important items under "Interaction" (discipline, staff-child interactions, interactions among children, etc.). For this reason, researchers who use the system sometimes combine its ratings with other quality measures that give more emphasis to teacher-child interactions or the other quality characteristics they are interested in studying.

Quality Care for Infants and Toddlers

Because babies and toddlers have needs that are very different from older children, the ECERS authors have developed a version of the rating system for this age group, called the Infant/Toddler Environment Rating Scale (ITERS).[18] We will see in chapter 5 that a large minority of these rooms are rated as poor, with an average score of less than 3 on the ITERS instrument, often because of poor sanitation practices and inadequate stimulation of the children.

In the low-rated rooms feeding and diapering conditions are usually unsanitary. Staff frequently forget to wash their hands before preparing food or feeding and after diapering or checking diapers. They may not sanitize the diapering surface or potties after each use or change diapers often enough. They may leave children on toilets too long, try to toilet train toddlers too early, or punish children for accidents. Staff do not keep children clean; runny noses abound, children's hands might not be washed after diapering; the same towel or washcloth may be used for different children. Emergency or other health records may be sloppy or nonexistant. Often, there are no written safety or emergency procedures. Babies can be left in cribs or playpens while awake, so they have no interaction with other babies. Infants may be put to bed with bottles rather than being held for bottle feeding. Staff do not talk much to children or respond to their bids for attention. They do not show much affection or they show favoritism; they provide very little physical contact. Staff members socialize with each other and this interferes with caregiving. Sometimes a caregiver will leave the children and cannot see, hear, or reach them. Usually, the rooms are understaffed.

In rooms rated "minimally adequate" (grade 3), sanitation has to be adequate. Diapers are changed as needed; caregivers wash hands after each diapering or diaper check, and wash children's hands after toileting and diapering. Staff talk and display affection to all the children and show warmth in physical contact. They help children who are hurt or upset. Bottle-fed infants are smiled at and held gently, not put to bed with a bottle. Cribs are used for sleeping, not extended play. Caregivers usually deal with negative social interaction among children. While there are discipline problems, staff usually maintain enough control to prevent children from hurting each other. There is some musical activity and some art materials, and books are used about three times a week. There is no safety problem.

Such centers are denied the rating "good" if staff do not focus attention on developing supportive, warm relationships with the children. They provide routine caregiving and do not focus on children's interests and development. They don't respond to infant signals and don't engage in responsive interaction. Talking in such centers is used mainly to control the child's behavior ("come here," "don't touch"). There is some response to children's attempts to communicate, but there is little talking with the child about objects and actions. In fact, there is little talking to the children at all.

For a rating of "good" (grade 5), sanitation problems must, of course, be absent. Staff members do a lot of talking to babies and toddlers, engage in verbal play, name and talk about objects and pictures and actions, read books to children and say nursery rhymes, respond to children's crying, gestures, sounds, words, and maintain eye contact while talking to the child. Children are taken from cribs when they are ready to get up. Caregivers are patient with a crying baby or an upset toddler. Staff are warm and affectionate, initiate verbal and physical play, and show delight in children's activity.

Babies and toddlers in care rated "good" use lots of age-appropriate toys to develop eye-hand coordination; they use toys and equipment indoors and outside in active physical play; are encouraged by staff to crawl and helped to walk; they play with blocks; they hear songs and are encouraged to sing along, clap, and dance as appropriate for their age. Babies get encouragement to feed themselves. At least one person with first aid training and CPR is on the premises at all times, and competent substitutes are familiar with children's special needs and emergency procedures

For a rating of "excellent," responsibility for a small number of children is given to one primary caregiver who develops a deep and long-lasting relationship with each child under her care. In many such centers the primary caregiver keeps a running diary with photos chronicling each child's development, and this journal is available for the parents to read/see and discuss. The caregiver varies her style of interaction to meet the children's individual needs. She encourages positive social interaction among the babies and toddlers, for instance, smiling and talking to babies who notice other children. Appropriate learning activities are planned and carried out with each child daily, alone or in a very small group. Caregivers work together in a team to create a nurturing environment and friendly safe place for children.

Quality in Family Child Care Homes

Family child care has been evaluated using criteria and instruments comparable to those used in centers. The authors of ECERS and ITERS have developed the Family Day Care Rating Scale (FDCRS), an adaptation of ECERS to the family child care environment.[19] The scale contains seven categories of care: space and furnishings for care and learning, basic care, language and reasoning, learning activities, social development, adult needs, and provisions for exceptional children. The values embodied in the ECERS approach also apply to family child care: warmth, attentiveness, lack of irritation and harshness, and emphasis on developmentally appropriate practices. It includes special sections useful to family providers, for instance, on safety precautions that may not be covered by state licensing rules, items on the use of TV, and balancing the provider's personal and caregiving responsibilities. The special section on caring for children with special needs is quite extensive.

Children have a different set of opportunities in a private home. Good family child care allows babies and children to experience family life and the kinds of activities that adults engage in in their own home—shopping, cooking, cleaning, repairing furniture and equipment, do-it-yourself projects, gardening, etc. Because the FDCRS derives from a system to assess child care centers, some critics argue it can lead to an unduly low evaluation of family child care providers who are more like good parents than good teachers. Children's experiences in family care may be just as developmentally appropriate, but they may be organized primarily around the daily activities of running a home or the special resources in the local neighborhood.[20]

Much of family child care is provided by members of the child's extended family, in particular by grandmothers. Using a FDCRS type instrument to judge the quality of care provided by a grandmother neglects the potentially most important part of relative care—the love and trust that builds up for a child, creating lifelong bonds of mutual caring and respect. Nevertheless, if early care is to include the educational opportunities of good, developmental preschool programs, then even care by a grandmother needs to be judged in part for its adequacy on the criteria used for centers. ECE professionals have yet to perfect appropriate criteria and identify benchmarks that will measure in these settings the same elements evaluated using the instruments for centers.

"STRUCTURAL" MEASURES OF QUALITY

To use the ECERS method, the evaluator must observe the actual *process* of caregiving and the environment that the children experience, and so these scales are said to measure "process quality." There are, however, a number of other measures that do not require observation, but rather reflect aspects of the provider's operation that might be expected to influence observed process quality. These include the ratio of caregivers to children, the size of the groups of children that are cared for together, the staff/provider education and training, the extent of staff/provider turnover, and the amount and quality of space used. They are called "structural quality" measures because they describe the structural features or inputs used in providing services.

Studies examining the relation between structural and process quality give reasonably consistent results. For centers, quality of services is strongly and positively related to the staffing ratio of children to adult caregivers, the education and training of center staff, and low staff turnover rates. In family child care where a provider cares for children in her own home, the provider's training and education are important predictors of process quality.[21]

There is an obvious connection between the ratio of caregivers to children and quality. If the adults are caring for more children than they have the capacity to handle with ease, we might expect to observe excessively strict discipline or no discipline, and few interactions that help children develop and learn. Centers with low ratios of staff to children have nobody to fill in for an absent staff person, or they may use a substitute who is totally unfamiliar with the children.[22] Overextended staff members tend to be harsh with the children and may be at risk of losing self-control as a result of constant stress. The staff are almost as victimized as the children under such conditions, and, consequently, many of them quit as soon as they find another job.

Traditionally, group size, or the number of children in a center classroom, has been considered an important contributor to good quality. Group size bears on, for instance, whether 2 groups of 8, each with a teacher, is better than 1 group of 16 with 2 teachers. Certainly, small group size and adequate space to separate sleeping areas from areas where babies are awake is important in the care of infants. Furthermore, many parents prefer to have their child in centers or family child care with small numbers of children in the same group. Although group size has not consistently been found to affect process quality, most early childhood professionals continue to consider it important, particularly for younger children.

The effect of group size and staffing ratios (usually the same thing) in family child care is not as clear-cut as in the case of centers.[23] In family child care, caring for one or two children should allow the caregiver to give the children a lot of attention and better quality services, and the NICHD study suggests that this is the case. However, another important study has found that professionally committed providers who engage in good business practices and care for close to the legal maximum number of children tend to provide better quality services than providers with less attachment to the field caring for smaller numbers of children.[24]

The level of general education and of formal ECE training also positively affect observed process quality.[25] Caregivers who lack training and education may react to children's behavior in ways that undermine the children's self-confidence and may have a poor repertoire of activities they can engage in with the children. A grounding in child development and language acquisition helps providers to tailor activities to children's needs and recognize signs of developmental delay. Recent research indicates that it is the *amount* of formal education that matters, and the more the better. It seems that the greater the percent of teachers with bachelor's degrees, the higher the center's process quality is likely to be. In particular, staff with bachelor's degrees are more sensitive to children's needs than are staff members with less education.[26] Some studies fail to find a relationship between process quality and the specialty training of the staff. However, most of those with a bachelor's degree working in the child care field have specialized in early childhood education, so it is difficult to separate the influence on quality of the specialized training from the influence of the general degree.

One would expect caregiver experience in child care to be a predictor of good quality services and positive caregiving behavior. Some studies have found that to be the case, but most have not.[27] The NICHD study found that for children at 24 and 36 months (but not at 6 and 15 months) caregivers with more experience gave more positive caregiving to study, children. On the other hand, Susan Kontos and colleagues' study Quality in Family Child Care and Relative Care found more experienced family child care providers to be slightly more detached from children in their care and to provide lower quality than less experienced providers.

High turnover rates in child care degrade process quality. If staff turnover is high, the children are less likely to be able to develop a warm, trusting relationship with their caregivers. Furthermore, continual turnover of staff inhibits development of a cohesive team of people working together to create a pleasant environment or carry out the center's educational philosophy.

Measures of structural quality have practical advantages over measures of process quality for some purposes. The information is more easily and cheaply gathered. (In fact it can be gathered in a short phone conversation or from written records, although the accuracy of such methods is by no means guaranteed.) They are more objective than the process quality measures, since the latter may vary depending on the skill, diligence, and judgement of the evaluator. Because of the ease of collecting the information, state regulators have depended heavily on the structural measures—their requirements typically concern staff-to-child ratios, group size, square footage per child, and safety features of the physical facilities.

Good early care and education is difficult to achieve without adequate staffing ratios, low turnover, adequate wages, and college-level training. The NICHD study has reported, for instance, that 36-month-old children have better achievement scores when they attend centers that meet more professional standards (staffing ratios, group size, caregiver education, and caregiver training).[28] However, these structural quality characteristics do not guarantee good care. They are preconditions for good process quality, necessary but not sufficient.[29] A staff, even if it is of adequate size, trained and well paid, may contain individuals who are harsh and have no talent for caring for children. Or a center may be poorly managed by a director who exerts little effective leadership. Only on-the-spot observation of process quality can detect problems of that sort. Nevertheless, a center without good ratios, trained staff, and low staff turnover will not achieve good quality.

CRITICS OF THE DEVELOPMENTALLY APPROPRIATE STANDARD OF QUALITY

Basing good quality on developmentally appropriate practice as interpreted by NAEYC and the authors of ECERS is widely but not universally accepted in the ECE profession. Some Christian fundamentalists object to aspects of developmentally appropriate practice as interpreted by NAEYC, as do some early childhood experts concerned about early education for ethnic and racial minorities and children with developmental delays.

The objections from some religious groups reflect a desire of these congregations to incorporate early childhood education into their spiritual ministry. Some of these groups are concerned with specific content and have been particularly critical of NAEYC for publishing a book that advocates an antibias curriculum for early care and education programs.[30] They do not want to condone divorce or homosexuality or even discuss these topics with children who are affected by them. Some are concerned with the maintenance of traditional sex roles and object to any efforts at encouraging the children to take part in activities that have in the past been reserved for the opposite sex. Efforts to teach children that there is more than one kind of family have been condemned by groups on the far right of the political spectrum as antifamily and anti-Christian and have led to the development of alternative training programs that include a Christian education component.[31] In some cases, as in North Carolina, Virginia, and Georgia, these attacks have been used by politically conservative groups to try to block state improvements in licensing standards.[32]

The main objection of these groups is not to developmentally appropriate practices, but to teaching about lifestyles that they consider to be anti-Christian or anti-American. To counteract the influence of the NAEYC, the Association of Christian Schools International (ACSI) has developed its own child care accreditation process that incorporates spiritual and age-appropriate educational objectives in its accreditation process.[33]

Another set of critics of developmentally appropriate practice has asserted that the standards as originally developed by NAEYC ignored the learning styles and needs of children from minority subcultures in the United States and of children with developmental disabilities.[34] They contend that children from different subcultures learn in different ways, that these differences may not be adequately accounted for within the standard model, and that failure to incorporate these approaches can inhibit learning by children from minority subcultures.[35]

One of these critics is Bruce Mallory, a developmental psychologist who considers the mainstream view of what is developmentally appropriate as overly psychological, building mainly on cognitive developmental theory and research. Mallory argues that other approaches to early childhood education grounded in different theoretical approaches may be applicable to children from deprived backgrounds or with developmental impairments. To encourage learning for children from other ethnic and racial backgrounds, cultural norms accepted by the children's ethnic or racial group may need to be understood and taken into consideration in organizing learning activities.

In particular, children with developmental impairments need to learn to adapt to their environment through training-oriented learning based on a more functional model of behavior change. Teachers need guidance in planning and evaluating programs for young children with special needs. Interventions to help these children need to be integrated into classroom activities and routines.

NAEYC has responded to these criticisms by revising their accreditation criteria to give a broader definition of developmental practice. It remains to be seen how effectively providers can incorporate these criteria into their daily practice.[36] Success depends on engaging providers in a serious study of cultural diversity, attracting more trained teachers into the field from culturally diverse backgrounds, helping teachers to learn from children and their parents, adopting a standard of diversity in staffing to assure role models of success for children, and avoiding the unconscious absorption by children of the dominant attitudes about minority cultures and developmental disabilities.

While we agree that early care and education needs to be both developmentally appropriate and culturally sensitive, we think it important to emphasize that children, whatever their racial or ethnic background or the income bracket of their parents, will need to be able to succeed in the mainstream culture of an industrialized society. In most cases, this is what their parents want for them. Children also will need to acquire the skills, manners, and sensitivity to others necessary to lead productive lives in a future society that will undoubtedly be more ethnically diverse than today's society, and their child care experience should help them to do that.

HOW CHILDREN BENEFIT FROM QUALITY CARE

Does child care quality, as defined by the experts, make a difference to children? There are really two issues here. The first issue, which we think particularly important, is the experiences and feelings of the children themselves. The second is the effect that quality has on children's development and future success in life.

A large fraction of the nation's children spend a considerable portion of their waking hours in care. We would argue that it is not asking too much that they be provided a happy, secure, and sanitary experience, one that is not boring and not frustrating. The descriptions we have given of care at various levels of quality earlier in this chapter can be used to make an informed judgement about the experiences children would have in care at each level. It is not difficult to come to the conclusion that children in facilities rated "inadequate" have a very bad time and actually suffer in such a harsh environment. The poor sanitation in such facilities is also likely to result in extra infections, contributing to the children's misery and both their parents' and caregivers' sick days and loss of time at work. Children in facilities rated "minimally adequate" are probably bored a good part of the time, many of them learning all too soon to just put up with, if not actively dislike, school. Children in facilities rated "good" are in care that is considerate of their feelings, and that keeps them interested, and that allows them to enjoy themselves while learning.[37] Such care is not, as some conservative critics claim, a lavish indulgence.

The authors visited a center that would have been rated "minimally adequate," which illustrates well why this level of quality is below the one we should aspire to provide. For the first hour, all the children at this center (33 of them) sat together on the floor in front of the three teachers who were sitting on chairs. Two of the teachers took no part in the proceedings, so there might as well have been only one. For almost an hour the children were made to sit still, listening to and singing along with an audio tape. If a child moved in any significant way or opened his or her mouth to do anything other than to sing, the lead teacher pointed at the guilty child and hissed loudly, disgracing the child in front of all the others. After the audio tape, the entire group traipsed into another room and proceeded to color, all using the same page in the same coloring book. The children, many of whom were sons and daughters of professional people and small business owners, were being kept safe, clean, and well fed. Clearly, however, they were bored and restless. A day spent that way is stagnating to their development and could be described as a punishment.

Good quality child care is especially helpful to children at risk of school failure. In particular, children from economically deprived backgrounds receive much less opportunity to develop their language skills. Child development psychologists Betty Hart and Todd Risley made extensive monthly observations of language interactions between parents and their youngest child for 42 families over the first three years of the child's life. They found an important relation between children's verbal abilities and the opportunities for language acquisition at home.[38] Utterances per hour and average number of different words used per hour by welfare parents were much lower than for parents who had professional careers, and the former were less responsive to or interested in their children's talk. The vocabulary size of three-year-old welfare children was less than half that of the three-year-old children of professional parents. Even more striking, the vocabulary size of the welfare-dependent *parents* was smaller than that of the three-year-old *children* in professional families. These handicaps acquired in early years by these young children persisted through age ten.

Hart and Risley emphasize that parents who are successful in cultivating their children's speech do so by continual encouragement, and that the emotional adult-child relationship is essential to the process. All children need that kind of encouragement, and those whose parents cannot provide it need to get it as part of their child care.[39]

The NICHD study findings indicate that sensitive and responsive caregiving, particularly language stimulation, are important to children's cognitive and language development throughout early childhood for all children. Even after taking into consideration home environment and children's attributes, children in better quality care tended to score higher on cognitive tests.[40] Furthermore, the longer children were in good quality nonparental care the greater the positive effect; at 54 months children who experienced better quality of child care over time scored higher on pre-academic skills, including language skills and performed better on short-term memory tasks than children who had had lower quality care. However, higher quality settings may not improve children's compliance or reduce behavior problems.[41]

Modest long-term effects of good quality center care on children's school performance and social-emotional adjustment were found in the Cost, Quality, and Child Outcomes study (CQO).[42] Children who had been in higher quality centers performed better at the end of the second grade than children who had been in lower quality centers, particularly with respect to their math skills. Closer teacher-child relationships in child care positively influenced children's social development through second grade.[43]

Initial evaluations of model early intervention programs—which have characteristics similar to high-quality child care programs, but which were mostly restricted to children from impoverished backgrounds—demonstrated that the children made significant immediate gains in their cognitive and language development.[44] However, these kind of gains tended to fade out over time.[45] This has been seized on by conservative critics who have argued against continuing appropriations for Head Start. But what these results suggest is not that help does these children no good, but that they need special help for longer periods of time than Head Start provides.

When researchers looked beyond IQ and looked at other kinds of benefits to the children in the early intervention programs they found important and lasting positive results. Grade retention and special education rates were lower for children in the programs than for those in comparison groups. The Abecedarian and High/Scope Perry Preschool programs involving poor, often low-ability children, had remarkably positive effects on participating children in terms of high school graduation and college attendance rates, employment as young adults, reductions in use of public assistance, and delays in giving birth.[46] Evaluation of the much larger Child-Parent Centers (CPC), an ongoing program in the Chicago public schools, shows similar effects.[47] Although achievement scores for CPC participants exceeded those of the comparison group only until 14 years of age, the percent of these children graduating from high school was significantly higher than for control group children, and they had less involvement with juvenile courts.

The preponderance of the evidence suggests that quality care has important and lasting benefits for children's development and school achievement and subsequent success in life.

The Importance of the First Three Years

Neuroscience has made major breakthroughs in the last 20 years in explaining the process of brain development and the extraordinary changes in brain structure and neurochemistry that begin before birth and continue through early childhood. Child care advocates have publicized this research to dramatize the importance of providing stimulating and caring environments very early in children's lives, when their brains are developing most rapidly.[48]

Brain development involves, among other things, the development and migration of brain cells to where they belong in the brain, and the formation of connections, or synapses, between nerve cells. These processes involve a complex set of interactions between gene activity and environmental circumstances both inside and outside the child. When the baby learns physical coordination, visual acuity, auditory responses, and language, synapses develop to embody those skills. The stability and strength of these synaptic connections seems to be governed by their use—the frequency of firing of the connections. These "wiring systems" guide the person's thoughts, memories, feelings, and behavior.[49]

Brain neurochemistry—the production and use of neurotransmitters—also affects brain development, both positively and negatively. Environmental conditions also play a role in regulating brain neurochemistry. In particular, abuse or neglect can create serious risks for healthy brain development. High levels of stress hormones such as cortisol have toxic effects, overactivating neural pathways that regulate responses to fear and stress. They increase activity in the area of the brain related to vigilance and arousal so that children who have experienced high levels of stress are likely to react even to the slightest stress via hyperactivity or anxiety. Continual and unpredictable stress can affect brain development so that the child grows up more fearful and less socially competent.

So far, less is known about the effect that exposure to rich experiences has on children. However, animal experiments indicate that such experiences have a positive effect on brain development and learning. Rats reared in complex cages containing play objects and other animals outperform other rats as adults and have more mature synoptic structures. Positive effects diminished over time when the animals were removed from the enriched environment, leading one set of reviewers to liken early intervention to a tetanus vaccine, which requires booster shots, rather than a smallpox vaccination, which provides permanent protection.

The research on the brain does not strengthen the case for mother care or for nonmother care. However, it does strengthen the case for care that emphasizes the development of deep relationships, responsive interactions, and stimulating experiences. In the case of children who do not receive adequate caring and stimulation at home, good quality care outside of the home has to be considered important. For children who have suffered from stressful home or community environments, interventions can help them compensate for deficits that might arise from these conditions. We can look forward to more guidance in the future from brain research. Existing research helps confirm that the early years of a child's life is a period of rapid learning, providing formative experiences that influence the individual in later life. A crucial part of early learning is becoming good at and learning to enjoy acquiring knowledge, developing the self-confidence of a good student. Mediocre early care experience can stifle this self-confidence and interest in school.

HOW HIGH A STANDARD SHOULD WE ADOPT?

As we have seen, the developers of the ECERS method of evaluating the quality of child care have attached the characterization "minimal" (meaning minimally adequate) to scores of 3. They have attached the label "good" to scores of 5. Academic researchers in psychology and education who specialize in child care issues generally advocate applying the term "developmentally appropriate" only to care that scores 5 or above.

These labels are judgmental, and, of course, that is the point of the whole evaluation exercise. They are intended to be used as signals to parents and to those considering public policy. They convey a message as to what kind of care should not be tolerated and what should be the ideal. If one accepts these standards, they define what constitutes moral behavior toward children and carry implications for what parents should do and for public policy. After all, it is not easy to defend care that is "less than minimally adequate." Nor is it easy to advocate anything less than getting all children into care that is at the very least "good," to say nothing of "excellent." Could the "quality care" that we are told we need be care that is less than "good"?

As we shall see in the next chapter, the CQO survey, which used the ECERS together with some other evaluative methodologies, found that the most common overall score for centers turned out to be 4, which was also the average grade. The ECERS authors did not attach a label to 4, but the CQO investigators decided to label centers with grades around 4 as "mediocre." They might have chosen a less pejorative term, such as "fair" or "middling." That they did not is a reflection of their judgement that a quality lower than 5 falls distinctly short of what is desirable for all children.

The question to which we now turn is whether this definition of "good" should be the standard we should recommend to parents, the standard we should demand in child care that public dollars are subsidizing, and the standard we should enforce in licensing or accreditation inspections. Not everybody agrees that we should strive for that level of quality in any or all of those cases. Some have accused the ECE professionals of advocating "Cadillac" care that dictates a standard that is beneficial to the profession but is extravagant in terms of real need.[50] As we have seen, the libertarians of the Cato Institute believe that parents' tastes and choices are the only ones that are pertinent.[51] Parents' "choices" are, of course, limited by what they can afford, but the Cato libertarians oppose any government help to parents of any kind. Libertarians also tend to oppose government regulation of privately run child care facilities. In effect, they argue for no publicly enforced standards at all.

Psychologist Sandra Scarr has argued that we should not set standards as high as those advocated by the ECE community. Scarr is a well-known academic expert on child care who served for a time as the head of KinderCare, the largest national for-profit chain of child care centers. The for-profit chains have generally lobbied against attempts to raise publicly mandated standards, even in states where the standards are relatively low. Most of their clients are middle-class people who, under current policies, get little help from government with their child care bills. The for-profit chains worry that higher quality standards would raise costs, force them to raise prices, and motivate some of their customers to seek cheaper and possibly lower-quality alternatives. Scarr argues that the type of care experts label as "mediocre" is all children really need, since much research seems to show that home environment counts most in promoting their development and school achievement. Her main concern is affordability.[52]

Scarr seems intent on defending for-profit centers, chains in particular, that provide medium quality care that working families can afford and in doing so implicitly limits the applicability of her assessment to the middle-class children who are KinderCare's main customers. She ignores the evidence about the success that quality early childhood programs have had in improving the in-school performance of "at-risk" children. Moreover, as we have seen, the CQO and NICHD studies indicate that benefits of high-quality care are not restricted to children from impoverished backgrounds. When middle-class children are given high-quality child care they have a decidedly better time, and they do better in school than those who have had inferior care.

However, even though quality care does improve children's performance, the argument that we must consider costs when setting quality standards is a serious one. It cannot be countered by saying "Nothing but the best for our kids." Common sense tells us that we can not disregard cost, and, indeed, we do not disregard it in any of the decisions, public or private, that we make.

To judge this issue, we need to consider what achieving the experts' standard of "good" might cost and to contemplate how children will be affected if they continue to be placed in care below that level. Choosing the appropriate level of care to pay for is not a scientific matter but a matter of values. Parents and government agencies must consider the price that has to be paid for various grades of care, as well as their taste, priorities, ethics, and the attractiveness of alternative uses of the funds.

We estimate that at present increasing quality from grade 4 to grade 5 on ECERS would raise center costs by about $2,000 per child per year. This is the estimated amount that would have to be added to a center's cost if the wages of center employees were to be brought up to market wage rates for people with their same amount of education and experience. (In chapter 8 we describe the scandalously low wages in this industry.)

Are parents interested in developmentally appropriate care? Surveys of parents reveal that they are concerned about the health and safety of their children. In addition, they want a nurturing, loving provider, particularly for their infants and toddlers. They want older, preschool-aged children in a program that will prepare them for school. The increasing use of center-based programs testifies to this parent concern.

Parents worry about the quality of care their children receive even though they may not be able to articulate clearly what makes good quality. Dr. Sheila Kamerman, a leading researcher on child care, provided a telling anecdote to one of the authors. A group of low-income working mothers all declared themselves initially quite happy with their children's care. But as the conversation went on, the mothers opened up about their unhappiness with the quality of care they were forced to settle for, and some of them wept.

Most parents cannot be expected to choose their child care on the sole basis of quality, and some cannot give quality a lot of weight. But there is little evidence that they disagree in any fundamental way with ECE experts about how to define good quality. What differences there are tend to disappear as parents learn more about the benefits of good quality services. For example, in a focus group study of parent discussions, initially good quality mainly meant that their children were being loved, were emotionally secure, and were receiving attention from the provider. They equated quality child care with good parenting and did not consider child care workers' training very important. However, after they were assigned the task of identifying specific outcomes they wanted from good quality, they realized that they were including components that required trained providers.[53]

Most simply, at present a considerable proportion of parents do not have the luxury of being able to purchase good quality services. Many parents, including those close to the poverty line, get no government help with their child care bills. One of the reasons we advocate large public subsidies for child care is to reduce the economic constraints on choosing care so that parents have less need to scrimp when buying care, have more choice, and can concern themselves with the quality of services. Another is that subsidies, together with better regulation and incentives for better quality, should have the effect of improving the quality of the supply of care.

What standards should subsidized care meet? While we generally agree with the rating scheme embodied in the ECERS method and consider the labels attached to the various levels as reasonable, there would be a severe problem in restricting public funding to providers rated "good" by such a method for the foreseeable future. As we shall detail in the next chapter, it would be unrealistic, given the current level of quality, to require subsidized programs to meet this standard. It is unlikely that the child care industry in the United States would be capable anytime soon of delivering care at that level to substantially all children. Rather, we will suggest in later chapters a series of measures to enable and encourage child care providers to work toward this goal and more stringent regulation to require those facilities at the bottom to improve.

In considering the longer term, it is important to look beyond existing funding constraints and to think what mandated quality might be desirable in an era when more government help to parents would be available. When and if that era arrives, the funds to finance high-quality care will be forthcoming if a good case for them can be made. The standard of 5 does not appear to be impractically high, and well trained providers should be able to meet it. Public money and stricter regulation ought to be devoted to getting as much child care as possible up to the "good" range. Among other things, that would mean subsidizing and requiring ECE education for those working in the child care field and higher pay for ECE teachers.

Obviously, everybody must come to his or her own conclusion. The authors do not consider the standards the experts specify as excessive. When we look at the kinds of centers that are assigned such scores, as we have done in this chapter, the labels seem to us reasonable and appropriate. We don't think it appropriate to label a level of quality that neglects children's learning and confines them to hours of boredom as "good." Readers might perform a small armchair experiment: Would you be willing to enroll a child of yours in a center rated as minimally adequate? Would you consider a "good quality" center rated near 5 on the ECERS scale as rather more than your child needs? For that matter, what standard of care would you have wanted for yourself?

Finally, in thinking about quality standards, the enjoyment and security that children experience in higher quality care and the boredom and frustration they feel in lower quality care need to be taken into account. European critics of U.S. child care public policy have commented on our need to justify public expenditures on child care on pragmatic, utilitarian grounds—that better child care will have an economic payoff. Americans, they say, are obsessed by economic results and evidently don't feel compelled to pay more for child rearing unless there is proof that the children will become more productive adults. In contrast, in Scandinavia and other European countries child care and early childhood education are fundamental rights of every young family and their children. High quality services are largely publicly funded and often publicly provided. Even in this era, when Europeans are questioning their social welfare programs, they are expanding rather than contracting public support for early childhood programs.[54]

Is the prevailing attitude in the United States a case of pragmatism gone amuck? Do we only care about children for what we can gain from them? Are they merely economic investment goods? Most Americans agree that children deserve happy childhoods. Unlike most European countries we haven't considered it a public responsibility to provide such childhoods, but now that the majority of children live their lives scheduled around parents' working hours, we argue that social policy should respond to children's needs and create appropriate settings for them.

CHAPTER FIVE

The Report Card: How Much of America's Child Care is Good?

"In 1996, after a year's maternity leave, I went back to work full time as a reporter at *The Denver Post*, and Will went full time to a family child care provider named Katherine. My husband and I had chosen Katherine after I interviewed 10 different providers. She was licensed by the state and had been in business 23 years. I thought her house was a little small for six children, but there were lots of toys and great outdoor play areas. She did things with the kids, like baking cookies, setting up a wading pool, and walks to the park. She was very safety conscious. Several current and former clients gave her great references.

Shortly after I got back to work, we started a team report about the federal welfare reform legislation that would take effect in 1997. I took on the story about child care. Everyone seemed to agree, without good, affordable child care, getting welfare moms permanently off the dole was going to be a real uphill battle.

I dove into the assignment, talking with welfare moms, child care center directors, folks from the state licensing office, people who talked about the shortage of qualified caregivers. ("Why would someone work in child care for $5 an hour when they can work in retail for twice as much and get benefits?" one source said.)

I found a 1995 study, *Cost, Quality, and Child Outcomes in Child Care Centers*, that had disturbing, close-to-home information. The researchers had evaluated child care centers in four states—Colorado, Connecticut, California and North Carolina—100 in each state. I was concerned that they ranked the overall quality of child care in my state as mediocre and observed very few good quality centers. The researchers found that Colorado's caregivers had less education and gave up more earning power than their counterparts in other states. And they said that Colorado kids in child care were behind in math and language skills.

But here's the fact that really floored me: Most of the care observed in the study was mediocre, but the vast majority of parents said their kids were getting excellent care.

Here I was, a professional with two college degrees who'd done a reasonably exhaustive search for good child care. What about parents who have less time, money, skill to spend on the task? And what about me? Was my son in mediocre child care and I didn't even know it?"

—Mary George, journalist and writer, Denver, Colorado

The quality of care that the children of working parents receive is not a minor issue—it affects the daily lives of almost 60 percent of our children.[1] Over 10 million preschool children in the United States are now in need of child care because their parents are working. In addition, 38 million school-aged youngsters have working parents and could benefit from after-school care. The 1996 overhaul of the welfare system requiring poor parents to take jobs has increased the number of children needing nonmaternal child care. Children in care spend considerable amounts of time there; preschool children of working mothers average 35 hours a week; younger infants and toddlers spend even more time in child care than older preschoolers.[2]

Child care and education services also serve many children whose mothers don't hold jobs. Increasingly, such families are sending their children to formal early education; in 1990 almost a third of nonemployed mothers had their three- and four-year-olds enrolled in center-based programs. Including all types of centers and preschools, about 41 percent of children are enrolled in formal programs by the age of three, 65 percent by the time the children are four years old, and 75 percent if they are five years old and not yet in school. Increasingly, school-aged children participate in center-based or before-and-after-school programs; the percentage rose from 7 percent in 1984 to 16 percent in 1990.[3]

In this chapter, we describe the different forms of nonparental child care in the United States and look at the research that has been done to see how much of this child care provides a safe and enjoyable experience, promotes social skills and cognitive development, and thus can reasonably be labeled "good." We also consider how much child care can be labeled poor because it inflicts a difficult, even painful, experience on the children, presents a danger to health and safety, and stifles development. Finally, we address how much child care falls in between these two extremes. As we shall see, there is a distressing amount of poor care and a paucity of good care. A great deal of the care that is given to American children is of an in-between quality, not low enough to deserve being called "poor" but not high enough to deserve the judgement "good." It is perhaps best characterized as "mediocre" or "fair."[4]

The state of our knowledge about the quality of care children in the United States receive is far from satisfactory. Most of the research done on quality has been concentrated on child care centers. Much less research has been done on the quality of care given by parents, other relatives, family child care (care by nonrelatives in the provider's home), and care by nannies, maids, and babysitters (nonrelatives who care for a child in the child's home). Moreover, few comparisons of the quality in these various modes of care exist. While it has become obvious that it would be desirable to upgrade the quality of the nation's child care centers and family child care provision, little attention has been paid to the possibility of quality improvements that might result from switching children from some modes of care to others—for example from nannies, relatives, and unlicensed family child care to licensed family child care, centers, and preschools.

WHERE DO CHILDREN RECEIVE CARE?

In 1994 of the more than ten million children under five with working mothers, roughly one-third were cared for primarily in their own home, one-third got care in someone else's home, and one-third got care in organized child care facilities (either child care centers or nursery/preschools).[5] An additional three and a half million children with nonemployed mothers also went regularly to some form of early education or care.[6]

Almost half of these preschool children spend time in more than one child care arrangement, with children of working parents using, on average, slightly over 2 different arrangements per week.[7] Each switch of a child from one arrangement to another in the course of a day contributes to the stress on both children and parents. The patched-together system that many parents are forced to use testifies to how far away we are from a hassle-free child care system.

Organized child care facilities (child care centers, nursery schools, or preschools) are the single most common form of care for those under five. The usage of centers has increased steadily, from 6 percent in 1965 to 32 percent in 1997.[8] Almost 20 percent of children under one year old were cared for in organized child care facilities, and the proportion of children cared for that way increases sharply with the age of the child. Centers enroll a larger percentage of children from middle- or upper-middle income than from poor families. Although parents in all income groups tend to prefer center programs for their older preschoolers, many cannot afford it.[9]

Care by the child's father was the second most common form of care, representing about 18 percent of cases in 1994.[10] The father who provides care while the mother works may be unemployed or out of the labor force, work part time, or work on a different shift than the mother.[11] Fathers provide more primary care in families with lower incomes, in families with a larger number of preschool children, and when the mother works part time. In addition to the children primarily cared for by fathers, 16 percent are cared for by grandparents, 9 percent by other relatives, and 5 percent by the mother herself while working (mainly at home). All in all, for almost half of the children of working mothers, a relative is their primary child care provider, either in the child's home or in the relative's home.

Relative care is used more extensively by mothers working a nonday shift, since most other sources of care are unavailable outside of standard business hours, and by the poor. About 40 percent of black and Hispanic children with working mothers are cared for by grandparents and relatives other than the parents, compared to 21 percent of white children.

Single parents are much more likely than couples to leave their children with a grandparent. Low-earning single mothers who have not secured a child care subsidy from the state need the free or almost-free care a relative might provide if they are to keep a roof over their heads and buy food. However, because, increasingly, grandmothers are also working away from home, single mothers making a transition from welfare to work may not be able to count on grandparents for child care to the same degree as mothers who were already working prior to the reform of welfare in 1996.[12] Many women have remained on welfare precisely because they have not had a grandparent or some other relative available to care for their children.

Many of the parents who rely on relatives to care for their children believe it is the most suitable arrangement. This attitude, apparently, is more common among Hispanic parents than non-Hispanic black and white families.[13]

Millions of parents rely on family child care provided by a nonrelative in her (or his) own home. The use of family child care as a percentage of total caregiving arrangements has been on the decline, from 22 percent of arrangements in 1977 to 15 percent in 1994. Increasingly, parents are shifting older preschool children out of family child care (and out of relative care) and into centers, which usually provide more structured educational activities. Family child care providers care for only 15 percent of subsidized children, suggesting that families who, thanks to the subsidy, have the ability to send their children to center care tend to do so.

About a fifth of the children under five years old are in unregulated family child care subject to no oversight other than that provided by the parents.[14] Family child care providers caring for no more than two or three children are exempt from licensing in many states, and of those required to have a license, many don't get one. Relative care is usually legally exempt from licensing and inspection. So is care given by nannies and babysitters in the child's own home.

As of 1995, 24 million of the 38 million school-aged children between the ages of 5 and 14 lived in families with working mothers who made arrangements for the children's out-of-school time.[15] Arrangements differed based on the age of the children and the family's economic circumstances. More than three-quarters of these children used multiple child care arrangements, averaging more than three per week per child. Parents rely heavily on each other. The Census Bureau reported that only three and a half percent of school-aged children are enrolled in formal center-based child care and about 12 percent are in family child care. Particularly in higher income families and for older children, families rely on out-of-school enrichment activities (sports, clubs, etc.) as a form of child care; 35 percent of children in the age group participate in these activities.

Finally, some children take care of themselves. Only one-tenth of one percent of children under five not cared for full time by their mother spent time alone in 1995, but that comprised 13,000 children. Nine percent of such children from 5 to 11 years old took care of themselves, and 41 percent of children ages 12 to 14 did so, on average, for seven hours per week.[16]

FULL-TIME CHILD CARE CENTERS

Almost half of the centers that provide full-time child care are operated as profit-making businesses, most of them owned by individuals or partnerships. National chains such as KinderCare, La Petite, and Children's World make up about 13 percent of the center market and 28 percent of for-profit centers.[17] The nonprofit providers are a mixture of public and private agencies. Nonprofit centers can be operated by individuals, by religious bodies, by colleges or universities, by hospitals, and by local public, charitable, or community agencies; a small proportion are operated by public schools. Some of the centers operated by individuals are nonprofit in name only—the chief operator gets the profits in the form of salary.

Almost one out of every six centers is housed in a religious facility (some of these are part-day preschools) and it is one of the fastest growing sectors. The Roman Catholic Church, with over 5,000 centers, and the Southern Baptist Convention, with 4,100, are the nation's largest providers of center care. Increasingly, these centers are being operated directly by the church or synagogue rather than by a separate nonprofit organization that rents or partners with the church. These trends reflect a growing interest in child care provision by the national denominational headquarters, who are concerned about expanding faith-based early education and making use of their physical facilities.[18]

Pros and Cons of Centers

Most child care centers today aim to incorporate traditional nursery school philosophy into a full-day program, and many offer part-day preschool programs to accommodate to needs of their clientele. Centers provide stability and dependability that help working parents get to their jobs reliably. Because of the organized nature of centers, and because generally they are licensed, they can provide the educational, health, and safety features parents want for their children. Since the staff consists of more than a single person, everybody who works in a center is subject to at least some degree of oversight.

Centers are normally safer than family child care for other reasons as well. Most centers follow (often due to state requirements) written and posted

health and safety rules; written identification of who can take the
center; daily records of infants' sleeping, eating, and diaper cha
weekly menus; and a special kitchen staff or established caterer
centers have a markedly lower rate of Sudden Infant Death Syndr
family day care homes, presumably because the caregivers in centers are instructed to put infants to sleep on their back.[19] Care is taken to protect allergic children, and centers can provide health and safety education for the families they serve. Moreover, they can promote immunization of children, and staff are trained to spot and report abuse.

Although children in centers are more prone to contracting infectious diseases, recent research suggests that infants in day care are at a considerably lower risk for asthma and allergies in later childhood. A possible explanation is that exposure to microbes early in life may help babies' immune systems develop properly. In the last 25 years there has been a marked reduction in childhood infections, and good health practices in centers can be very effective in controlling communicable diseases.[20]

As a result of an institutionalized approach to safety, children in centers have less exposure to sharp knives, poisonous materials, fire, and excessively hot water; therefore, they are less prone to accidents and accidental death than children in family child care, who, in turn, are safer than children in their own home.[21] Many states require centers to have doors locked from the outside to protect children from intruders, or they have a receptionist who monitors visitors. Parents and staff move about in centers freely, so that child abuse, particularly sexual abuse, is less likely to occur there than in a home where the provider is not as subject to observation.

Center services are preferred by many families for the early education experiences they can provide. Other modes of care have a hard time competing with centers when it comes to the provision of toys, outdoor play equipment, books, and learning materials. Centers have scheduled activities where children hear stories, sing and play games together, and go on field trips. Centers serving mainly children of working parents may provide before- and after-school programs, transportation to and from school, summer programs, and music and swimming lessons.[22]

Centers can have some distinct disadvantages. Children may get less individual attention, and there can be less intimacy or affection displayed in a center than in a family child care home or with a relative. Also, being with a sizeable group of other children for long hours may be a harassing experience for some children, and this is a particular danger if the staff allows the center to become chaotic. Larger centers take on an institutional quality that many parents want to avoid for their children. Centers have inflexible hours, ordinarily operating 10 to 12 hours a day, often from 7:00 A.M. until 6:00 P.M., and sometimes for a shorter time period, so they may not fit the scheduling needs of parents. Very few are open at night or on weekends.

Center Quality

How good are centers in the United States? How many of them actually nurture children, promote their development, contribute to their sense of well-being, and prepare them for success in school? How many centers are places where children are happy to be? Four large studies of centers based on evaluations of quality using the methods described in chapter 4 have been completed since 1990.[23] All four report similar results. In addition, the NICHD study looked at the quality of the centers and of the other forms of non-maternal care received by the children in that study, using different methods of assessment.

The most recent of the four studies of centers using the Early Childhood Environment Rating system (ECERS) methodology was the Cost, Quality, and Child Outcomes Study (CQO), based on evaluations made in 1993 on 100 randomly selected centers in each of four states. For-profit centers made up half the sample. Trained observers intensively and systematically studied two rooms in each center, one containing preschool children and a second containing infants and toddlers, if the center served children of that age.

For care given to preschoolers (three years old and above) most of the rooms were rated as at least minimally adequate (an average score of 3 or more on a 7 point scale). But high quality care—as opposed to minimally adequate or mediocre—was relatively rare. Only 24 percent of preschool rooms and 8 percent of infant or toddler rooms received care rated "good" or "developmentally appropriate" (an average score of 5 or more). Unfortunately, the study found that downright poor quality care—care that may be harmful to children's development and even their health—is far from rare. Of the rooms for preschool age children (two to five years old), 10 percent were rated "poor" (an overall score of less than 3) and a shocking 40 percent of infant/toddler rooms were rated as providing poor quality.

The poor ITERS scores given to infant rooms are due in large part to poor sanitation practices—failure of providers to wash their hands after diapering each child or to wash diaper-changing surfaces and children's hands and toys—and to careless feeding practices. The average score for health practices in infant rooms in the CQO study was 2.5, a rating below the minimally adequate rating of 3. At least 50 percent of all infant/toddler classrooms received a score of 1 for general health practice, indicating that tasks were not handled in a sanitary way to avoid spread of germs. This disgusted comment by one of the evaluators in the CQO study graphically describes a commonly-observed practice: "I went into an infant room and a very young girl was assigned to change the diapers. She changed seven diapers and washed the pad down; she didn't wash her hands. Then it was time for snack. She went and got the snack. She gave the food with those hands that had just changed seven diapers. You cringe."[24]

While sanitary problems in infant and toddler care were a major concern, they were by no means the only problem. In poor quality rooms there was little use of toys to foster physical, social, emotional, and intellectual growth; children were rarely held, cuddled, talked to, played with, encouraged to sit up or take a step or say a word. Toddler rooms were particularly problematic. This is a difficult, willful, and confusing time for many children, and it is important to help toddlers learn to talk, gain self-control, and learn about the world. Evaluators commented that in the lower quality centers staff don't expect enough of toddlers and don't offer them enough variety of things to do or play with.

Observers in the CQO study saw numerous centers in which children spent a lot of time waiting for the next schedule change—waiting for lunch, waiting for the teacher's attention, waiting for nap time, waiting to get up from nap, waiting to go outside to play. They observed centers where children wandered about aimlessly with no adult attention and where children were unfairly reprimanded. They saw centers with too many large group activities that interested only a fraction of children, regimented mealtimes when adults ignored children except to discipline them, and excessively long nap times in which children were required to remain on their mats long after they had awakened.

Observers gave grades below "good" when they noted missed learning opportunities and the inability of well-meaning staff members to extend play or encourage problem-solving because of lack of training. In such centers, they saw staff undoing a child's initiative or belittling the positive things children had learned on their own.

Because, as we have noted, the ECERS/ITERS method of evaluation puts a relatively low weight on the sympathy, attention, and kindness with which the adults treat the children in their care, the CQO researchers also used the Arnett

Caregiver Interaction Scale (CIS) to evaluate these caregiver behaviors. Lead teachers were rated on their sensitivity, harshness, detachment from children, and permissiveness.[25] They found that teachers in a majority of centers were treating children for the most part in a kindly fashion. Other studies have also reported that children are more likely to receive adequate caregiving than developmentally appropriate services.[26] Nevertheless, in over a third of infant rooms and almost half of the preschool rooms in the CQO study, positive caregiving behavior was not often observed.

Another source of information on quality in child care centers, as well as in other forms of child care, is the study sponsored by the National Institute of Child Health and Human Development (NICHD) referred to in chapter 4.[27] This research team has evaluated the quality of nonmaternal care experienced by study children at regular intervals up to 54 months of age. Their main evaluation tool (similar in emphasis to the Arnett Caregiver Interaction Scale) assessed the degree of "positive caregiving" given the child being studied, employing detailed criteria in the use of which the evaluators were trained and tested. (See note 41, chapter 4 for a description of the positive caregiving measure.)

The "positive caregiving" measure used by NICHD and the Arnett scale (CIS) used by the CQO study differ considerably in detail and so are by no means fully comparable. Nevertheless, the NICHD evaluators seemed to give a considerably lower rating to caregiver behavior in centers than did the CQO evaluators. In their assessment, positive caregiving behavior with the target child was "not at all characteristic" or "somewhat uncharacteristic" in 67 percent of the centers when the child was 15 months old and in 63 percent of the centers when the child was 36 months old.

In focusing on the caregiver's interaction with the target child, the evaluation of "positive caregiving" does not measure many of the significant characteristics of child care evaluated by the ECERS/ITERS procedure. These include sanitation and other health-related concerns, the program of activities, the extent of developmentally appropriate practices, the toys and equipment, the physical setup, safety concerns, the nature of disciplinary practices, and the quality of the supervision. NICHD evaluators did make an overall assessment of caregiving at the end of the observation period, rating the quality of the setting on a five point scale from 1, or terrible, to 5, or excellent, based on their own common-sense interpretation (they received no training). Based on these ratings, 48 percent of children in centers were getting care rated as "good" or "excellent," a far higher evaluation than those given in the CQO study of centers, in which evaluators determined ratings based on specific criteria. These "common sense" ratings, however, were inconsistent with the more carefully derived positive caregiving ratings. Half of the centers given a global rating of "excellent" did not receive the highest rating for "positive caregiving," and half of the centers given a global rating of "good" by the NICHD observers were places where the same observers judged that "positive caregiving" was "somewhat *un*characteristic."

Given the frankly impressionistic method used to assign these ratings, we must reach the conclusion that the NICHD results on center care tend to corroborate earlier findings that indicate that a considerable majority of centers are delivering care that does not deserve to be called "good" and that a distressing proportion provide care that is minimally acceptable or worse.[28]

Quality in For-Profit and Non-Profit Centers

Since for-profit child care centers are businesses concerned with earning a rate of return on investment, it is commonly believed that they give care that is on average of lower quality than the care given by the nonprofit centers. Most studies tend to substantiate this view. However, in the four states studied in the CQO study, for-profit centers provided lower quality than nonprofits only in North Carolina, a state with relatively low licensing standards. Further, the CQO data reveals that while for-profit centers generally provide relatively low quality, some nonprofit subsectors do too.[29]

Table 5.1 compares indicators of quality for groups of centers within the for-profit and nonprofit sectors, classified by type of ownership or sponsorship.[30] It is certainly not true that just any type of nonprofit center is likely to be better than a for-profit center. Church-operated centers and centers operated by community agencies provided significantly lower quality than public centers and nonprofit independent centers.

The nonprofit centers surveyed in the CQO study with the very best quality ratings were those run by public agencies and by private schools or colleges.[31] Somewhat lower in quality were the nonprofit independents and the church-affiliated centers located in churches but not directly operated by them. These four categories of nonprofit centers had more educated staff, payed them better, and provided better quality than the other four categories of centers.

In thinking about the reasons that average quality differs by sponsorship or ownership, table 5.1 indicates that for-profit centers and church-operated centers overwhelmingly serve families that do not receive subsidies to help with their child care costs. So these centers, serving middle-class working families, are dependent for their revenue on parent fees and have to be concerned about

TABLE 5.1.

Clientele, size, fees, and quality by type of ownership or sponsorship of child care centers.

	CHAIN	FOR-PROFIT INDEPENDENT	CHURCH OPERATED	CHURCH INDEPENDENT	NONPROFIT INDEPENDENT	PRIVATE SCHOOL OR COLLEGE	COMMUNITY AGENCY	PUBLIC
NUMBER SURVEYED	77	124	49	27	57	10	25	27
CLIENT CHARACTERISTICS								
% SUBSIDIZED CHILDREN	12%	14%	9%	12%	42%	22%	73%	57%
% INFANT/TODDLERS	29%	33%	16%	21%	29%	17%	11%	14%
% REVENUE IN PARENT FEES	88%	85%	86%	85%	54%	69%	35%	36%
FAMILY INCOME PER YEAR	$64,000	$60,000	$54,000	$62,000	$43,000	NA	$32,000	$31,000
FINANCES								
PRESCHOOL FEE PER HOUR	$2.06	$2.03	$1.80	$1.96	$2.00	$2.82	$1.98	$2.16
WAGE, TEACHERS & AIDES	$6.38	$6.50	$6.50	$7.15	$7.17	$9.64	$6.49	$9.37
QUALITY								
% CLASSROOM STAFF WITH BA	24%	29%	24%	32%	34%	46%	20%	35%
PRESCHOOL STAFF-CHILD RATIO	.13	.14	.16	.21	.19	.18	.17	.23
CENTER QUALITY INDEX	3.89	3.86	3.74	4.16	4.19	4.50	3.82	4.71

Source: John Morris and Suzanne Helburn, "Child Care Center Quality Differences: The Role of Profit Status, Client Preferences, and Trust," *Nonprofit and Vountary Sector Quarterly,* 29:3 (September 2000), 225-247.

Note: These are least squares means that eliminate the effects of unbalanced sample sizes among the four states in the study.

keeping costs under control. Church-operated centers may occupy rent-free space. But instead of using the freed-up funds to improve quality, they appear instead to pass cost savings on to customers, some of whom may be parishioners, in the form of lower fees. Some church-operated centers may also serve as income-earning arms of the church. Community agency centers receive most of their funding from vouchers or contracts from state and local government, and the reimbursement rates may be too low to provide the resources needed to give quality service to this group of children. They may, for instance, have trouble attracting talented staff. Some of these centers can count on contracts from local social services agencies, and that may encourage lax management and lower quality.

Of the nonprofit groups that provide higher quality services, most centers operated by private schools cater to parents who are willing to pay higher fees for a trustworthy provider, often designing their preschool curriculum around a particular educational philosophy to which the parents subscribe. Centers operated by public agencies on college or university campuses serve faculty and students, often acting as ECE training programs, or are intervention programs for at-risk children. Church-affiliated centers, unlike the church-operated centers, are run by professional directors independent of the churches that house them and are little different from other nonprofit independent centers.

A major expansion of center care, which would result from the adoption of a government subsidy program to make affordable care available to all parents, would in all likelihood mean a major expansion of for-profit centers and church-operated centers. Even without increased subsidies, it is likely that these kinds of centers will grow relative to other subsectors. So it is especially important that state licensing standards that affect quality be brought into line across the states.

Quality of Employer-Sponsored Centers and Military Child Development Centers

Employer-sponsored centers represent a niche in the child care center market and tend to provide good quality child care services. It is one of the fastest-growing segments of the market, although it represents a very small percentage of all centers.[32] The CQO found that on-site child care centers provided significantly higher overall quality than non work-site centers, averaging a full point higher on the ECERS scale.[33]

The 1990s economic expansion created an increasing demand for large employers—mainly in pharmaceuticals, finance, insurance, and health care—to offer services as an employee benefit. In addition, the federal government has set up about 240 child care centers for civilian employees, many sponsored by the General Services Administration. Most of these centers are operated by corporate child care chains, and the field is increasingly dominated by a few large companies. Employers with work-site centers are aware of the need to deliver high-quality services in order to satisfy their employees' needs. Accordingly, wage and benefits packages for center staff are somewhat higher than prevailing market rates. Bright Horizons Family Solutions, specializing in high-quality, employer-sponsored centers, is the largest operator with 325 centers, and it is the fifth largest for-profit child care provider in the country. Bright Horizons cofounder, Roger Brown, attributes his success to viewing the employers, rather than the parents, as the customers.[34] Most of the national child care chains are trying to follow suit by creating special departments to serve corporate sponsors. The success of these chains in providing generally good quality services shows that they are able to ante up the quality when the demand exists.

The United States military runs the largest and possibly most successful employer child care operation in the country, serving over 200,000 children, and it, too, tends to provide good quality services. Since the passage of the Military Child Care Act in 1989, enacted in response to a national scandal about the low quality of child care in military installations, the U.S. Military Child Development Program has built an exemplary system of child care provision. It includes funding for child development centers, parent fees based on sliding fee scales (that don't exceed 10 percent of family income), training requirements for child care staff and family providers, better wages for the highly trained, improved staff-child ratios, careful monitoring of centers and family child care providers, resource and referral services, strict enforcement of standards, an accreditation initiative, a child abuse prevention program, and parent programs.

The program has subscribed to the NAEYC guidelines for providing developmentally appropriate early care and education. Each center has a training and curriculum specialist who gives technical assistance and helps in program evaluation. The program enforces a strict oversight routine that includes four unannounced inspections per year and a policy of "fix, waive or close." Centers are encouraged to seek NAEYC accreditation. The military child care program is an example of what can be accomplished in a relatively short time period, admittedly by an organization that can institute change from the top down and can successfully garner public resources.[35] Interestingly, cost per child is not much higher than cost in good quality centers in the civilian sector.[36]

FAMILY CHILD CARE

There are three distinct groups of family child care providers: (1) providers licensed or registered in their state to provide child care in their home; (2) family child care providers who care for few enough children to be legally exempt from regulation in their state or who reside in a state that does not require any family child care providers to be licensed; (3) illegally operating family child care providers who care for more children than their state allows without a license.

The majority of family child care providers are women—women who are mothers who value mothering and the traditional role that women have had in family life. Providers can be young mothers with a child at home, middle-aged mothers with school-aged children, empty-nest older mothers and grandmothers, but almost always mothers.[37]

Most family child care providers have a husband with a job outside the home so that family income is not completely dependent on child care earnings. Sometimes the husband's job provides family health insurance and retirement benefits. These women contribute about a quarter to a third of family income. Median family income of family child care providers is somewhat lower than for the nation as a whole. Many of these women say they started doing day care in order to earn money while still staying home with their own children. Half of the providers have a preschool child of their own at home. They average about 40 years in age and have about 6 years of experience in family child care.

There is high turnover in family child care; estimates range from 30 to 40 percent per year.[38] Evidently many who enter the field do not stay long. Most have had previous labor market experience. Family child care providers normally like their work and enjoy being with children, even though a large proportion do not intend to make a long-term career of family child care and do not see their work leading into the broader field of children's services. Most providers have little contact with the professional child care community.

There are substantial racial and ethnic differences in the economic and family situations of family child care providers. White, non-Hispanic providers are more likely to be part of a married couple with relatively good family incomes. Black and Hispanic providers tend to be older and to care for one or more grandchildren as well as unrelated children.[39] Their lower income can translate into a less comfortable environment for the children.

Caroline Zinsser's ethnographic study of child care arrangements in an unidentified small Northeastern "rust-belt" city illustrates the nature of much family child care.[40] Zinsser focused her interviews on a neighborhood of lower-middle-class white but ethnically diverse working-class families. Most of the providers had been born and raised in the neighborhood. Most of the adults in the family were high school graduates; the women had stayed home and raised children, and the men were employed in service and blue-collar jobs. For these women, who call themselves babysitters, child care was an extension of their lives as housekeepers and mothers.

The caregivers Zinsser observed take care of relatively few children and raise them much as they did their own children. Their view of child tending is to lay a blanket in the kitchen or living room floor and put the children and their toys on the blanket to play by themselves with instructions, quickly learned, not to stray off the blanket. They value a clean house and have learned the tricks of keeping it that way even with children in it. They love kids and mothering. Their main interaction with the children is in changing them, feeding them, and taking them to the park for long periods, both in the morning and afternoon, where the children find other children to play with and the babysitters can chat with their friends. They see their function as custodial, not educational. They are very careful to keep the children from harm and give them plenty of fresh air and nourishing food, just the way they raised their own children. These women reported some problems accommodating their husbands' desire to have the house to themselves, which may explain why many family child care providers limit care to weekdays and daytime.[41]

Most of the babysitters Zinsser studied had no special training and saw no need for it. None of them were licensed and none reported their income to the IRS. They saw their babysitting as an extension of their service as housewives, as a way of prolonging their period of active motherhood. Zinsser's caregivers said that they communicated very little with the parents about the children, evidently because both parents and caregiver saw the arrangement as purely custodial. There wasn't much to talk about unless the child got ill, or fell, or was off his food.

Pros and Cons of Family Child Care

In family child care, children get to spend their time in a homey environment. They can do the same things they do at home—watch and sometimes help with the laundry, cleaning, cooking, and shopping. Older children can take their naps in a real bed. They can get home cooking. Usually children are cared for by a mother who can provide love and affection. The children can get continuity of care and can form a secure attachment to her, provided, of course, she stays in business.

There may be somewhat more scheduling flexibility with a family child care provider. Child care centers are open set hours only during the day, while at least some family child care providers will take children early in the morning and keep them late into the evening, possibly overnight. They may accept a sick child.

Prices for family child care are somewhat lower than prices fo. care, particularly for infant care. Unregulated homes charge lower fee regulated ones, perhaps 25 percent less.[42] Family child care homes ﹍ .ﺍﺍ residential neighborhoods, and many families will find them more convenient than the nearest center. The only care in rural areas and low-income urban areas may be family child care.

The disadvantages can outweigh the advantages, however, particularly for preschool-aged children. Because of the more informal nature of family child care, it may be difficult to gauge the actual quality of care. In a center, a parent can sit somewhat unobtrusively and watch the organized activities and the interactions of the adult caregivers with the children. This is harder to do in the home of a family child care provider.

Many family child care providers do not have the resources to create as rich a learning environment for the children as centers do—providers often have only a few toys, little in the way of materials for creative play and cognitive learning, and not much outdoor play equipment. They may depend on the TV to occupy the children much of the day. Most providers have less education and training than center teachers.

Many family day care providers are not licensed, so standards, including the number of children cared for, light or heat, space for the children to play, training, sanitation, and lack of criminal record, are unregulated. The homes may be lacking smoke detectors, fire extinguishers, covers over electrical outlets, effective barriers to the busy street outside or the steps inside, and protection against stoves, heaters, kitchen poisons, or family medications. Most parents probably lack the energy, savvy, and nerve to do their own checking. Besides, they have to try to stay on the good side of the child care providers they use, for their own and for their children's sake. Even among licensed family child care providers, inspection and the enforcement of mandated standards by the state agency is likely to be lax compared to center regulation.

There is likely to be no backup when the provider or someone in her family is sick. The children may come in contact with other members of the provider's household, or with sexual partners, neighbors, and friends whom parents do not know and over whom they have no supervision. It is not uncommon to read in the newspapers of a death of an infant due to shaking by the boyfriend of a caretaker who has left him in temporary charge of the child.

Most family child care providers work alone. If cruelty, bad temper, or inattention occurs there is nobody to witness it. In centers, the presence of witnesses and supervisors inhibits to some degree bad behavior of caregivers and results in the firing of employees who act inappropriately.

Quality in Family Child Care

It is far more difficult to study quality in family child care than in centers. With large numbers of providers legally exempt or operating illegally, there is no ready-made list from which a representative sample might be drawn. Many providers don't want to be evaluated and won't grant access to researchers. It is certainly likely that the ones who won't grant access are on average worse than the ones who are willing to be studied and evaluated. Finally, the presence of the evaluator in the home is more obtrusive than in a center, so that what goes on in the evaluator's presence may not be representative of what goes on when no evaluator is there. Thus, the few studies that researchers have struggled to produce in the face of these difficulties may well provide a picture that makes family child care look better than it actually is. Even so, most of these studies suggest that poor quality is quite common in family child care.

The National Day Care Home Study of 302 providers in Los Angeles, Philadelphia, and San Antonio carried out in the late 1970s found that providers on average spent 37 percent of their time uninvolved with the children.[43] They spent very little time talking with the children. Compared with regulated providers, unregulated providers and providers whose own children or children of relatives were present spent less time in direct interaction with the children and more time doing house work; they used fewer child-centered and structured activities.

More recent studies have measured quality using the Family Day Care Rating Scale (FDCRS) described in chapter 4.[44] In the largest, recent study, regulated homes appear to be roughly comparable to centers in quality. However, downright poor care was common in the nonregulated family child care homes, which are in the vast majority in many communities. Fully half of these nonregulated homes were rated "inadequate"; only a tiny minority were rated "good." Unregulated providers were less sensitive, more detached, and less responsive to children's bids for attention than regulated providers.[45] These results confirm earlier findings about the level of quality and differences based on regulation.[46]

One study of family child care gives meaning to the term "custodial" and to what children are missing in mediocre quality settings. Researchers found no instances of reading to infants; providers read to toddlers in only 38 percent of the homes and to preschool and school-aged children in only 29 percent of the homes. Very few of the providers gave preschool-aged children the chance to do arts and crafts projects that are commonplace in centers. Infants and toddlers had materials to play with in only 40 percent of the homes and in over two-thirds of the homes observers found instances where infants were restricted and unoccupied.[47]

The NICHD study reports positive caregiving as "not at all characteristic" or "somewhat uncharacteristic" in 50 percent of the cases for 15-month-old babies and 66 percent of the cases for three year-olds in family child care (see note 44 chapter 4 for a description of this quality measure). This suggests that it is probable that an infant placed in family child care receives little or no positive caregiving.

Indicators of Quality

Children put in the care of family day care operators who are licensed and regulated, better educated, and with some training have a better chance of getting adequate care than children left with untrained and unregulated providers. Providers who consider themselves family child care professionals running small businesses give better quality care than those who consider the work temporary or mainly as a help to the mothers. Those who see family child care as their chosen profession tend to have training in child development and early childhood education; they are devoted to and take pride in helping children grow up. They are more likely to belong to their local or national professional associations, be licensed, use contracts with parents that include specific rules defining financial arrangements, care for a larger number of children, have a waiting list, earn a reasonable living, have back-up help when they need it, and have invested in their home and backyard to create a good environment for children.[48] Providers with good quality scores (FDCRS of 5 or more) planned several activities per day for the children, used more age-specific activities, engaged the children in more conversation, read to them more, and did less housework.[49]

Professional, business-like providers, while providing better quality, cared for more children. Nevertheless, the ratio of children to adults does matter. A recent study of the impact on quality of adding two school-aged children in a child care home found that while the FDCRS score did not change, there was a decrease in provider sensitivity and a shift in her attention to the older children.[50]

CARE FROM RELATIVES

Placing children into the care of relatives has a long history in human societies throughout the world. As we have seen, it is still widespread today in the United States. It is a common form of mutual aid that many people consider a normal part of private life. Governments don't regulate care by mothers or fathers (except when things go badly awry and serious abuse or neglect is suspected). That trust is extended to care by relatives, which is viewed as the nearest thing to parental care. It is simply not considered anybody's business if a mother decides to have her own mom or her sister watch her child. If some money changes hands, well, it's all in the family, and, many people would say, not something that the Internal Revenue Service necessarily has to be told about.

Relative care costs considerably less than family child care. About 70 percent of nonparental care by relatives is given free; others charge mainly for their expenses or are paid in kind. For those who do pay, the average price of relative care is about 20 percent below that of family child care and 34 percent below that of care in a center.[51] Beyond that, care by a relative has many of the same advantages and disadvantages we listed for family child care.

Many people would assume that a relative would be more concerned with the well being of a child than a stranger would and would care for the child more lovingly. Most would assume, in short, that relative care would, on average, be high quality care. The very limited research that has been done on care by relatives provides contradictory evaluations. Relative care, when rated by trained observers using FDCRS and CIS, was graded even worse than unregulated family child care. Almost 70 percent of the people observed caring for their relatives' children were judged to be giving care of a quality that was below "minimally acceptable." Virtually none were judged to be giving care rated "good." However, evaluations of relative-child interactions based on Arnett ratings were less negative.[52]

The NICHD study, which did not evaluate overall quality and the early education aspect of care but just positive caregiving, reported relatively high positive caregiving ratings for relatives. Sixty percent of fathers (not covered in other studies) and 71 percent of grandparents were judged to be delivering "positive caregiving" to children aged 15 months. That gets reduced, however, to 47 and 45 percent, respectively, when the children get to be 36 months. Even these results indicate that over half of three year-olds are not receiving positive caregiving.

Relatives apparently pay less attention to the early education aspects of child care but may provide the emotional support young children need. In truth, early childhood professionals have not yet created instruments specifically designed to measure quality of care given by relatives. Relative care needs to be evaluated by standards appropriate to it.

NANNY CARE

In-home care by a nonrelative was the primary arrangement for about 5 percent of preschoolers in families with an employed mother in 1994, some 9 percent of the children whose family income was over $54,000.[53] About 500,000 children are cared for in this way. Not surprisingly, employed mothers with infants make more use of nannies than do families with older children. In the last 20 years the percentage of children cared for through such arrangements seems to have been on the decline as centers gained in popularity.

The now-popular term "nanny" derives from the term used for a woman who lived with a well-off British family and cared for their children. She was not of lower-class origin and did no housework; the families had other servants for that. Thirty years ago, one heard little of nannies in the United States, and those using the term would have been considered stuck-up. "Babysitter" was the term commonly applied to a nonrelative who cared for a child in the child's own home but was expected to do little or no housework. A person who was paid to care for the children but also to do a substantial part of the housework was called "housekeeper" or "maid."

In the United States today, the job of a nanny is generally low-paying and low status. It usually subjects the nanny to sometimes-capricious supervision from someone with no experience as a supervisor, provides no opportunity for advancement, and is socially isolating. Since people with other opportunities naturally shun such a job, the present-day American nanny often comes from the lowest rung of the social ladder. The nanny is likely to be a recent (possibly illegal) immigrant with little or no education and little English, or a young woman from the midwest eager to get away from home.

The chief advantage of hiring a full-time nanny, especially if she lives with the family, is the flexibility it allows the parents. There are other advantages as well. The children don't have to be carted from home to a provider and back home again; they have care at home when they are sick. The parents' commutes to work are not complicated by delivering and picking up their children from providers; parents think they can have more control over their child's routine and standards for care; they can enjoy household help in cleaning, cooking, errands, etc.

On the down side, parents' privacy is infringed upon; they become employers and must spend the time and emotional energy necessary to make that relationship work; they need more space to accommodate the nanny if she is to live in. If the family has only one child, hiring a nanny will be expensive, compared to other modes of care, even if hired from the lowest tier of the labor pool. As with family child care or relative care, and unlike center care, most of the caretaker's work will not be directly observed by any other adult. In some well-publicized cases, parents have resorted to using hidden video cameras, but this is a symptom of a lack of trust rather than an effective method of supervision.

A somewhat more subtle problem with hiring nannies is brought out by sociologist Julia Wrigley of Columbia University, who interviewed 177 mothers and their nannies in the early 1990s. Wrigley gives a disquieting view of the social relations in families that employ nannies.[54] The parents expect and want the nanny to develop a loving relation with the child and to care for the child with the same solicitude a family member would. Yet the nanny cannot consider herself a family member. The parents are her bosses—they order her around, feel free to criticize her roundly, and feel free to pile extra tasks on her. They also feel free to fire her when they decide the child is old enough to need more stimulation, or for any other reason. This inconsistency in many cases sours relations, prevents the nanny from attaching to the child, and affects the care the child gets.

Hiring a nanny to take care of a child at home may have some unintended negative consequences for the child's social development. The nanny-child relation, if not skillfully managed, can produce a pattern of learned helplessness and class prejudice in the child. Often children see nannies as people who are at their beck and call and whose job depends on their good will. This can breed dependence, aggressiveness, and selfishness. They learn early about privilege and exercise it.

American parents don't enjoy becoming employers of household servants. The mothers usually have little experience hiring domestic help. They don't know how to screen potential employees, how to structure the job, or how to manage the social relations. With nannies from a much lower socioeconomic stratum, there is sometimes an underlying distrust—a fear of boyfriends, theft, or their child's safety.

The low pay and the problematic social relations in close quarters produce high turnover rates in nanny care. Nannies often leave unannounced. The frequently revolving door creates instability for the children. When there is a sudden departure, job-holding parents have to find a replacement in a hurry. They may have been careful and taken a lot of time in the search for the first nanny they hired. But if a nanny quits on short notice or has to be fired, and the parents feel a strong pressure to be at work, they will not be able to be as careful in choosing the second nanny, or the third, forth, or fifth, for that matter.

Many nannies work from 6:00 A.M. until 10:00 P.M. for low cash wages plus room and board. Although hired as child care workers, Wrigley reports that mothers expect these women to do housework and, over time, tend to add more and more household responsibilities. The job can become truly onerous for "live-ins" who have little contact with other adults or the outside world. If they are immigrants, their restricted lives make it difficult for them to learn English and to drive a car, which keeps them at the lowest rung of the economic ladder.

When the nanny comes from a much lower social stratum than the parents, cultural differences worry the parents, who want the child to be attuned to their brand of culture, not the nanny's. The nanny may have to learn to subordinate her views of appropriate child-rearing practices to those of her employers, a process that can be painful and ultimately unsuccessful. The cultural differences may cause the parents to want to reduce the care giver's responsibility to the custodial chores of diapering, feeding, overseeing sleep, taking the child to the park, attending to the child's safety, and giving the child "love." The parents try to reserve the more interesting child-rearing tasks for themselves. They do the storytelling and reading, supervise homework, and organize outings and parties in order to spend "quality time" with their children. This division of labor, while understandable, further limits the autonomy and quality of the work experience for the child care provider. To the extent that this reduces the care giver's interest in or ability to do a good job, the children's well being can be compromised.

Families who want their children cared for by someone with a middle-class background and habits may hire a student from a local college or import a European au pair through an agency. The latter will be a young person whose motive for coming is to experience life in America. These arrangements don't provide the convenience and flexibility that the lower-class full-time nanny provides and may not serve when the mother has a full-time job. Using an au pair is not cheap. Expenses quoted by one agency that supplies families with au pairs covered services for a 50-week year and included room and board, plus about $13,000 for agency fees.[55]

One grave problem with the au pair arrangement is that the au pair must be engaged, and fees paid for, before the family has had a chance to meet her. Refunds are partial and uncertain. Hiring someone to care for one's child for a year (especially someone from a different culture) without benefit of a face-to-face interview must surely be classed as a highly risky procedure. If the parents are disappointed when they do meet her, they may allow the money and time they have sunk into importing her to overcome their better judgement that she will be bad for the child. A second grave problem is that an au pair who proves satisfactory is obligated to go home at the end of a year, so the child must relate to a new caregiver, and the risk of getting an incompatible person must be run all over again.

Wrigley's research provides no direct evaluation of the quality of in-home care. She turned up no cases of actual child abuse, but she did find three cases of known neglect. In one case, parents became suspicious of their nanny. When they installed a hidden video camera they observed a severely depressed person who was able to turn on a pleasant tone and enthusiasm when the parents were present or called but who spent most of her time lying on the couch ignoring the baby. In another case, a mother came home unexpectedly in the middle of the day to find that the nanny had gone out, leaving the child in the care of the cleaning woman. To her horror, the mother found the baby crying in the crib with soaked pajamas and diapers.

Nanny care was included in the kinds of care studied by the NICHD researchers, but they were not singled out for special analysis. In the report, they were classified as part of a group that provided care in the child's home, a group that also included relatives other than grandparents and fathers. That group received generally high marks for "positive caregiving," a finding that might be expected of paid employees when they are being observed.

COMPARISONS OF CHILD CARE QUALITY
BY MODE IN THE NICHD STUDY

The NICHD study was designed to give a comparison of the quality of all of the various types of care. Table 5.2 presents in summary form the percentage of caregivers in each of five kinds of care for whom "positive caregiving" was highly or somewhat characteristic. When the children were 15 months old, these evaluators rated center positive caregiving lowest, and family child care next lowest. Fathers were rated higher still and grandparents highest of all. As the children got older, the evaluations of family child care, fathers, and grandparents declined considerably. By 36 months, positive caregiving was rated about equally for family child care and centers.

TABLE 5.2.

Summary of NICHD evaluations of child care, by type of provider and age of child

(percentage of providers getting rating
"positive caregiving somewhat characteristic" or "positive caregiving highly characteristic").

TYPE OF CARE	15 MONTHS	24 MONTHS	36 MONTHS
CENTER	28	22	34
FAMILY CHILD CARE	50	41	35
FATHER	60	51	47
GRANDPARENT	71	64	45
OTHER IN-HOME CARE	61	58	57

Source: Source: NICHD Early Child Care Research Network, "Characteristics and Quality of Child Care for Toddlers and Preschoolers" *Journal of Applied Developmental Science* 4, no.3 (2000):116-135.

A fifth group, "other in-home care," included nonrelatives (nannies) and relatives aside from fathers and grandparents giving care in the child's own home. The caregiving of this fifth group was rated relatively highly, although almost half of these providers were giving little positive caregiving. The ratings of this group declined hardly at all as the children aged. In fact, by the time the children were 36 months old, the NICHD observers gave this fifth group the best ratings of all, by a considerable margin. Surely, this result must be treated with skepticism unless confirmed by further studies. One source of the problem may be that the observer is much less noticeable in a child care center room than in the child's or relative's home, where the caregiver is constantly aware of being evaluated.

As we have seen, the studies that used the ECERS type instruments to assess global quality gave low ratings to unlicensed family child care providers and even lower ratings to relatives on average, suggesting that center care, at least for three- to five-year-olds, is on average better. NICHD findings seem to go against the bulk of these previous studies. Unfortunately, the emphasis in the NICHD study on caregiving rather than on developmentally appropriate practice and activities preclude giving it a great deal of weight. We conclude from our survey of the research that centers and regulated family child care providers are likely to provide better quality services than the other forms of care. None of these modes of care, however, have been shown to dependably deliver good quality services.

NURSERY SCHOOLS, PREKINDERGARTENS, HEAD START

The end of the nineteenth century saw the appearance of nursery schools whose primary purpose was early education rather than care for the children of job-holding mothers. These programs were aimed at promoting children's cognitive, physical, social, emotional, and moral development and at getting them ready for a successful school career. The operators of nursery schools were eager to show that their services were different in every way from those provided in facilities caring for children of working mothers, virtually all of whom, at that time, were extremely poor. Working mothers' wages were very low, and the day care centers that served them were run as charities. They kept the children for the whole working day. By contrast, the part-day nursery schools charged fees, were aimed at middle-class children, and kept the children only for half a day, often just a few days a week. They emphasized educational rather than custodial services.[56]

The huge advance in the number of mothers of young children with jobs—many of them well above the poverty line—has eroded the sharp differences between child care centers and nursery schools. Fee-charging, full-time child care centers now exist to serve the children of job-holding middle-class parents, and most claim to give an educational experience. Many of these centers also provide a preschool program for children who attend two or three days a week or mornings only. Still, however, about a quarter of all centers still run on a part-day basis (and in many states are exempt from licensing), so that the tradition of the part-day nursery school is still with us.

The quality of preschools and their effectiveness in preparing children for school, except for Head Start, have not been the subject of much research. This may be due to the fact that the performance of these schools has not been a public policy issue, since they serve children from more affluent families and generally are not publicly subsidized

The half-day schedule of the early private nursery schools, and of many still-surviving ones, has been adopted as standard in many publicly supported programs where the avowed primary purpose is an educational experience for children under six—kindergartens, prekindergartens, and Head Start. Programs that can be represented as serving solely an educational function are apparently far easier for politicians to advocate and defend than programs that also work to facilitate maternal job-holding. Yet the implementation of the welfare reform legislation of 1996 that prescribed job-holding for single mothers is forcing some changes. Some of these programs, especially those targeted toward poor children, are moving to full-day schedules, and presumably more will do so in the future.

Head Start

The federal government's major effort in early childhood education is the Head Start program, which aims to promote the social competence and school readiness of low-income children and others at risk of school failure. The program is intended to further all areas of children's development—their physical well-being, social and emotional development, language usage and literacy, approaches to learning, and cognition and general knowledge.[57] Children with special needs must constitute 10 percent of enrollment. Head Start also provides family support and health services, and local programs are encouraged to link the children and their families to needed community services. Families with special problems, such as drug or alcohol abuse, or job loss, can receive help through Head Start.

Head Start programs started out serving only three- and four-year-olds through a half-day, school-year program. To accommodate the increased demands on poor women to work, half of the programs now provide some full-day programs, becoming, in effect, part of the child care supply.[58] However, Head Start programs provide wrap-around child care arrangements (child care services before and after the hours children are in their Head Start program) to only 27 percent of children needing it. Since 1994, Head Start was authorized to serve infants, toddlers, their families, and pregnant women, but this program remains very small, accounting for only 6 percent of overall Head Start enrollment in 1999-2000. Most of the Head Start programs are based in centers, but about 668 grant recipients operate home-based programs for about 48,000 children and their families, provided by home visitors who work with parents to provide comprehensive services to children and their families. Parents are encouraged to participate as volunteers and to take paid jobs with the program. Parents of current or former Head Start children must be given preference in filling job vacancies, and they occupy about 32 percent of the staff jobs.

Federally funded Head Start programs are organized at the local level through grants to nonprofit organizations and public school systems. Initiated in 1965 as part of the Johnson administration's War on Poverty, Head Start is one of the few programs from that era to remain popular. In Congress it is one of the sacred cows, not unlike Medicare and the Social Security system, and difficult for conservatives to dislodge. Even with this popularity Congress has not seen fit to fully fund Head Start; the program still serves slightly less than half of the eligible children. It enrolled 858,000 children in fiscal year 2000 with an appropriation of 6.2 billion dollars.

Center-based programs operated by Head Start grantees must meet standards set by the U.S. Department of Health and Human Services (HHS) that include educational components similar to those identified in the ECERS and ITERS instruments. Teachers must obtain a Child Development Associate (CDA) or equivalent within one year of employment as a teacher, and by 2003, 50 percent of all Head Start teachers must have college degrees.[59]

Despite the lofty Head Start objectives, severe resource limitations have compromised the ability of the programs to deliver all these services. Many programs have insufficiently qualified staff, inadequate facilities, and limited coordination with community health professionals. Low salaries have made it difficult to attract qualified teachers.[60] Funding for salaries increased considerably after 1994, but average Head Start wages are still lower than those in comparable job categories in the public schools. Nevertheless, turnover rates are considerably below those reported for other child care centers.[61]

In 1995 Head Start initiated a longitudinal study to assess program quality and effectiveness. ECERS evaluations in over 400 classrooms show somewhat higher global quality than that found in CQO preschool classes (with 72 percent of the rooms rated "good" or better).[62]

Evaluations of the effectiveness of individual Head Start programs following children into grade school have shown mixed results. While some studies showed gains persisting through the third grade compared to children in the control groups, others showed that short-term gains declined quickly in early elementary grades.[63] Studies have tended to focus on cognitive gains, not on social skills and attitudes, which Head Start also tries to improve. A recent long-term evaluation of Head Start participants in Florida and Colorado suggests that the program may have particularly good effects on girls. A higher proportion of girl participants in the Florida Head Starts completed high school and a smaller proportion were arrested than was true of the girls in the comparison group.[64] The latest assessments indicate that children do need and benefit from Head Start experience, and that the more exposure the more they benefit.[65]

Some fade-out effects of early intervention should be expected unless interventions continue, particularly in Head Start graduates who subsequently attend the poorest schools.[66] Nevertheless, the studies suggesting fade out of cognitive benefits have been seized on by conservative groups opposed to spending money on Head Start as demonstrating that "essentially, children end up back where they started."[67] The most sensible interpretation of the evidence suggests that more, rather than less, money and effort over longer time periods needs to be spent on these children. One can make an analogy to an experiment giving children with deficient diets vitamin pills for a single year. If health gains were made but faded in later years, the obvious lesson to be drawn would be that the vitamins should be given over a longer period, not that vitamins do no good for such children and are a waste of money.

State Funded Preschools and Prekindergarten

All 52 states spend some of their own revenues on early childhood education. Thirteen of them have chosen to use state money to supplement Head Start programs. The rest fund prekindergarten programs of various sorts for four-year-olds, using a combination of federal and state funding sources.[68] Many of these, like Head Start, are aimed at children who are deemed to be at risk of starting school with serious developmental and cognitive deficits.[69] Some states are moving toward providing prekindergarten services free to all of the four-year-olds whose parents want them enrolled. This move to universal provision, while represented as strictly and solely an educational project, represents also a potentially substantial new contribution from government to the finance and organization of child care for working parents.

The Children's Defense Fund has estimated that in the 1998-99 school year, the states were spending $1.7 billion on prekindergartens.[70] These programs are currently serving about 725,000 children, or about 19 percent of the country's four-year-olds. We can roughly guess that more than five times as much would have to be spent if all states were to make programs like these free and open to all.[71]

Georgia, a state whose educational system had previously ranked low both in expenditure and results, has led the movement to state-funded universal prekindergarten.[72] Through skillful advocacy, Governor Zell Miller was able to establish a state-run lottery, whose proceeds went toward education. The state devoted the lottery profits to a series of brand new educational ventures, rather than putting the money into the state's existing education budget. Universal prekindergarten was the most conspicuous and expensive of the new programs financed by the lottery.

The already-existing private child-care industry, which would have lost a considerable share of its customers and revenues, would have opposed and been able to defeat a prekindergarten program based solely in public facilities. Furthermore, public schools did not have the necessary physical plant capacity. So the Georgia program was set up to allow private providers—for-profit as well as nonprofit—to apply for a contract with the state to establish prekindergarten units. Currently, 57 percent of the children in prekindergarten are in programs other than those run by public schools.

In Georgia, the standard program runs on a 6 and a half hour day, 5 days a week, 180 days a year, or 8.3 months in the year. Some facilities have extended hours and run all year round; some have wrap-around care arrangements for which they charge fees to the parents.

Providers of prekindergarten services must employ teachers with one of several permissible credentials, including a CDA credential, teacher certification, or a college degree in early childhood education or elementary education. Aides must be at least 20 years old and high school graduates. The state offers financial incentives to providers to hire teachers with high qualifications. A survey taken in 1996-97 showed that 85 percent of the teachers in the program had a four-year degree, and most of them held certification in early childhood education. Providers must choose and adopt one of the prescribed standard curricula for four-year-olds previously developed for use in nursery schools and centers.

As of 1997, Georgia was spending $3,516 per child in prekindergarten. For the year 2000, assuming proportional per-hour costs, this would work out to $7,885 on the basis of a day care center's provision of a 9-hour day for a full year.[73] The programs are subject to periodic inspection, and some revocations of contracts have occurred. Evaluations of the state prekindergarten program by experts at Georgia State University suggest that most prekindergarten teachers are using developmentally appropriate practices.

Together, Head Start and prekindergarten serve 80 percent of four-year-olds in Georgia; in some counties, 90 to 100 percent are served. The prekindergarten program has brought many children away from maternal care for at least part of the day and has changed the kind and quality of care received by those children who would have been in nonmaternal care in the absence of the program. The program has probably helped the children of job-holding mothers receive a considerably higher quality of care than they would have otherwise obtained. Further, large numbers of children will enter school more ready to learn; this is the official rationale for the program. Georgia is in many ways a conservative state, yet the prekindergarten program is overwhelmingly popular: a survey taken in 1997 showed 85 percent of respondents supporting the use of lottery funds for prekindergarten.[74]

The state-funded prekindergarten program and the federally funded Head Start program obviously overlap to a considerable degree in function and seek to serve the same age group. The prekindergarten authorities in Georgia have made an effort to avoid competition with Head Start and have contributed funds to the program. As the Georgia prekindergarten administrator put it, "We have made a commitment to [the federal Head Start administrator in Georgia] that we will not try to usurp any of his clients. . . . we cannot afford to absorb the 17,000 four-year-olds in this state."[75] While this may be seen as a canny way of preserving two funding streams and disarming the opposition of Head Start providers to the prekindergarten program, there is a less attractive side to this situation. One must wonder whether in the future poor black parents trying to enroll their children in the state-funded prekindergarten will be turned back and told to go to Head Start. The continuation of Head Start may have the effect of segregating poor black children away from the prekindergarten classrooms. It is not unlikely that the popularity of the prekinder-garten program in Georgia stems at least in part from that segregation. If the movement of states to create universal prekindergarten programs continues, the existence of the two programs side-by-side in Georgia and in the rest of the country is likely destined to be a source of difficulty.

Head Start provides some important health and social services that the prekindergarten programs typically do not provide. If the prekindergarten programs became universal and enrol the low-income children that the Head Start program has traditionally served, it would certainly be desirable to continue the provision of such services to families that would benefit from them (probably a wider group of families than have been able to benefit from them under Head Start). It would be tragic if the valuable services of Head Start were to wither on the vine as a result of the advance of the prekindergarten movement. The prekindergarten movement could also threaten some centers and family child care homes by drawing away their four-year-old children from their client base.

BEFORE- AND AFTER-SCHOOL CARE

The American school day usually ends midafternoon, and schools typically schedule long summer vacations. That kind of scheduling seems quite natural and normal to American children, parents, and teachers. But it is our lifelong familiarity with these practices, not their conformity to the needs of children and parents, that make them seem to be the right way to schedule schooling. The length of the school day and the school year we have today derive from an era that is more than a century in the past, when the vast majority of mothers were at home and could supervise their children when they were out of school. The United States was mainly rural so that most families lived on farms, and farm families wanted their kids to have time at home to help with the chores. Today, with a high proportion of mothers of school-age children holding jobs, and less than 3 percent of the population left on the farm, the customary school schedule, like our system of caring for preschool children, is out of touch with current family needs.

One in five children between 6 and 12 years old and 35 percent of children between 10 and 12 are on their own before and after school. In the after-school hours, many children and young teens without supervision may be in unsafe situations or use their time unproductively—watching a lot of television or spending hours playing video games. Some of them hang out with companions likely to get them into trouble. Juvenile violent crime rates soar in the hour after school lets out.[76] Youngsters in the K-9 levels are in some ways more at risk than their younger siblings.

The desperate need for programs providing constructive and attractive programs for children of working parents has only been recently recognized but has become a priority with Congress as well as some state governments and private philanthropic foundations. In 1999 Congress appropriated $200 million to establish the Twenty-First Century Community Learning Centers. Some of the initiative comes from the law enforcement community looking for ways to reduce juvenile crime. Fight Crime: Invest in Kids, a national organization of police and other law enforcement officials, considers quality educational child care for preschool children and after-school programs two of the most powerful crime deterrents. They argue, "it is time to cut crime's most important supply line: its ability to turn American's kids into criminals."[77]

In 1995 almost 40 percent of the nation's children in kindergarten through third grade received some form of nonparental care before- and/or after-school care on a regular basis. They spent an average of 14 hours per week in this care.[78] A wide variety of sponsors operate out-of-school programs—child care centers, private schools, youth and service agencies, churches, recreation centers, and public schools—often in widely dispersed locations that can create transportation problems for children and their parents. The number of school-based programs has increased substantially in the 1990s, since new public funding is being channeled mainly through the schools.

Programs are expensive for many parents, even though perhaps half of them use sliding fee scales or offer scholarships. Even with increased public funding, parent fees probably still constitute a larger percent of revenue for these programs than they do for preschool programs.[79] Staff are predominantly part time, on duty 17 to 28 hours per week. Four out of ten have other jobs as well. Most are women. Despite high staff turnover (35 percent per year) and low earnings, more than 60 percent of the directors, 37 percent of senior staff, and 21 percent of other staff hold at least a bachelor's degree. Staff retention is a major problem.

Most out-of-school-time programs use shared space, and this reality can create serious limitations. For programs located in schools, cafeterias and gyms are often off limits for after-school programs, and if they are available they are hardly very cozy places to relax. Regular daytime teachers don't appreciate sharing their rooms with messy before- and after-school programs. As for programs located in churches, the space is not usually designed for school-age children, and older children do not normally want to hang out with little kids enrolled in the church child care center.

Research indicates that, compared to children in other types of after-school care, children enrolled in formal programs tend to engage in less antisocial behavior, score higher on math and reading achievement tests, develop better work habits, and have better relations with other children. Participation in less formal after-school activities, including tutoring, has similar effects. These programs may help compensate for poor schools and home environments. One group of researchers studying patterns of after-school care and their influence on success and adjustment in grade 6 concluded that "high amounts of self care in the early grades . . . appear to place a child at risk . . . and this risk was heightened for children from lower socioeconomic status, for children already displaying high levels of behavior problems prior to the self-care experience, and for children not participating in extracurricular activities."[80]

Most of the children enrolled in out-of-school programs are in the third grade or younger. Children's participation in these formal programs declines as they get older (about 22 percent of kindergarteners are in programs but only 1 percent of seventh graders). Out-of-school enrichment activities (sports, lessons, clubs) take their place for many children from higher income families, but much less so for children from poor families whose parents cannot afford the fees or provide transportation. This is unfortunate since tutoring and participation in after-school activities can produce many benefits in better work habits, better relations with peers, and better emotional adjustment.[81] Fewer of these special

activities-based programs exist in low-income areas; parents often do not know about the services that are available and are more likely to work odd hours when programs are not available.[82]

Quality criteria have recently been established for the voluntary accreditation program initiated by the National School-Age Care Alliance.[83] Good quality programs must meet the expectations of the children they serve, parents, and often public or private funders, all of whom may make somewhat different demands. Children, particularly as they get older, want programs that are fun and that allow them to be with their friends and to develop some autonomy. Parents want safe, goal-directed programs. Policymakers want programs that prevent problem behaviors and promote learning.

Program excellence depends on good community outreach, child guidance, recreation planning, and group facilitation. In middle childhood, from age 7 to 11, children are learning to be competent and productive by building their skills and developing good work habits. They are also becoming self-aware and can develop a sense of inferiority and low self-esteem if they are not successful in school. Out-of-school programs can provide a noncompetitive environment and help children develop a good self-concept by giving them opportunities to explore and develop their own talents and interests.

Not much systematic information exists about the quality of out-of-school programs. The evaluation of 75 programs in the pilot test of the accreditation system carried out in the late 1990s showed wide variation in quality among states, probably related to differences in licensing standards and the availability of technical assistance. A few other, smaller evaluation studies found mostly poor to mediocre quality of programs. Many of the observed programs were too thinly staffed to provide adequate individual attention to children; often they involved inflexible scheduling, inadequate planning, or not enough varied activities to keep children engaged.[84]

RACIAL AND INCOME DIFFERENCES IN CHILD CARE QUALITY

Are there class and racial or ethnic differences in the availability of good quality early childhood care and education? This is a complicated but answerable question. Since paid-for child care for just one child can potentially eat up a considerable proportion of a low-income family's income, such families typically look for inexpensive solutions to child care. The Census data quoted at the beginning of this chapter tell the story. Many couples in low-income families care for their children in shifts. Or the mother takes her child to work, uses relative care, or leaves the children to care for each other or themselves. Even where an adult is involved, he or she may not be primarily watching out for the children, who are often on their own in many of these arrangements. Since informal care arrangements are not likely to emphasize developmental activities, a high percentage of children forced to depend on such arrangements are not receiving the benefits of early education and may not even be getting good custodial care.

Middle-income and white families tend to use regulated care, while minority and low-income families are more likely to use unregulated, relative, and cheaper care. Thus, it is not surprising that in the NICHD study for children in family child care, higher quality care was associated with higher family income.[85] In the Quality in Family Child Care and Relatives Care study, white providers were rated more sensitive to children's needs and less restrictive with children than black and Hispanic providers. Children from low-income families were significantly more likely to be unoccupied than children from middle-income families. Latino children were more likely to be unoccupied or watching television than European American children.[86]

As we have seen, centers are more likely to give better early care and education than unregulated family child care providers and relatives. Because low-income families often have to rely less on centers and more on informal child care arrangements and unregulated family child care, their children receive poorer care than children from more affluent families. However, those poor children who are in centers are usually enrolled on a subsidized basis in nonprofit and publicly-operated centers. Except for centers operated by community agencies, these centers tend to provide services that are superior to for-profit and church-operated centers that enroll children from middle income two-earner families who are not eligible for subsidies. The NICHD study results also indicate that infants from lower and higher income families received better quality center care than infants from moderate income families.[87] So those relatively few children from the poorest families who are lucky enough to be in subsidized centers and preschool programs generally receive higher quality care and are more likely to receive developmentally appropriate care than children from middle-income families.

Head Start and state preschool programs appear to be of relatively good quality, but eligibility standards and funding limitations prevent these programs from serving the near-poor and the middle-income families that are also struggling financially. Furthermore, most of these programs are part time, do not satisfy the child care needs of working parents, and are usually restricted to serving four-year-old children.

While a child from a poor or near-poor family is unlikely to receive care rated as good and is more likely than not to receive care that is less than even minimally adequate, the quality problem is by no means restricted to such families. Relatively few of the centers patronized by middle-income families deliver high-quality care, so quality is a problem in all income ranges. Very few children—whatever their race or economic circumstances—are getting very good care, even children of the rich. Only the children of discriminating, well-educated parents or those lucky poor children in certain centers are enjoying the high quality of services we know how to provide but seldom do. Differences in parents' preferences about child care arrangements by race and ethnicity add to the complexity of designing public policies that suit all parents and their children.

MUCH IMPROVEMENT NEEDED

Our review of the various modes of child care suggests that a majority of children in the United States do not receive care that deserves the title "good," and that a substantial number, especially infants, receive care that is unacceptable. The review leads us to argue that from the point of view of children's needs, public policies should encourage parents to use center and licensed family child care and make it unnecessary for them to depend on informal, and often illegal, providers out of financial necessity. The benefits of programs that provide early education are important, particularly for children at risk of performing poorly in school, but these opportunities need to be available to all children, regardless of family income.

Expanding public subsidies for child care in the form of vouchers would enable low-income parents to put their children in a mode of care more likely to be of average quality or better and middle-class parents to upgrade their children's care. Giving help to parents with their child care bills will allow many to shift from more informal arrangements to licensed care. If help is only given to those parents using licensed care, the shift would be all the greater.

The Regulations: How Much Quality Control in Child Care?

Slip into an alley off New Hampshire Avenue NW. Turn at the dirt lot—the one with the swing set without swings. Climb the broken stairs, pass the screenless open window high above concrete. Survey the rooms stocked with scores of toddlers and infants, who are here at public expense while their parents try to find work and get off welfare.

Follow these directions and check on these children, and you will do what the city inspectors responsible for their safety haven't done in years, according to D.C. records.

The private Humpty Dumpty infant center is one of 180 Washington day care centers—more than half of all city facilities— operating with an expired license. D.C. officials say that most renewals have been held up because of serious health and safety problems. Overcrowding, infestations of roaches and rats, inadequate supervision, filthy cots and kitchens: All are part of the landscape of D.C. day care as seen in city records and visits to the facilities by the *Washington Post.*

Municipal efforts to protect children in day-care centers have ranged from haphazard to non-existent. The Department of Consumer and Regulatory Affairs (DCRA) routinely fails to visit each center once a year, as required by law. The agency has only five inspectors—half the number of three years ago—to fulfill its public charge of monitoring 350 centers and hundreds of home day care operations. . . .

Records indicate some centers have had their licenses delayed by bureaucratic backlog, not quality issues. But Ellen Yung-Fatah, who oversees DCRA's day-care inspectors, attributed the majority of lapsed licenses to "serious" and "systemic" deficiencies, from overcrowding to fire-safety problems, many of which have persisted for years. "Since we discovered the problems," she said, "we've been trying to work with owners to fix them without closing centers and creating massive upheaval. . . ."

—Katherine Boo,
"Most D.C. Day-Care Centers Have Expired Licenses,"
The Washington Post, 6 October 1997

~&   ~&   ~&

The system of greatly expanded subsidies for child care that we are proposing should be accompanied by significant changes in the system of quality control. There are providers who deliver low-quality services, even unsafe ones, and children and their parents need greater and more consistent protection against them. Without improved protection, there is danger that large quantities of public money and parent fees would be going to poor programs.

In this chapter we discuss the major mechanisms for achieving better quality assurance in child care—state licensing, enforcement of federal funding standards, professional accreditation of programs, and differential reimbursement schemes that reward providers of good quality services. Each mechanism serves a different and important function in promoting better quality, and no single procedure can provide the silver bullet that will "solve" the quality problem in child care. We outline changes in the quality control system that we consider desirable; they would require additional spending, and we estimate what those costs would amount to.

State licensing typically works by requiring all licensed providers to meet minimum standards for such things as staffing ratios, group size, staff qualifications and training, and practices that affect health and safety. State licensing is a form of consumer protection designed to reduce the risk of harm to children. However, such matters as the qualifications and ratios of staff to children obviously affect the quality of children's experience in care as well as their safety. Licensing standards differ considerably from state to state. Some norms are developing that provide an adequate floor under safety and quality, and a majority of the states apply most of them. However, in almost a third of the states standards are low enough to allow situations that are dangerous to children's physical safety and their healthy development. Of course, in all states many providers exceed their state's mandated standards.

Yet many providers also violate their state's mandated standards. Effectiveness of licensing depends on how well the standards are enforced. Without conscientious monitoring of providers, regulations are useless. Even when licensing standards are relatively low, good enforcement can do a lot. Unfortunately, most state licensing agencies are underfunded, leading to infrequent monitoring inspections and enforcement of penalties.

One way of compensating for the unevenness of state licensing systems is for the federal government to set "funding standards," requirements that must be met by those who wish to receive federal funds. This mechanism can raise quality requirements for these programs and create greater standardization of practices throughout the country, affording more equal treatment of children regardless of their state of residence.

Incentives are needed for providers to increase quality above the minimum that the licensing or funding standards require. One approach is for states to provide higher rates of reimbursement for subsidized services to providers giving higher quality. As of this writing, 24 states are trying this approach and are creating funding standards that programs must meet to qualify for higher reimbursement. We believe this should be part of a federal program that significantly expands child care subsidies.

Professional accreditation is another part of child care quality control. Programs that are accredited provide consumers with an indicator of good quality services. In child care the major accrediting agency, the National Association for the Education of Young Children (NAEYC), has accredited about 7,500 child care centers. Some states are using accreditation as the funding standard that determines eligibility for higher reimbursement. We will compare current accreditation programs and discuss the potential of accreditation for improving quality. We will also discuss potential problems that will need to be resolved as accreditation becomes a funding standard for higher reimbursement.

Finally, we consider the question of the proper role of government in creating an appropriate regulatory environment for the child care industry. Even in this era of backlash against government regulation, most people consider child care licensing an important safeguard. Not everyone, however, agrees. Objections to regulation come from those who generally oppose any kind of market regulation. They claim it reduces options for parents, raises prices, and reduces quality. We will consider the strength of the case that has been made for this point of view.

STATE LICENSING

States set minimum requirements for child care programs to protect children from injury, unsafe buildings and equipment, fire, infectious disease, and developmental impairment. All 53 states and territories (including Puerto Rico, the Virgin Islands, and the District of Columbia) license centers and regulate some family child care homes through a licensing or registration procedure. Coverage is far from complete, since some states exempt certain categories of centers. Family child care regulation is even more sketchy, as many states exempt a large percentage of homes from regulation.

Norms are developing in certain areas of regulation, to which many—but by no means all—states adhere. Licensing rules are developed through a consensus-building process among interested parties so that they reflect the values and actual practice in each state. Even if regulators want to increase standards significantly in weak-regulation states, realistically they cannot do so unless most licensees are willing and able to meet the higher standards. If states set licensing rules so high that they cannot be met, the result will be the issuance of many waivers to the regulations. Furthermore, states cannot require higher quality unless they are willing to pay for it in the programs they help finance.

State Licensing Standards for Centers

All states require licensing for certain child care centers, but only 21 states require licenses for all of them. Twelve states exempt some religious centers and 20 states exempt half-day nursery schools. In some states, child care programs that are part of public schools are not licensed since the state department of education is responsible for regulating the schools.

Overall, states have been increasing minimum requirements for centers in recent years, particularly for infants, where the staffing ratio of 4:1 has been adopted in 30 states (including the District of Columbia) and a ratio of 3:1 has been adopted in 4 states. There is considerable evidence that the staffing ratio is one of the most important determinants of quality. In the 1993 Cost, Quality and Child Outcomes study, North Carolina required staff/child ratios considerably below the other states studied, and its centers had lower quality by a considerable margin.[1] The National Child Care Staffing Study, conducted in the late 1980s, also found lower average center quality in states with lower licensing standards.[2]

In the last 15 years, an increasing number of states have begun to regulate group size, require preservice training, and increase ongoing staff training minima. All states now require children in child care centers to be immunized; most states outlaw corporal punishment; all but two states require staff to complete first aid training or to have at least one trained person on site at all times. Most states require center staff to undergo criminal checks, and states are increasing the stringency of these rules. All but four states prohibit smoking (although several states allow designated smoking areas).[3]

States still have a long way to go, however, if we are to provide uniform and adequate quality control over the entire country. We would recommend that all states adopt the maximum child:staff ratios recommended by NAEYC, specifically, 4:1 for infants and 10:1 for three year olds, that teachers be required to have substantial preservice training, and that all centers come under regulation.

Table 6.1 highlights weaknesses in the current system. It identifies states that exempt either church-operated centers or part-day centers from regulation, as well as states that currently do not require acceptable minimum levels of regulation of staffing ratios, staff training and staff qualifications, and square footage.[4] It reveals some obvious weaknesses:

- Eighteen states still permit an infant:staff ratio of 5:1 or more, and 20 states permit a ratio for three-year-olds of 11:1 or more.
- Twelve states still do not require TB testing, and 22 do not require staff to pass a medical examination.
- Nine states do not require staff to undergo criminal checks, and 13 do not check child abuse registries.
- Nine states do not require centers to meet the nationally recommended indoor space requirement of 35 square feet per child, and 21 do not require the recommended 75 square feet per child using the outside playground space at one time.

Almost half of the states currently allow either high ratios of children to staff, or low training requirements, or both. Fourteen of these states allow both, mostly southern states or states from the intermountain west and the great plains.

State licensing standards ignore the importance of staff education and training in protecting children. Only 12 states require teachers to have a high school diploma or equivalent, only two states (Hawaii and Rhode Island) require them to have a B.A., and only 2 states require directors to have a B.A. (Indiana and New York). Most states allow centers to substitute experience in the field for post-secondary education and training. Table 6.2 shows that

- Thirty-two states require no preservice training for teachers except possibly an orientation session; most permit experience in lieu of training.
- Fourteen states require no preservice training for directors.
- Thirty-one states require 12 or fewer clock hours of annual ongoing teacher training.
- Twenty-two states have no preservice or substantial ongoing training requirements for teachers.

Most states require minimal amounts of ongoing training for teachers and some require it for assistants and aides: 10 to 15 clock hours is the norm. Only Minnesota requires as much as 40 clock hours a year for full-time teachers, roughly equivalent to the class hours spent in a three-credit hour college course.[5] Thirteen states require six clock hours a year or less. Equally troubling, these training requirements are not integrated into any sequential curriculum that is tied to career advancement.

Regulating Family Child Care

There is even more variety in state regulation of family child care than of centers, and, generally, standards are lower. Although licensing family child care has positive effects on quality, finding an effective approach to regulation is not easy. It is difficult to enforce licensing, since family child care providers can evade the law so easily, and the stricter the licensing requirements, the greater is the incentive to do so. Providers may consider inspection of their home an unnecessary intrusion and making alterations to meet standards an unnecessary expense. This is particularly true of a woman caring for only one or two children other than her own, who may foresee doing it for only a few years.

TABLE 6.1.

Do states require that child care centers meet important standards? (year 2000)

STATE	ALL CENTERS REGULATED	MAXIMUM NUMBER OF CHILDREN PER STAFF MEMBER		STAFF QUALIFICATIONS						INDOOR SPACE > =35 SQ FT
		INFANTS 4:1 OR LESS	3YRS OLD 10:1 OR LESS	TEACHERS REQUIRE PRE-SERVICE TRAINING	DIRECTORS REQUIRE PRE-SERVICE TRAINING	TEACHING STAFF INSERVICE TRAINING > 12 HRS/YR	MEDICAL & TB EXAM REQUIRED	CRIMINAL RECORDS CHECK	CHILD ABUSE REGISTRY CHECKS	
ALABAMA	NO	NO	NO	NO		NO		NO	NO	NO
ALASKA	NO[1]	NO		NO			NO[5]			
ARIZONA		NO	NO	NO		NO	NO[5]		NO	NO
ARKANSAS	NO[2]	NO	NO	NO	NO	NO				
CALIFORNIA			NO			NO				
COLORADO		NO		NO		NO				NO
CONN.									NO	
DELAWARE	NO		NO							
D.C.						NO		NO	NO	
FLORIDA	NO		NO			NO	NO[5]			
GEORGIA	NO	NO	NO	NO[3]	NO	NO	NO		NO	
HAWAII			NO			NO				
IDAHO	NO	NO	NO	NO	NO	NO	NO			NO
ILLINOIS	NO									
INDIANA	NO			NO		NO				
IOWA	NO[1]			NO		NO	NO[5]			
KANSAS			NO			NO				
KENTUCKY		NO	NO	NO[3]	NO	NO	NO[5]		NO	
LOUISIANA	NO	NO	NO	NO[3]		NO			NO	
MAINE				NO		NO				
MARYLAND						NO	NO[6]			
MASS.	NO[1]									
MICHIGAN				NO		NO			NO	
MINNESOTA							NO			
MISSISSIPPI		NO	NO				NO			
MISSOURI	NO			NO	NO	NO		NO		
MONTANA	NO			NO[3]	NO	NO	NO[5]			
NEBRASKA	NO			NO	NO[3]	NO	NO	NO		

TABLE 6.1 (CONTINUED)

STATE	ALL CENTERS REGULATED	MAXIMUM NUMBER OF CHILDREN PER STAFF MEMBER		STAFF QUALIFICATIONS						INDOOR SPACE > = 35 SQ FT
		INFANTS 4:1 OR LESS	3YRS OLD 10:1 OR LESS	TEACHERS REQUIRE PRE-SERVICE TRAINING	DIRECTORS REQUIRE PRE-SERVICE TRAINING	TEACHING STAFF INSERVICE TRAINING > 12 HRS/YR	MEDICAL & TB EXAM REQUIRED	CRIMINAL RECORDS CHECK	CHILD ABUSE REGISTRY CHECKS	
NEVADA		NO	NO	NO³		NO	NO⁵			
NEW HAMPSHIRE						NO				
NEW JERSEY				NO³	NO	NO		NO		
NEW MEXICO		NO	NO	NO	NO		NO⁵		NO	
NEW YORK	NO					NO		NO		
NORTH CAROLINA	NO²	NO	NO							NO
NORTH DAKOTA	NO			NO			NO⁵	NO		
OHIO		NO	NO	NO		NO⁴			NO	
OKLAHOMA	NO		NO	NO³	NO	NO	NO⁵		NO	
OREGON	NO			NO	NO		NO			
PENN.	NO			NO		NO				
R.I.	NO									
SOUTH CAROLINA	NO²	NO	NO	NO	NO					
SOUTH DAKOTA	NO	NO		NO	NO		NO			
TENNESSEE				NO³		NO	NO⁷	NO	NO	NO
TEXAS	NO	NO	NO	NO³			NO			NO
UTAH	NO		NO	NO³						
VERMONT						NO	NO			
VIRGINIA	NO			NO		NO	NO			NO
WASH.	NO						NO⁵			
W. VIRGINIA	NO			NO						NO
WISCONSIN	NO¹									
WYOMING		NO		NO	NO	NO		NO	NO	

Source: The Children's Foundation, *2000 Center Licensing Study* (Washington, DC: The Children's Foundation, 2000).
    Also, consultation with Sheri Azer, Center for Career Development in Early Care and Education, Wheelock College.
Notes for Table 6.1
1. Exempt school-based programs.
2. Exempt some centers from licensing but not from regulation for health and safety.
3. The state requires only an orientation meeting.
4. Requires 45 clock hours over 3 years for those with no previous training.
5. No medical examination required.
6. No TB test required.
7. Tennessee will require background checks as soon as the system can be put in place.

Most states distinguish between small family child ca large or group child care homes. Small homes, which are the \ are those where one provider cares for one or more unrelated chi provider's residence. Large family child care homes are those in w are enough children to require two or more caretakers. In some state., such a home may serve as many as 20 children. Most states require large family homes to be licensed or certified, and minimum standards are somewhat more stringent than for small family child care homes, though still less demanding than for centers.

The best states—11 in all—require that all small family child care providers be licensed regardless of the number of children they care for. Other states exempt providers who take care of only one child, still others exempt those taking care of only two, and still others exempt those taking care of only three. The worst—the 19 identified in column 1 of table 6.2—exempt most family child care providers.

Full coverage of all family child care providers is expensive for a state and requires a lavish expenditure of the time of a large staff. An inspector monitoring 20 family child care homes is serving at most 80 to 100 children whereas one monitoring 20 centers is serving more than 1,000 children. We recommend that all states require licensing of any family child care home caring for 3 or more children. This would increase the number of regulated small family child care providers in all but 16 states. Those caring for 1 or 2 children should be required to register and undergo background checks for a record of criminality or child abuse. However, we would reserve the right to receive public funds to licensed providers.

Other weaknesses of the regulation of small family child care providers are shown in table 6.2. Column 2 shows that 14 states permit one provider to care for 9 or more children. In all, based on information in columns 1 and 2, we would have to rate about 30 states as having inadequate regulation of small providers of family child care. In addition, there are a considerable number of states that do not require:

- TB tests for providers
- criminal record checks
- child abuse registry checks
- first aid and CPR training

TABLE 6.2

Do states require that small family child care homes meet important standards?
(year 2000)

STATE	REGULATION REQUIRED FOR MOST PROVIDERS*	MAX. GROUP SIZE < 9	QUALIFICATIONS (REGULATED PROVIDERS)						INSIDE SPACE REQUIREMENTS
			PRESERVICE TRAINING (OTHER THAN ORIENTATION)	INSERVICE TRAINING >= 6 HOURS/YR	CPR/FIRST AID TRAINING	TB TESTS	CRIMINAL RECORD CHECK	CHILD ABUSE CHECKS	
ALABAMA			NO	NO	NO		NO	NO	NO
ALASKA	NO		NO			NO			NO
ARIZONA	NO		NO					NO	NO[7]
ARKANSAS	NO		NO		NO				
CALIFORNIA			NO	NO					NO
COLORADO			NO			NO			
CONNECTICUT		NO[2]	NO	NO				NO	NO
DELAWARE		NO[2]							NO
D.C.			NO	NO			NO	NO	
FLORIDA		NO[2]		NO					NO
GEORGIA			NO			NO		NO	
HAWAII			NO	NO	NO				
IDAHO	NO[1]		NO	NO	NO	NO		NO	NO
ILLINOIS			NO	NO					NO
INDIANA	NO		NO	NO					NO
IOWA	NO		NO	NO		NO			NO
KANSAS			NO	NO					NO
KENTUCKY								NO	
LOUISIANA	NO		NO	NO		NO		NO	NO
MAINE		NO	NO					NO	
MARYLAND									NO
MASS.			NO	NO				NO	
MICHIGAN			NO	NO				NO	
MINNESOTA		NO	NO			NO		NO	
MISSISSIPPI	NO		NO			NO			
MISSOURI	NO	NO	NO		NO		NO	NO	
MONTANA				NO	NO				
NEBRASKA		NO[2]	NO			NO	NO	NO	
NEVADA	NO[1]		NO					NO	
NEW HAMPSHIRE		NO[2]	NO[3]			NO			
NEW JERSEY	NO			NO	NO		NO	NO	NO

TABLE 6.2 (CONTINUED)

STATE	REGULATION REQUIRED FOR MOST PROVIDERS*	MAX. GROUP SIZE < 9	QUALIFICATIONS (REGULATED PROVIDERS)						INSIDE SPACE REQUIREMENTS
			PRESERVICE TRAINING (OTHER THAN ORIENTATION)	INSERVICE TRAINING >= 6 HOURS/YR	CPR/FIRST AID TRAINING	TB TESTS	CRIMINAL RECORD CHECK	CHILD ABUSE CHECKS	
NEW MEXICO	NO		NO					NO	
NEW YORK			NO		NO		NO		NO
NORTH CAROLINA			NO						NO
NORTH DAKOTA	NO	NO[2]	NO			NO	NO		
OHIO	NO		NO	NO[5]				NO	
OKLAHOMA			NO		NO				
OREGON		NO	NO	NO		NO			NO
PENN.			NO						NO
RHODE ISLAND				NO		NO		NO	
SOUTH CAROLINA	NO				NO	NO	NO	NO	NO[8]
SOUTH DAKOTA	NO	NO	NO				NO		NO
TENNESSEE	NO		NO	NO			NO[6]	NO	NS
TEXAS		NO[2]	NO						NO
UTAH	NO	NS	NO						
VERMONT		NO[2]	NO			NO			NO
VIRGINIA	NO[1]		NO						NO
WASHINGTON		NO	NO	NO				NO	
WEST VIRGINIA			NO	NO	NO			NO	NO
WISCONSIN			NO[4]		NO				
WYOMING			NO				NO		

Source: The Children's Foundation, *1999 Family Child Care Licensing Study* (Washington, DC: The Children's Foundation). Gwen Morgan and Sheri L. Azer, "Trends in Child Care Licensing and Regulation, 2000. Center for Career Development in Early Care and Education, "Definition of Licensed Family Child Care Homes in 2000." Correspondence with Sheri Azer, November 2000.

* Six of the 19 states marked "NO" only regulate providers receiving public funds, one state exempts all small family child care providers (Idaho), one state exempts providers caring for six or fewer children (Iowa), four states exempt providers caring for five or fewer children, and seven exempt providers caring for four or fewer children.

1. City or county may require licensing or registration.

2. One provider is permitted to care for nine or more children at the beginning or end of the day, but only 6 during the school day. An additional 3 or more children can be present before and after school.

3. Providers between 18 and 21 years of age must have completed an approved vocational course.

4. Wisconsin does not require preservice training but does require 40 clock hours of early childhood education within 6 months of licensing.

5. In Ohio regulated providers must take ongoing training for 4 years only: 12 clock hours the first year and 6 hours per year up to 30 hours total.

6. In Tennessee, checks are now required but a system is not yet in place.

7. Inside space requirements for providers with five or more children: 30 square feet/child.

8. 35 square feet inside and 75 square feet per child outside for the 10 licensed centers in the state, no requirements for the 1,528 registered small family child care providers in the state.

NS means not specified.

All but five states and territories require children in licensed homes to be immunized. Corporal punishment is prohibited in all but six states. Most states prohibit smoking in rooms used by the children and where food is prepared, but 11 states permit smoking in family child care homes without restrictions.

States pay less attention to family child care physical facilities than to center facilities, although family child care homes are often subject to local building codes and health inspections. Twenty-six do not regulate minimum indoor space per child, and 32 do not require outdoor play space. Very few states test homes for the presence of radon, asbestos, and lead or address the issue of pesticide use near family child care homes in rural areas.

Standards for provider qualifications and ongoing training in licensed small family child care homes are nonexistent to low. Table 6.2 shows that 18 states require no training whatever, or training that involves at most 6 clock hours a year. Providers who enter the industry without training are not required to make up for their lack of knowledge in any substantial way in many states. Only four states require small family child care providers to have a high school degree or equivalent (GED), although they all require large group providers to have a high school diploma. In most states small and large group providers can be as young as 18 years old; some states allow family child care providers to be 16 years old.

While there have been some improvements recently in training requirements in some states, persisting low or nonexistant training requirements in others suggests official acceptance of family child care as babysitting in these states. However, they also reflect practical realities. Higher training requirements discourage providers from getting licensed, tending to push family child care underground. Again, increased funding should make it possible to raise training requirements. Adequately reimbursed licensed family child care providers would be more willing to invest in training and in a career in family child care.

Enforcing the Standards

Enforcement practices are at the heart of effective regulation. In addition to routine inspections of existing centers and providers, licensing staff handle applications for licenses. Initial license approval can be a time-consuming process involving several site visits by the licensing inspector to help the center or child care home come up to licensing standards. In many states licensing staff provide training and briefing sessions, particularly for prospective family child care providers, on legal requirements and other aspects of the work.

Inspectors/consultants follow up on complaints, which can require multiple site visits. They must initiate and participate in legal actions against providers whom they consider to be seriously out of compliance and endangering children.

At present most licensing agencies are understaffed and cannot adequately monitor providers.[6] For family child care homes, the caseload ratio is over 100:1 in 70 percent of the states reporting this information, and well over 300:1 in populous states like California and Massachusetts. For centers, where inspections are much more time-consuming, the average reported caseload is also over 100:1, reaching over 200:1 in Maine, Michigan, and Vermont.[7] Experts in the field consider caseloads of 75:1 for family child care and 60:1 for centers to be appropriate.

Compliance with minimum standards is improved when facilities expect periodic unannounced inspections. Table 6.3 shows the states that did not require even one unannounced inspection per year in the year 2000. At least 18 required either no unannounced inspections or fewer than one a year for both family child care providers and centers, among them several densely populated states: New Jersey, Maryland, Massachusetts, Michigan, New York, Pennsylvania, and Washington. Nine states required inspections of licensed centers only when a complaint was filed.

A recent case in Alexandria, Virginia illustrates the value of unannounced visits. A family child care operator was licensed to care for 6 children, but when an infant in her care died, it was revealed that she was (with some assistance) caring for 28. All inspection visits to her were announced ahead of time, and on the rare occasions when the inspector was expected, she told the parents of the extra children to keep them home.

The unfortunate effect of infrequent state inspections was addressed in a study done in Vermont by political scientist William Gormley of Georgetown University. The state instituted a system in which the licensing period varied depending on the center's record of code violations. Over a five-year period, Gormley compared the performance of centers that had previously been rated as "good," and thus were only inspected once in two years, with the performance of the centers previously rated "poor," which received an inspection every year. The formerly "good" centers got worse reports than the formerly "poor" ones.[8] Results from the NICHD study also substantiate the need for more frequent unannounced inspections. A quarter of the centers observed in that study were out of compliance with their state's group size standards, and noncompliance ran as high as 60 percent in some states.[9]

TABLE 6.3.

Do states require at least one unannounced inspection per year in the year 2000?

STATE	CHILD CARE CENTERS	SMALL FAMILY CHILD CARE HOMES	STATE	CHILD CARE CENTERS	SMALL FAMILY CHILD CARE HOMES
ALABAMA			MONTANA		NO
ALASKA	NO	NO	NEBRASKA		
ARIZONA			NEVADA	NO	
ARKANSAS			NEW HAMPSHIRE	NO	NO
CALIFORNIA		NO	NEW JERSEY	NO	NO
COLORADO	NO	NO	NEW MEXICO	NO	NO
CONNECTICUT	—	NO	NEW YORK	NO	NO
DELAWARE	NO		NORTH CAROLINA	NO	NO
D.C.		—	NORTH DAKOTA	—	
FLORIDA			OHIO		
GEORGIA	—	NO	OKLAHOMA		
HAWAII	NO	NO	OREGON	NO	NO
IDAHO	NO	NO	PENNSYLVANIA	NO	NO
ILLINOIS			RHODE ISLAND		NO
INDIANA		NO	SOUTH CAROLINA	NO	NO
IOWA		NO	SOUTH DAKOTA	NO	NO
KANSAS		NO	TENNESSEE		
KENTUCKY		NO	TEXAS		NO
LOUISIANA	—	NO	UTAH		
MAINE	—		VERMONT		
MARYLAND	NO	NO	VIRGINIA		
MASS.	NO	NO	WASHINGTON	NO	NO
MICHIGAN	NO	NO	WEST VIRGINIA		NO
MINNESOTA	NO	NO[1]	WISCONSIN		
MISSISSIPPI		NO	WYOMING		NO
MISSOURI		—			

Source: The Children's Foundation, *2000 Child Care Center Licensing Study, 2000 Family child Care Licensing Study* Washington, DC: The Children's Foundation, 2000).

1. Counties may make unannounced visits.

— means information was not provided by the Children's Foundation.

Effective enforcement requires states to respond quickly to licensing violations by imposing sanctions and, when necessary, by shutting down providers. Traditionally, states have revoked very few licenses. Most licensing offices have a large backlog of allegations and insufficient numbers of staff to take many cases to court. Revocation of a license usually requires an administrative hearing and an appeal procedure that can take four or five years. Appeals require state departments of justice to prosecute cases, and with their own backlog to manage, some states are reluctant to move against even serious violators of child care rules. Recent increases in staffing in some states and in the District of Columbia are leading to more revocations. However, the problem illustrated in our opening account of enforcement in the District of Columbia still remains in many locations; licensing agencies may be loath to close down providers and create a shortage of child care slots.

License revocation, while the essential ultimate threat, is nevertheless a crude tool. States need intermediate sanctions such as fines or public notice of violations to induce providers to comply with standards. Unfortunately, some states have not developed their laws and regulations to allow these intermediate sanctions.

Ideally, state licensing agencies would combine enforcement with consultative services to correct problems and improve performance, although combining these roles does have potential costs in terms of the rigor of the regulatory function and may produce conflicts. In many state agencies professionally trained licensing staff often have considerable bureaucratic discretion. With the right enforcement tools as well as adequate budgets, staff could do much to help providers improve quality.[10]

In many states inefficiencies exist because of parallel and sometimes conflicting inspection systems. In addition to facility licensing, state fire marshal and health department permissions and monitoring are often required. Local governments enforce building and zoning regulations, occupancy permits, and sometimes require separate fire and health inspections. In 1990, according to one account, family child care providers caring for six children had to obtain business licenses in 31 percent of U.S. cities, an occupancy permit in 36 percent of U.S. cities, and a zoning permit in 25 percent of cities.[11] Local occupancy and zoning requirements that limit commercial activities in residential neighborhoods tend to discourage family child care providers from getting licensed. In most states more coordination is needed to increase efficiency and reduce the burden of inspections on providers.

Does Regulation Help or Hurt?

Many political conservatives and some economists oppose any licensing at all for child care providers. (They tend to oppose licensing in all fields, not just child care.) Some detractors of regulation claim that any mandated minimum standards are unnecessary because consumers are the best judge of safety for their children. They argue that regulation itself is expensive, a waste of the taxpayers' money.

Opponents of regulation in child care claim that there are serious unintended consequences that defeat the initial purpose of protecting children from harm and that put more children at risk than would be the case if there were no licensing.[12] They argue that regulation keeps some potential providers out of the market, reducing the choices that parents have. It also raises the start-up and operating costs for regulated providers, and therefore parent fees. If the government actually were successful in preventing unlicensed providers from operating, then some families would be shut out from the market for child care services by the higher prices.

If the regulation applies to some but not all providers, as is the case with child care in many states, or if there is widespread flouting of the regulation requirements, then families can pass up the licensed care and patronize legally exempt or illegal providers. Opponents of regulation argue that enforcing standards does not permit lower-priced centers to operate and that children who might have been accommodated in them would be placed instead with relatives or boyfriends, where the children would be given care of a still lower quality. This kind of argument leads to the position that lowering standards is always a good thing, raising them always a bad thing.

Is there substance to these objections? The existence of regulation and inspection reflects the common sense public view that to do without them would pose an unacceptable risk for some children. The reasoning is much the same as requiring inspection of restaurants or elevators, which few people would object to. Licensing assures that the 80 to 85 percent of programs that fall short of good quality nevertheless provide acceptably safe services. We do not know how child care providers would react to the complete elimination of all standards. The Cost, Quality, and Child Outcomes Study (CQO) provides some indication that many of these centers would lower quality considerably if they were free of regulation but not from price competition.

There is evidence that higher standards improve the quality of the regulated portion of the industry and that the regulated portion gives better quality care than the unregulated part. The National Child Care Staffing Study and the CQO both found that, on average, center quality in states with more stringent regulations had higher process quality than centers in states with lower standards.[13] In the Family Child Care and Relative Care study, regulated family child care homes provided considerably higher quality than nonregulated homes and relatives.[14]

On the question of diversion of children away from regulated providers, although research results are mixed, some studies of centers did find that higher licensing standards reduce usage and availability.[15] In three early studies higher required staff:child ratios had a negative effect on usage or availability but higher training requirements did not, except in one study. Fuller and Lian, in *The Unfair Search for Child Care,* found no relation between center availability and stringency of regulations. In more recent studies higher required staff:child ratios reduced use of centers in two of the studies and higher training requirements reduced usage in all three studies. However, Hotz and Kilborn report that higher training requirements were associated with more center use by nonworking mothers (who, presumably, are mainly concerned about good quality preschool education).

Lower standards should induce more for-profit centers to enter the market, so that in states setting relatively low standards, a higher proportion of care is provided by centers. However, little effect on the quantity of services supplied was observed when Georgia raised standards, reducing the number of infants cared for per staff member from 7 to 6 and increasing the requirement for ongoing staff training.[16] About half of the reporting centers improved staffing ratios and hired on average one additional teacher. Although average cost per infant increased some, there were no changes in center closures statewide or in program turnover rates.

Minimum required staffing ratios, group size, and training have little effect on availability of family child care homes or on parent choice.[17] Licensing small family child care homes may make them more visible to parents looking for care and may alert potential providers of the service to the opportunities available. This may have a positive effect on the number of places available and on the ease with which a parent can find an appropriate provider.

More frequent inspections have been found to increase parent usage of regulated services, suggesting that parents may have more confidence in child care when there is more enforcement.[18] Inspections may, however, discourage providers from getting licensed.[19]

Not surprisingly, regulation of group size, training requirements, and number of inspections have large and significant effects on price, quality, and quantity (the number of child hours) of services provided.[20] Further, regulations that directly affect centers indirectly affect family child care. For instance, higher family child care training requirements increase the use of center care.[21]

Because affordability is so crucial to most families, we have to be concerned about the diversion of children from licensed to unlicensed care. Until there is considerably more help with fees for families, minimum licensing standards should not be set higher than necessary to reduce the risk of harm to children. If, as we urge, we were to provide much higher levels of subsidization of child care, it would be possible to institute higher licensing standards without jeopardizing low- and middle-income children. However, to reduce parents' tendency to substitute unregulated for regulated care, the solution is not to deregulate but to make licensed services affordable through the kinds of subsidy programs we are advocating.

We Need a Better-Financed Licensing System

Most states have either low standards for centers or family child care, or infrequent monitoring in one or both of the sectors. Some states with low standards for one or both categories of care have reasonably good enforcement. Some states have reasonable policies for centers, but not for family child care. Currently, states are hampered by inadequate funding in their attempts to provide quality control. Adequately funded state licensing enforcement is crucial to the success of the voucher program we are recommending. Vouchers give parents maximum flexibility in choosing services, but the options available need to be of acceptable quality, and public subsidies should not be used, as they are today, to purchase poor quality care. In our plan, only licensed programs with an acceptable level of compliance would be eligible to receive vouchers. Providers in categories that are currently exempt in many states—preschools operating part-time, centers operated by religious groups or schools, and family child care providers (even relatives)—would have to be licensed in order to receive federal funding.

To provide adequate licensing enforcement, staffing in most state licensing agencies needs to be increased to create appropriate inspector caseloads. Some states take six months to process applications. When inspectors are overtaxed, there is a reluctance to initiate legal actions when they are warranted.[22]

In many states salary scales need to be increased to reflect the professional training and experience required of inspectors/consultants. Licensing inspectors do more than check off compliance and noncompliance. They have to make judgements about program adequacy and apply the intent of the rules to the situations that exist in a given facility. Inspectors must know the law, decide if legal action is warranted in a particular case, know how to create the factual base for legal action, and serve as credible expert witnesses in a judicial setting. They also serve as consultants to providers, helping them solve noncompliance problems. Ideally, jobs as inspectors/consultants should require experience as a licensed child care provider, specialized legal and policy training, a master's degree in either social work or early childhood development or education, and ongoing training to keep inspectors abreast of relevant legal cases and procedures and child development research.[23]

We estimate the extra cost of providing an adequate staff to be about $335 million per year. It would correct current inadequacies and also meet the needs created by voucher expansion. It is based on caseloads of 60:1 for centers and 80:1 for family child care providers, which would permit at least two unannounced inspections per year plus other inspections required for new applicants, relicensing, and complaints. A ratio of six licensing specialists to one field supervisor was used, which represents current practice in several states. In addition to lower caseloads, the estimate allows for an across-the-board increase of 33 percent in supervisor and licensing specialist salaries.[24]

Actual costs could be lower since more effective enforcement through lower caseloads might also bring increased efficiency in the inspection process. Oklahoma found that noncompliance dropped with lower caseloads. Then when caseloads doubled in the early 1990s, negative sanctions increased 213 percent, increasing the number of complaint investigations and follow-up inspections that had to be done.[25]

QUALITY STANDARDS FOR
PROVIDERS RECEIVING FEDERAL FUNDING

Even an adequately financed system of state licensing will not guarantee access for all children to reasonably good quality early care and education; it merely reduces the risk of harm to children. One way to promote higher quality standards for the nation as a whole, at least for publicly subsidized projects, is through federal rules that prescribe quality standards and restrict eligibility for public money to those providers who meet them.

At present, the federal government imposes funding standards on many of the goods and services it purchases. Even in the child care field, there are funding standards for Head Start contractors, and the Department of Defense monitors its centers based on standards developed in the Military Child Development Program. However, for the two major federal programs providing subsidies for child care—the Child Care and Development Fund (CCDF) block grant and the tax credit for dependent care—no specific federal standards of quality have been set.

The idea that federally funded early care and education programs should be required to meet specified quality standards has been highly controversial. Ideologically based opposition to federal funding and regulation of child care programs comes from conservatives who resist any support for child care as an alternative to maternal child care, by those who argue that the child care market already operates efficiently, and by those who advocate devolution of power to the states. From a practical standpoint, instituting federal standards increases the cost of programs. Since the impetus for federal child care subsidies has been motivated by a desire to get poor parents off welfare and into jobs, cost containment of government child care subsidies has been a high priority.

Attempts to establish federal funding standards have over a 60-year history.[26] The U.S. Office of Education issued the first federal day care standards in 1941. After World War II and the withdrawal of funds for child care, child care disappeared from the national agenda. It resurfaced again in 1962 welfare reform legislation, an early attempt to move from welfare to "workfare" by providing employment and training services for clients of Aid to Families with Dependent Children (AFDC). The law required child care programs receiving federal funds to be licensed, inducing a number of states to pass their first licensing laws. The welfare reform legislation in 1967 mandated a common set of program standards for the child care it funded, including Head Start. The affected federal departments all agreed to implement a common set of standards, the Federal Interagency Day Care Requirements (FIDCR), to be created by a panel of experts.

In 1970 Democrats in Congress introduced the Comprehensive Child Development Act to establish a comprehensive child developmental care program based on the Head Start experience; it would extend federal assistance to the nonpoor as well as the poor. President Nixon vetoed the bill asserting that it was "family weakening," but he did sign legislation calling for a revision of FIDCR. The revisions, however, were opposed from two sides: Child development advocates considered them an attack on quality, and the Office of Management and Budget considered them too costly. The revisions were buried, leaving the 1968 version in place.

During the 1970s, there were various attempts to revise the 1968 FIDCR regulations. In practice, the regulations were widely waived. However, they were written into Title XX child care funding legislation in 1975, becoming law. When they were widely enforced, new opposition arose from providers whose programs served both subsidized and unsubsidized children in states where FIDCR had previously been waived because the standards raised costs and, therefore, fees for unsubsidized families. Congress declared a moratorium on enforcement of FIDCR staffing ratios and mandated a study of the appropriateness of federal day care standards. Results of the National Day Care Study indicated that group size had more effect than staffing ratios on outcomes for preschool-aged children and helped defuse arguments over appropriate staffing ratios. However, Congress, worried over the costs of implementing the regulations, temporarily suspended enforcement of FIDCR. Regulations were eliminated permanently in the 1981 legislation that also cut federal child care subsidies.

Later, in the 1980s, national publicity and uproar over child abuse created a new opportunity for regulatory action. In 1985 Congress directed the Department of Health and Human Services to create model child care standards to be advisory to states. The department issued a series of regulatory guidelines; however, the department concluded that, because of the differences in state approaches and the lack of public consensus, that a single set of standards could not be applied in all states. When, in 1990, Congress increased funding for subsidized child care significantly, it left responsibility to the states for the use of public expenditures on child care. Federal standards had become a dead issue.

At the present time, under CCDF, although federal funding standards are essentially absent, a state can choose to impose more stringent standards than state licensing regulations require on child care providers receiving federal funding as long as the standards do not significantly restrict parent choice. The 1996 Temporary Assistance to Needy Families legislation (TANF) requires states to permit parent choice of type of care, and regulation of providers is construed to interfere with parent choice. Child care advocates and members of Congress sympathetic to increased funding for child care have given up on tying funding to funding standards, fearing that fights over quality standards would reduce appropriations for child care. Furthermore, enforcing funding standards on providers who serve both subsidized and unsubsidized children is a major practical stumbling block as long as subsidies are limited to a small percent of the population of children in paid nonparental care. This problem would be minimized if, as we are suggesting, the federal government were to expand subsidies to include all children whose costs of care exceeded 20 percent of their parents' income over the poverty line.

To provide some national guidelines, the Maternal and Child Health Bureau of the Public Health Service collaborated with the American Public Health Association (APHA) and the American Academy of Pediatrics (AAP) to publish performance guidelines. A shortened version of key items, including recommendations on staffing ratios, group size, and staff qualifications was published as *Stepping Stones to Using "Caring for Our Children."*[27] A new version of the standards is under development at this writing.

While establishing funding standards at the federal level has not been politically feasible, some states are moving to use them to try to improve quality. About half of the states are creating tiered reimbursement systems, paying higher rates to providers who provide better quality. Most just use two tiers, allowing one rate for licensed providers and a higher rate for accredited centers. North Carolina uses a star system with five levels that makes use of the ECERS rating system and also looks at compliance with regulation requirements, the director's education, staff training levels, and compensation.

ACCREDITATION

Traditionally, in U.S. health- and education-related services regulated by states, national quality standards have been established and enforced through voluntary accreditation by professional associations. With the growth of federal funding in higher education and medical care, accrediting agencies became quasilegal entities, gatekeepers determining which institutions are eligible for federal funding. In practice, accreditation is mandatory for any college, university, or hospital desiring to receive federal funding. Schools are hard put to recruit students, and hospitals to recruit staff and patients, without it.

Accreditation institutionalizes program characteristics and training requirements considered important by professionals in the field and signals to purchasers that the provider meets these standards of quality. Accreditation, if widely accepted, can create nationwide standards of good practice. It has its own limitations and is subject to failures and problems of various sorts, and so is far from a panacea. However, its potential contribution is certainly an important one.

There are many potential benefits of extending accreditation to child care. If properly administered, accreditation makes shopping for child care more efficient by identifying programs that have met professional standards for good quality. This information is important to consumers who have trouble evaluating service quality. Just like star systems for restaurants and hotels, knowledge about accreditation is an efficient first step in finding good quality services. As in higher education, accreditation could also be used as an eligibility criterion for receiving public or philanthropic funding. Accreditation gives providers an incentive to improve their service and help in doing so through a self-study process that enables them to evaluate their program against the standards of the profession. In terms of improving the overall quality of child care, this self-educational function is the most important aspect of accreditation.

Center staff members in military child development centers who have gone through accreditation have reported that the most significant effect was in using more developmentally appropriate, child-initiated activities.[28] Accreditation also improves center organizational climate in encouraging more innovation, consensus on goals, opportunities for personal growth, levels of job commitment, and tenure on the job.[29]

The largest association of child care professionals, the National Association for the Education of Young Children (NAEYC), is the current leader in the accreditation field. Starting in 1980, the association invested heavily in developing an accreditation system. This effort involved building a consensus within the profession regarding appropriate accreditation criteria, ensuring the validity of these criteria, designing and field-testing the accreditation system, and training volunteer validators. The NAEYC goal has been to provide a process to facilitate lasting improvements in program quality and then to reward these centers with accreditation, a kind of Good Housekeeping seal of approval. Self-study has become the lynchpin in that process, which requires one or two years to complete even for centers ready for accreditation.[30]

NAEYC accredited its first programs in 1986, and in 2000 approximately 7,500 programs were accredited, with another 7,500 in the process of self-study. Of the more than 106,000 licensed, center-based early care and education programs, roughly 7 percent are accredited and 7 percent are moving toward accreditation.

The accreditation process has been supported financially by corporate employers concerned about the availability of good quality services for their employees. IBM was the pioneer in facilitating center accreditation, paying fees for centers, and setting up supportive group discussions, consultations, and mini-grants to help the self-study process. The child care centers that serve the military, centers sponsored by the federal General Service Administration, Head Start programs, and public school prekindergartens are being encouraged or required to achieve accreditation. Some national child care chains—Children's World Learning Centers, Bright Horizons, and, more recently, the largest of them all, KinderCare—are emphasizing accreditation. In addition, most states introducing differential reimbursement rates for publicly subsidized children base eligibility for higher reimbursement on accreditation.

NAEYC Center Accreditation

The NAEYC system is designed for child care centers. More specialized accreditation programs have also been developed for family child care and out-of-school programs for school-aged children by their respective professional organizations. NAEYC accreditation is based on a set of standards that define good quality. They include 93 criteria classified into ten categories. Table 6.4 lists the categories and selected criteria in each category. In contrast to state licensing standards these accreditation standards include classroom process characteristics (similar to items assessed by ECERS and ITERS, described in chapter 4) and administrative effectiveness as well as structural quality and health and safety practices.[31]

NAEYC recommendations on staff qualifications represent an advance over most state licensing standards but reflect realistic goals, given present realities. They recommend that assistant teachers and teachers have at least a Child Development Associate (CDA) credential and that programs have at least one staff member with a B.A. degree in early childhood education.[32] NAEYC recommends a range of acceptable staffing ratios and group sizes, depending on the age group being served. However, it is possible for some centers to gain accreditation if they do not have ratios within the recommended range.

In the self-study phase of the application process, the program staff and the director review their program and observe classes to rate staff-child interactions and other program characteristics that bear on quality, correcting deficiencies in the program prior to the review by outsiders. This may involve hiring more trained staff, providing training for existing staff, or increasing ratios of staff to children. An outside validator designated by NAEYC visits the center for at least one day to check the accuracy of the self-study, making direct observations of classrooms, examining records and procedures, and interviewing the program director. The self-study surveys of parents and staff and the validator's report are submitted to NAEYC, where a commission conducts a blind review and makes the accreditation decision. If the program is found deficient, accreditation is deferred. Deferred programs may make recommended improvements and request another verification visit and accreditation decision, or they can appeal the decision. Accreditation is valid for three years with annual reporting of progress on improvements recommended by NAEYC and on major changes such as location or ownership.

TABLE 6.4
Selected criteria from NAEYC accreditation procedures

1. INTERACTION AMONG TEACHERS AND CHILDREN:

Frequent respectful, affectionate interaction

Teachers are available, attentive and responsive

Teachers encourage independent functioning

No corporal punishment or humiliating or frightening discipline.

2. CURRICULUM:

Written statement of goals for center and for each child

Balance of activities in and out of doors, variety and choice

Developmentally appropriate materials and equipment

3. RELATIONSHIPS AMONG TEACHERS AND FAMILIES:

Regular, collaborative communication between teachers and families

Parents are welcome visitors, cultural differences respected

Center uses community resources

4. STAFF QUALIFICATIONS AND PROFESSIONAL DEVELOPMENT:

Formal education requirements at different staff levels

Orientation and in-service opportunities

Availability of specialists

5. ADMINISTRATION:

Written policies with annual review

Salary scale and benefits

Record keeping

6. STAFFING:

Group sizes and child staff ratios by age

Continuity both of groups and staff

7. PHYSICAL ENVIRONMENT:

Adequate safe, clean, attractive space, both indoors and out

Spaces for individual, small group, and larger group activities

Age appropriate materials and equipment

8. HEALTH AND SAFETY:

Compliance with all state and local codes

All adults free from hazardous psychological and medical conditions

Sick child attendance policy

Emergency plans

General cleanliness and universal hand washing

9. NUTRITION AND FOOD SERVICE:

Appropriate kinds, amounts, and frequency of snacks and meals

Parents informed of menus

Meal and snack times are pleasant learning experiences

10. EVALUATION, BOTH STRENGTHS AND WEAKNESSES:

All staff, including the director, are evaluated at least annually

All staff, parents, and school-age children do program evaluation

Children's progress recorded and analyzed, used in planning.

Source: *Accreditation Criteria and Procedures of the National Association for the Education of Young Children, 1998 Edition* (Washington, DC: National Association for the Education of Young Children, 1998).

NAEYC accrediting commissions exercise some discretion in their final decisions, but approved programs must be in "substantial compliance" with accreditation criteria. However, NAEYC has not developed criteria describing degrees of compliance other than "professional judgement." In making the accrediting decision, NAEYC gives the greatest weight to staff-child interactions, curriculum, staff-child ratios, group sizes, and health and safety.[33] They rely most heavily on classroom observations for evidence of compliance. In the year 2000 commissioners deferred or held back only 12 percent of programs under consideration.[34]

Accreditation Under Non-NAEYC Auspices

Accreditation has become highly salient in the child care field, largely thanks to the NAEYC's activities. However, NAEYC does not have the field all to itself; six other systems of accreditation are currently operating under other auspices, including the two specialized ones designed for the accreditation of family child care and after-school care. The major potential rival to NAEYC is the National Early Childhood Program Accreditation (NECPA) set up originally by the National Child Care Association—a trade association with membership mainly from the for-profit sector. In addition, the Association of Christian Schools International (ASCI) accredits centers sponsored by evangelical Christians. These groups have seen fit to establish and use accrediting agencies that they control. The Council on Accreditation (COA), operating since 1977, accredits social service agencies and the child care centers they run.[35]

NAEYC leadership has generally welcomed the presence of other accrediting agencies as a means of encouraging more providers to go through the accreditation process. Yet questions certainly must arise as to the adequacy of the latter's standards and procedures and their comparability with those of the NAEYC. These alternative bodies have as yet accredited only a few hundred centers, and to date there has been no systematic assessment of their procedures and overall effectiveness.[36]

The NECPA system was created to provide a more user-friendly alternative to NAEYC accreditation. The system is based on the "key indicator" approach (originally developed to streamline the monitoring of licensing compliance) that uses a short list of quality indicators that predict overall quality. This simplifies the evaluation process by cutting many items that the NAEYC would require to have evaluated and reported on. The set of key indicators of center quality were statistically identified from NAEYC and the APHA/AAP Guidelines. A study that NECPA sponsored showed that if a center had passing ratings on a certain core group of key indicators, it was likely to have passing ratings on the rest of the NAEYC list. Unfortunately, once certain items are habitually omitted from the evaluation list, the incentive to perform well in those respects may evaporate. This shortcut is built into the self-study manual, which is designed around the indicator checklist, not the full list of criteria. The self-study is also relatively simple to use compared to the NAEYC procedure, requiring the director to give a "yes" or "no" answer to a set of straight-forward questions. In principal, a center must receive "yes" responses to all questions in the self-study; however, NECPA evaluators do allow for some deviation from 100 percent compliance.[37]

NECPA accreditation criteria are strong on health and safety and the characteristics of the building and equipment. They are weaker than the NAEYC on quality criteria related to child/staff interactions and the abilities of staff to work sensitively and intelligently with children to encourage their development. The standards relating to staffing ratios and group size are more stringent than those of NAEYC, but the NECPA teacher education qualifications are lower. NECPA requires only one teacher in the center to have at least a CDA certificate; other members of the teaching staff must have 30 clock hours of instruction within a year of being employed. The low education requirements has an effect on the bottom line: they make it easier to hire staff for the relatively low salaries that for-profit centers tend to pay.

Accreditation by the Association of Christian Schools International (ASCI) is designed to be used by Christian preschools that base their philosophy of education, goals, and mission on biblical sources.[38] Accreditation requires that center board members and staff members evidence a personal relationship with Jesus Christ and identify with the evangelical mission of the preschool, although the ASCI includes developmentally appropriate practice as a goal as well as religious practice. The staffing and teacher-training standards it prescribes are significantly below those prescribed by the other accreditation agencies, often merely requiring that the center meet state licensing standards.

The Council on Accreditation (COA), in accrediting a broad range of social services for families, uses criteria that emphasize management and the effectiveness in organizing service delivery. They are less specific about the quality of services. COA, however, uses higher structural quality requirements than NAEYC, for instance, higher staff:child ratios and staff education qualifications.[39]

Accreditation of Family Child Care and Before- and After-School Programs

The National Association for Family Child Care (NAFCC) and the National School-Age Care Alliance (NSACA) inaugurated accreditation programs in 1999 after several years of identifying standards and testing the systems. They have adapted the general NAEYC strategy for developing an accreditation system as well as the standard procedures for going through the process. They both emphasize a self-study process that encourages continuous improvement of programs. They require comprehensive program critique, direct observation of services by an outside validator to rate quality, and improvement plans that must be acted upon before requesting a validation visit. Both accreditation systems go to great lengths to make their quality criteria sensitive to the concerns of ethnic and racial groups.[40]

Assessing Accredited Programs

Several studies provide evidence that while NAEYC accreditation is associated on average with relatively good quality, it does not guarantee it. Findings from the National Child Care Staffing Study, based on evaluations using ECERS, ITERS, and Arnett instruments, revealed that, compared to other centers in the study, accredited centers had higher average overall quality, provided a more developmentally appropriate environment, employed more highly trained staff who were more sensitive to children's needs, and paid them higher wages.[41] The Cost Quality and Child Outcomes study confirmed these results.[42] In both of these studies, however, not all accredited centers had scores in the "good-quality" range.

In a more recent study the Center for the Child Care Workforce reported similar results in evaluating quality in 92 centers, 55 of which were observed before and after seeking accreditation. Compared to centers that did not achieve accreditation, centers that did become accredited had higher overall classroom quality at the beginning of the self-study process and showed greater improvement in overall quality, staff-child ratios, and teacher sensitivity scores.[43] Nevertheless, almost 40 percent of these NAEYC-accredited centers were rated mediocre.

The fact that so many accredited centers have been found to produce less than good quality services indicates the need to establish more effective screening practices. Currently the NAEYC is engaged in a thorough evaluation of their system to refine procedures and increase their capability to handle the increased requests for accreditation. NECPA is similarly concerned and is experimenting with employing a paid validator in an effort to assure reliable verification of center self-studies.[44]

Current child care accreditation programs may be allowing mediocre programs to receive their seal of approval because they are failing to adequately screen programs for quality at one or more steps of the accreditation process: (1) the agency may not have developed criteria that incorporate high enough standards; (2) validators may be too lenient in applying the standards; (3) the commissioners may not apply criteria uniformly, or may not have clear criteria for exercising discretion in their decision whether or not to grant, defer, or deny accreditation; (4) child care quality may deteriorate during the three-year accreditation period between renewals; and (5) the accrediting body itself may have been created to make it easier to legitimate certain classes of centers.

There are significant differences in criteria. Only NAEYC accreditation stresses detailed standards related to developmentally appropriate services. Self-study manuals vary in the way they describe acceptable observable behavior. In the ECERS instruments, for instance, specific behavior thresholds must be met for a room to merit a score of five, or "developmentally appropriate." This is rarely the case in the self-study manuals. The less specific the description of appropriate characteristics, the more leeway there is for center staff to give themselves passing grades and for validators to agree with them. Accrediting agencies need to work out effective ways to encourage both objective program evaluation and program improvement.

Validators need to discriminate between programs that do a good job of self-assessment and those that do not. In addition to checking records, validators must spend enough time in classrooms to verify the center's own view of itself, which does not always happen in some accreditation programs. They should be highly trained and devote the time necessary to do a thorough job. All agencies use volunteer validators, not unusual for accrediting associations. In child care, in contrast to university accreditation visits, validators must observe and evaluate the actual delivery of services. The problem of training the army of validators and assuring inter-rater reliability is an enormous task, and the volunteer status of this army makes it difficult for the accrediting agency to enforce its own standards. One improvement, which would raise costs significantly, would be to move to paid staff validators.

Commissions, in exercising discretion, may approve accreditation programs that are not really qualified. There are understandable extenuating circumstances that can explain granting accreditation to rather mediocre centers. Regional differences in quality may account for accrediting programs that do not meet standards. For instance, programs in states with low licensing requirements operate in a region where the public perception of what constitutes good quality is lower than in other regions. However, funding agencies and parents still want to use the best services available. Should this need to identify better quality programs influence commission decisions? If so, such policies and actions should be explicit and accompanied by other policies that induce these regions to raise standards. Other tough calls arise when previously accredited programs come up for renewal and do not pass muster but nevertheless expect to be reaccredited. Problems arise in borderline cases, particularly if there are legal ramifications for the accrediting agency. It is not clear to us how these thorny problems can be mediated except by moving to a strict reliance on standards and reducing the commission's discretionary power.

Finally, the quality of services in programs may deteriorate after the programs are accredited. The three-year accreditation period may be too long in an industry that experiences so much turnover of personnel, including directors. Even in the hospitality business, which is more stable than child care, the red Michelin guides to restaurants and hotels are revised annually, as are AAA (American Automobile Association) ratings in the United States. Accrediting agencies should consider interim evaluations, possibly on a random sampling basis, through relatively inexpensive professional evaluations using an instrument such as ECERS or a key indicator checklist of items that predict whether or not a program is maintaining accreditation standards.

Accreditation as a Funding Standard

Accreditation status can be used as a funding standard in two different ways. It can be the standard all programs must aspire to in order to receive funds, meaning that all programs have to be accredited in order to be eligible for public dollars. Alternatively, it can be the funding standard that must be met by providers identified as giving good quality and, therefore, eligible to receive reimbursement at a higher rate.

Under present conditions, a policy requiring accreditation as a condition for the receipt of public funds in child care would create chaos, as a large proportion of the supply would suddenly be declared ineligible. Some centers do not even meet state licensing standards. Many are not close to good enough for accreditation. There is a big gap between centers providing minimally adequate custodial care and those providing good, developmentally appropriate services—in terms of center leadership, staff abilities, and financial resources available to the center. Improving quality in these programs probably involves basic changes in leadership, funding, and staff competence as preconditions for entering the accreditation process. If the CQO study is any indication, only about

15 to 20 percent of centers could get accredited rather easily because they already provide good quality. Possibly another 30 percent of centers—mediocre to good quality ones—are ready to start the process and could achieve accreditation in a reasonable amount of time with a modest investment. The percentage of family child care providers who might get accreditation is much lower. Many of these providers do not expect to remain in the field for very long. In family child care, only about 12 percent of the approximately 300,000 regulated family child care providers would deserve accreditation, about 36,000 providers.[45] This policy would place enormous pressures on the accrediting organizations to relax standards, particularly in geographic regions where there is very little good-to-excellent care.

While accreditation as a standard for getting *any* public funds is unlikely in the foreseeable future, some states are experimenting with incentive systems that give higher reimbursement to programs providing higher quality. Of the 24 states with differential reimbursement rates, several states include both center and family child care programs. All but one of these programs (in North Carolina) use accreditation as the standard for higher rates. A few states accept only NAEYC or NAFCC (for family child care) accreditation, but most accept NECPA accreditation and some accept all forms of national accreditation.

We think that tying the level of public reimbursement to a provider's demonstrated level of quality has great promise. However, using accreditation as the funding standard presents some problems that will have to be addressed by accrediting agencies. Assuming that the reimbursement differential is high enough to offset the costs of accreditation and of improved quality, state policies that raise the rates they pay for good quality services will encourage more centers to become accredited.[46] This creates at least two potential problems for accrediting agencies. Many centers may choose the accrediting agency that shows the most leniency in awarding accreditation. In addition, since there is a clear financial cost of being denied accreditation, accrediting agencies could be under greater pressure to award accreditation and under increasing threat of legal action from disgruntled providers.

State differential reimbursement based on accreditation makes it important for accrediting agencies to come to agreement about core criteria for accreditation and uniform standards for determining substantial compliance. Unless all the accrediting agencies use roughly comparable standards of quality and decision-making procedures for awarding accreditation, many centers will seek accreditation from the agencies with the weakest program. To some extent, this is already happening. Accreditation could become diluted and a questionable indicator of quality, reducing its effect on improving quality.

Helping Providers to Get Accredited

Using accreditation as a funding standard also raises questions of fairness. Gaining accreditation is expensive in terms of money and time in an industry where profit margins and family child care income are low. There can be extensive initial costs and long-term increases in operating costs associated with accreditation. These costs are higher the lower the level of quality provided before accreditation. Some states recognize this problem. For instance, a task force studying the situation in New Jersey pointed to the immediate need for funds to pay for application and validation fees and to pay for upgrading programs.[47]

Centers need technical and financial help to complete the self-study process and to follow through on changes necessary to improve their program. The latter can include reducing child:staff ratios, providing for staff training, hiring some more qualified staff, and making significant improvements in the physical plant or playground. Some of these are one-time expenses; some require ongoing budget increases. Assumimg higher reimbursement rates were adequate to cover these expenses, the center would have to make the initial investment, which many nonprofit centers and family child care providers are not in a position to do.

Several models exist around the country that give varying degrees of assistance to programs seeking accreditation. The most successful and the most ambitious is probably the Chicago Accreditation Project, which grew out of the McCormick Tribune Foundation's accreditation initiative. In the 1990s the foundation spent $8 million over a five-year period to help 150 early childhood programs in low-income Chicago neighborhoods achieve accreditation. Building on this success, in 1998 the city of Chicago launched the Chicago Accreditation Project as a private-public partnership to pay for all costs of accreditation for another 400 early childhood programs in low-income communities in the city.[48]

The Chicago project indicates how costly it is to raise inner city programs to accreditation standards. The current budget of $16 million for this project suggests that it takes, on average, $30,000 to $40,000 for a center to achieve accreditation. Projects sponsored by the American Business Collaboration have had similar experiences, indicating that converting such centers into good quality programs can involve several stages of quality improvement and a large investment that these centers cannot afford to make.

POLICY RECOMMENDATIONS

Large increases in public funding will make child care affordable to all families, but will not assure good quality. For that, direct government action is needed to create a more effective, better financed quality control system. Based on our discussion in this chapter, we recommend the following.

- Eliminate exemptions to center licensing requirements, e.g., for religiously affiliated centers, part-day preschools, and prekindergarten programs. Requiring part-day programs to be licensed could encourage some of these programs to extend their hours if there were no regulatory reason not to. There is no logical reason to exempt centers operated by religious organizations. Hospitals and nursing homes operated by religious groups are not exempted from being licensed. Extending licensing to child care centers is particularly important given the findings reported in chapter 5 that church-operated centers have, on average, relatively low quality.
- Limit licensing exemption for family child care providers to those serving no more than two children or just children from one family. However, eligibility to receive public subsidies should be restricted to licensed providers.
- Encourage licensing (and accreditation) by family child care providers through public funding. This should expand family child care networks that could perform functions related to licensing, such as technical assistance to providers preparing for licensing and some monitoring. To encourage providers to join networks, they should offer providers useful services that would improve quality: training, lending libraries, access to the food program, licensing and accreditation consulting, health insurance, and provision of substitutes. Network affiliation would be voluntary but a useful way to recruit and train new providers and bring providers up to licensing standards.
- Require states to introduce differential reimbursement rates for public child care subsidies, with higher quality programs getting higher rates. Eligibility for higher rates could be based on accreditation status, percentage of staff with advanced degrees, or other evaluation criteria.

Rate differentials need to reflect the cost of providing higher quality. Using differential reimbursement as an incentive to improve quality of services should be evaluated for its impact on program quality and accreditation standards.

- Encourage providers to seek accreditation and provide financial assistance for the initial investment to achieve accreditation. Public financial support of accreditation is justified because: (1) it is a source of increased consumer information in an industry with poorly informed consumers; (2) it is a mechanism for improving the quality of services received by children, and, in particular, children subsidized by public funds; and (3) it would make access to accreditation widely available to all providers.

- If accreditation status is to be used as a funding standard in a differential reimbursement system, then accrediting agencies must move toward standardization of accreditation requirements and evaluation procedures. A first step would be a national study comparing current accreditation standards and practices among the accrediting agencies and evaluating their effectiveness in screening for good quality. If the systems differ significantly, assessments, procedures need to be standardized: core evaluation criteria, quality indicators, validator training, validation procedures, and accreditation decisions. It may be necessary to substitute permanent staff validators for volunteers and reduce the discretion given accrediting commissions. The accrediting bodies must stand behind their accreditation and defer programs that do not meet certain structural quality, whether or not the missing quality is due to cost constraints.

- The accrediting agencies or state licensing agencies also need to create an effective annual interim monitoring system involving on-site program evaluations. These could employ a short form of an ECERS-type instrument composed of indicators that predict whether a program will meet accreditation standards.

The Federal Role

Much of the responsibility for establishing an effective quality control system lies with the states in their licensing and quality improvement functions and with the child care industry in setting and enforcing professional standards. For two key reasons, federal funding is nevertheless necessary to help finance the system:

- to subsidize state licensing agencies so they can increase monitoring and provide more technical assistance, particularly to new family child care providers and centers. This involves additional funding of at least $335 million per year.
- to increase subsidies for accreditation. A reasonable, modest program could subsidize 5,000 grants per year of $25,000 each to centers as accreditation readiness grants; 5,000 grants per year of $10,000 each to centers going through the accreditation process; 15,000 grants of $5,000 each to family child care providers to get ready for and go through the accreditation process, requiring additional funding of $250 million per year.

A new approach to creating federal funding standards should be devised and implemented. To raise standards in the states with low standards, it would be desirable to put in place federal funding standards to promote at least acceptable quality. At a minimum, to be eligible to accept vouchers, providers should be licensed and in compliance with state licensing regulations. To overcome political resistance, federal funding standards should be limited to achieving modest objectives. Common practice among states could be taken as the guide, requiring states to adopt practices that already exist in most states, for instance, the 4:1 infant:staff ratio now required in 34 states. However, funding standards should be used to increase staff and provider training requirements. States with higher training standards could be eligible for extra federal funds as a bonus for requiring higher quality. These funds could be used to finance tiered reimbursement policies to finance higher wages. With a vastly expanded voucher system, the major practical objections to federal funding standards would no longer hold, since the majority of families would be eligible for vouchers, and all families would be able to afford good quality care and pay the higher fees.

If it is not politically feasible to establish federal funding standards, states could be required to set their own funding standards for eligibility for federal funds based on federal guidelines. The federal government could develop and publish funding standard guidelines and quality rating systems based on the latest research findings. The federal government could require periodic reporting by states and compile, compare, and publish data on state licensing/enforcement practices and on monitoring procedures for publicly funded services, and identify states with inadequate licensing and funding standards. Thus, the federal government could play a leadership and educational role by expanding and making generally available public information.

CHAPTER SEVEN

The Marketplace: What is Peculiar About The Child Care Industry?

"I was afraid to go further. I just knew that I felt good about this and I just didn't want the hassle of interviewing. I just prayed that everything would work out."

"I went through all my leads. Nothing checked out. Then I really started getting desperate. A friend of a friend agreed to take the baby. I really liked her. It seemed it was going to work out okay. Then, two days before I had to go back to work, she called me and said she couldn't do it."

"I felt I had a very limited choice. I was completely uneducated [about child care] and I was the first in our family to have a child in Hartford. None of us knew anything about child care at all. The place we ended up at we just took on decent recommendations."

"One of the main things that I looked for in finding nursery/daycare was convenience for me as far as my work schedule went. [The place]

is only three minutes from my house. I work from six to six, so there
were a lot of things I would have given up [for the convenience of
having a provider] only three minutes away."

—Comments from a working mothers focus group
in *Choosing Child Care: A Qualitative Study Conducted*
in Houston, Hartford, West Palm Beach, Charlotte,
Alameda, Los Angeles, Salem and Minneapolis
EDK Associates, January 1992

～○～   ～○～   ～○～

Child care and the child care market have peculiarities that call out for regulation
and subsidy. The industry does not produce uniformly good care. Some providers
produce abysmal care that should not be tolerated. This chapter explains why we
can't rely on consumer choice and competition to create acceptable quality child
care for all children who need it.

Traditionally, child care has been considered a service to mothers, so they
can go to work, rather than an educational and developmental service to children
that should be provided publicly, like schools are for older children. Parents
wanting child care have had to purchase it on their own, mainly from private
individuals or businesses, and local child care markets have grown up to satisfy
this demand. Thus, parents' ability to pay for care, as well as their preferences
for certain types of care, have determined the amount and quality of services
produced. Of course, in a modern economy most goods and services are
provided by private entities, and the usual assumption is that they do a tolerably
good job in most cases. Competition is supposed to motivate private suppliers
to keep costs down, to keep prices close to costs, and to offer a line of goods
that are of a kind and quality that consumers want to buy.

Conservatives who oppose any government intervention in the marketplace
argue that the child care industry should be unregulated and unsubsidized. They
claim that child care markets provide the wide variety of services that suit the tastes
and budgets of parents, and that poorer parents have inexpensive options like using
relatives or sharing child care responsibilities between husband and wife. They say
that parents are the best judges of what their children need and claim that child care
quality is almost uniformly good, based on surveys reporting that parents are
satisfied with their child care arrangements.[1]

If we say that there is a public interest in seeing that all children get good
care (and that their family budgets are not devastated by the amount they have

to pay for it), then the market does not automatically guarantee that. There is no guarantee that a low-wage family will have a relative who can be pressed into service or, under our present policies, that there is a vacancy in a local subsidized center. The invisible hand of market competition does not miraculously create services of acceptable quality suitable to every family budget.

For markets to operate efficiently, buyers must be well informed about their alternatives. They must make decisions that are in the best interests of the user of the product. As we shall see, this is frequently not the case in child care markets, where parents are often poorly informed, where searching for the right provider is difficult, and where parents' top priority is often to find convenient, reliable, affordable services rather than high quality services.

We argue that there is a public interest in good quality child care provision. Studies show very clear gains to society from high quality early education for children at risk for poor school performance. They demonstrate the serious negative effects on these children when they receive poor quality care. Recent studies are beginning to show that all children receive long-run benefits from high quality child care. So all children who need it *should* have access to good quality child care. We accept that luxury goods should not have to be provided to everybody, but we do not accept that good quality child care is a luxury that some children should have to do without. As a wealthy society with an overwhelming percent of mothers in the labor force, we should provide children with a pleasant, constructive, and safe environment purely for the sake of the children, if for no other reason.

Significant increases in public subsidies will alleviate the affordability problem and finance the public demand for services. If these subsidies are to be distributed through vouchers to parents (as is mostly the case today), then parent choice needs to be limited to safe options with regulated providers to prevent spending public tax dollars on harmful care. In addition, public policy needs to be directed toward efforts to create effective quality control, market coordination, and incentives to increase quality.

WHY PARENTS CANNOT BE IDEAL CONSUMERS

Peculiarities in the child care market stem partly from the nature of child care as a commodity. Efficient market allocation requires users of a product to act in their own best interests in making consumer purchases. But children, who are the direct users of child care, do not choose their own care; rather, parents act as their agents in the market transaction. The choice of provider must satisfy two sets of often contradictory needs—the needs of the child and the needs of the parents. To make working outside the home viable, parents have to be concerned about expense, convenience, and reliability. For children to develop their potential, their needs for education, socialization, and stimulation must be met. Usually, some compromise between the two sets of needs must be struck. Recognizing this reality is not a criticism of parents' devotion to their children.

Quality Versus Convenience, Reliability, and Cost

Most families do not have the luxury of pursuing high-quality child care as their top priority. They report that their major concerns are location, hours of service the provider is available, convenience, the child's safety and comfort, and cost.[2] Working parents must buy child care every working day. Employers do not tolerate absenteeism for any reason, including an employee's unreliable child care arrangements. Working families are short on time, even with convenient child care. Inconvenient and unreliable care makes life a nightmare. Of these three locations—where you work, where you live, and where your child care is— it is usually impractical to change the first two.[3] Often, it is difficult to adjust child care arrangements because it takes major juggling just to cover the hours when care is needed. More than a third of families depend on more than one child care arrangement.[4]

Low-income parents, often with few transportation alternatives, are particularly stressed and short of time. Picking up their children from child care on time after work at the time set by the provider is a particular source of stress.[5] For mothers without enough hours in the day, convenience of location and the provider's flexibility in fitting into the parents' work schedules weigh in as crucial concerns.

Cost is clearly a big consideration. The fact that purchased child care, even the cheapest, is a large expenditure means that buyer decisions are quite sensitive to the price of services.[6] A modest percentage difference in fees translates into a lot of dollars. Decisions about purchasing licensed child care are particularly sensitive to the level of fees because of the availability of cheaper, unlicensed or illegal substitutes. Parents in one focus group study, while claiming that they wanted the best care they could afford, lapsed into sharing how much they paid, names of low cost providers, and how to pay less.[7] An indication of the relatively low priority given to quality is that parents will not pay much more for higher quality.[8] Unless providers operate in a niche market serving well-off parents mainly concerned about high quality, providers of good quality services cannot usually charge much of a premium.[9]

The lower the family income, the less able a parent is to give much weight to quality considerations without help from a subsidy program. If the parents' legitimate needs severely limit their ability to buy good quality child care services, as is the case with low-income parents, then this is an argument for public help. Public subsidies targeted specifically to pay for child care can free parents to be more concerned about quality.[10]

Parents Are Often Poorly Informed Buyers

Trading off one objective for another is at the heart of all economic transactions, but to accurately calculate the benefits of the alternative choices a person must be adequately informed. Parents may purchase lower-quality services than they would if they had full information about alternatives and the potential benefits to their child and themselves of good quality child care.

In fact, parents have a limited understanding about the characteristics of good quality and have difficulty judging the quality of the care that providers offer.[11] As mentioned earlier, in judging quality parents are concerned about health, safety, and attentive, loving care of their child. For preschoolers they also want a program that will prepare their child for school, but they are relatively uninformed about the process of child development and the ingredients of high quality, developmentally appropriate early education. Most parents do not have a formal or informal checklist of necessary characteristics of good care, and even with one, accurately evaluating the quality of child care is beyond many parents. (We provide such a checklist in appendix B.)

Cost, Quality, and Child Outcomes (CQO) provides a striking example of the difference between experts' assessment of quality and that of parents. Parents of children in rooms evaluated by observers were asked to evaluate the quality of the care in their child's room on each characteristic in the ECERS and ITERS instruments. Disturbingly, they significantly overestimated the actual quality of these characteristics in their child's room. Not a single parent rated the care of their children as poor. Of the parents of infants and toddlers who were in poor care, 88 percent rated their children's care as good; the remaining 12 percent rated their children's care as fair. Parents of children in poor care were almost as likely to rate their children's care as good as parents whose children actually were in fair care or good care.[12]

Why are parents relatively uninformed about quality? Most parents have little prior experience buying child care services until they need them, and they need them for the relatively short time their children are young. Unlike food and clothes that they have shopped for since childhood, they did not tag along as a child while their mother picked out a child care center. Some of today's parents did not experience nonmaternal child care when they were young, so they do not even have a child's eye view of what to expect or avoid.

Parents are at a disadvantage in purchasing child care because they are not the direct consumers of the services. Their children receive the services, usually in their parents' absence. This makes it difficult for parents to personally evaluate quality. They cannot even rely too much on their child's reactions. Even with the best of intentions, there is plenty of room for parents to think that all is well when it is not.

Lacking direct experience in consuming the service slows down the learning curve for parents. It takes time to judge the adequacy of the care. A mother decides after one haircut whether or not to go back to the hairdresser again. With child care, it takes parents longer to understand what goes into good child care and to recognize whether or not they've bought a lemon.

It is interesting to speculate about the reasons most parents do not take the time to learn more about child care quality. If parents have little choice of child care providers because of their financial limitations, they have little reason to learn about the benefits of excellent care. Most parents have never seen quality care and cannot even imagine what it would be like. Parents might think there is not too much to learn. They might see it as just a purchased form of what mothers have always done without any advanced training, so they may think that anyone can do it. Compared to other services purchased by families—medical care, legal consultation, and tax return preparation—many parents do not consider training important for the people giving care to their children. Possibly, they feel confident in their ability to know when they find a trustworthy provider.

Many low-income and minority families prefer using relatives and neighbors they trust from their own racial or ethnic community, not just because of cost considerations. This seems to be particularly true of Latino families.[13] Indeed, these arrangements may assure that children get loving care, good food, and are kept from harm's way; however, the children may not get the preschool experience they need.

Lack of Consumer Information

Child care markets do not generate the kind of information parents need about alternative sources of services or service characteristics. In other important, costly purchases of complex goods and services—buying a car, renting or buying a house—buyers have no trouble getting the information they need. In real estate, agents provide clients with full appraisal information and comparables. Car lots are lined up along major thoroughfares; dealers advertise in the newspapers and in want ads, on radio and television. *Consumer Reports* and specialized magazines provide specifications of cars and evaluate their performance. Blue book values of new and used cars are easily available.

By contrast, in child care markets, ordinarily there is not a lot of money to be made selling child care, so there is little incentive for providers to mount advertising campaigns touting the superiority of their services. Moreover, there are few market intermediaries—like real estate agents—that provide technical assistance to buyers and sellers and facilitate the purchase. The exceptions are local resource and referral agencies (R&Rs, to be discussed later in the chapter) that exist in most big cities. As yet, most parents do not know about or use resource and referral agencies, and their services are not available in many parts of the country. Moreover, many R&Rs have not yet offered the kind of help that parents want.

Prices provide important signals to potential buyers. In highly competitive markets where prices reflect cost of production, price differentials between competitors indicate a difference in quality. In child care, cash and in-kind donations to nonprofit centers permit them to offer higher quality services at fees comparable to those charged by centers offering lower quality. To the extent that parents assume that a higher fee signals higher quality, they could be misled by price, adding to the difficulty in making an informed decision.

The High Cost of Finding Good Quality Care

Undertaking a thorough search for suitable child care is costly in terms of time consumed and stress involved. The search involves getting a list of potential providers, screening the list for suitable providers with vacancies through extensive telephone calls, and visiting a short list of them for an hour or two to observe classes and to conduct interviews. While parents that do this kind of comparative shopping become much better informed, most parents do not.

Even if most parents do not go through a painstaking process to locate the best provider they can afford, it still takes time to find a suitable arrangement, and parents often have to repeat the process several times before their children no longer need child care or supervision. Particularly in low-income areas— rural areas or low-income neighborhoods in cities—it is hard to find a child care situation that is convenient, suits a family's specific needs, gives reliable services, and is in one's price range. Transportation and nontraditional work schedules create problems for young mothers and there are not as many child care providers in these low-income neighborhoods.

Many parents feel they have little choice, and they report that the search process itself is so stressful that they want to get it over as quickly as they can. Authors of one study comment: "Looking for child care was such a stressful experience that most mothers were desperate to see the problem resolved and feared that they would not find a good arrangement for their child. They settled on the first place that seemed 'acceptable.'"[14]

Child care markets would work more effectively if parents had access to more information about program quality and help finding a suitable situation. This would cut the cost of searching for care and increase the likelihood of more comparison shopping by parents. The industry needs marketing intermediaries to make it easier for customers to shop intelligently. Ready access to adequately funded resource and referral services can serve this function; widespread program accreditation or easily accessed program rating systems could provide reliable signals about quality that would decrease search costs.

CHARITABLE AND PUBLIC DEMAND FOR MORE QUALITY CHILD CARE

Even if parents were ideal consumers with complete information about market alternatives, child care markets could not be relied upon to provide enough good quality services. Markets ration supply based on the ability to pay. If deserving families cannot afford good quality or if society as a whole benefits from more early care and education, then charitable or public funding is necessary to finance the increased supply; otherwise it will not be produced.

Child care, education for school-aged children, college for the bright, medical care, and immunization are all examples of *merit goods*—services that some people in the community or the whole community consider important for others to have regardless of their ability or willingness to pay for it. They believe in the value—merit—of the service and are willing to pay for it so others are not deprived of the benefits.

Providing free or low cost access to merit goods is a time-honored way of promoting equal opportunity in the United States. The Declaration of Independence assures all citizens the right to life, liberty, and the pursuit of happiness, and as a nation we have advanced these rights mainly through programs that improve opportunities for disadvantaged groups. The ideal may often be abridged, yet it still has real meaning to Americans, particularly with respect to children, who play no part in their conception but who suffer the consequences of early disadvantages. These charitable impulses are expressed through private giving and public spending.

Child care is widely recognized as a merit good in the United States. Many child care centers began as charitable organizations, and today United Way subsidizes slots for low-income children in local child care centers across the country. Opinion polls have consistently shown that Americans think children deserve a healthy start in life and that they are willing to contribute to providing child care and other services necessary to help accomplish this.[15] In the debate about welfare reform—and the need to get single mothers into jobs—many politicians expressed the view that those mothers should have the support they need, including help with child care. Private charitable impulses and public programs have not, however, come close to making affordable care available to all children who need it.

Early childhood care and education also creates external benefits—advantages to others not involved in the market transaction—that justify public spending. Parents purchasing child care will only pay for the perceived benefits to their own family, which may not even include long-run advantages such as the effect on their child's future earning capacity. If, like education for older children, good child care creates external benefits, then public spending is justified in augmenting private spending to assure the availability of enough good quality services to provide these benefits.

Child care programs provide external benefits that reduce public spending in the long run if the savings associated with the program are greater than the cost of the program. This seems to be the case, at least, for children at risk of doing poorly in school. Two longitudinal studies of the effects of early intervention that involved both good quality early care and education as well as parent involvement have shown considerable long-term cost saving by the public. In the High/Scope Perry Preschool project (described in chapter 4) the project savings to government have been estimated to be more than twice the cost of the program: 40 percent of the reductions in criminal justice costs, 26 percent in taxes on increased income earned by participants as adults, 25 percent in education services, and 9 percent in reductions in welfare costs. For society as a whole, the monetary benefits are higher than these savings to government because of benefits enjoyed by the participants from higher income, and the savings of persons who would have been crime victims.[16]

Similar estimates of government savings and benefits to society have been found for children enrolled in Chicago's Child-Parent Centers (CPC) described in chapter 4. Compared to a group of children who did not participate in the program, the CPC participants had 26 percent greater high school graduation rates, were left back in school 35 percent less often, and were less than half as likely to have been arrested two or more times. The program has been estimated to have saved the government $2.31 for every dollar invested and to have saved the participants and the public $5 for every dollar invested.[17]

For these two programs the estimated savings include only those related to the participants and are tracked only through their early adulthood. They do not include savings from increased income of the mothers of participating children. Benefits may be greater still for children in good quality early childhood programs that last from infancy through entry to school.

Law enforcement officials who organized Fight Crime: Invest in Kids to advocate public spending on good educational child care understand the terrible financial cost to society when a person adopts a life of crime: it is estimated at between $1.7 million and $2.3 million per hardened criminal.[18] At a public cost of, say, $50,000 per child in good child care, preventing 3 percent of the beneficiaries from going wrong alone would make the investment in child care worthwhile.

Subsidized child care provides other external benefits. For instance, young women may be more willing to invest in their own education and future careers if they know they can rely on good quality care for their children. Particularly with low-income women, access to good quality, reliable child care can be an incentive to get the training and experience necessary to take jobs that might lead to middle-class status. Mothers in the Abecedarian project achieved higher educational and employment status than mothers of control-group children.

Both the merit good and social benefits justifications for public spending mesh with another argument for increased public subsidy of child care. The nation benefits from the child rearing of those who bear and raise children, but not everyone raises children. Child rearing can be seen as a gain to society as a whole because all members of society benefit from the services and sacrifices of those who raise the next generation. If parenting is seen as a public service, there should be an equitable distribution of costs of child rearing, of which the cost of child care would be a major part.[19]

In European countries there is concern that the costs of care may decrease the willingness to bear children. This fear creates support for the substantial subsidies for child care and family services provided by countries like France, where pronatalism is a tradition. However, the French, who have found that free child care does not induce large numbers of births, also value highly the developmental benefits that good preschools confer. In the United States, fears of a declining population are less. Moreover, many Americans take the attitude that single or low-income people should not have as many babies as they do, and that they should not be encouraged in this behavior by government help of any kind. The view of the authors is that it is in the public interest that children who have been brought into the world get good care, whatever the behavior of their parents.

In determining the appropriate level of public spending on child care, another fairness issue must be taken into consideration. Most arguments favoring public spending on child care are justifications for subsidizing services for low-income families. However, as we have seen in chapter 5, middle-income working families who use center care tend to receive the relatively low-quality center services. This hardly seems fair, particularly since one reason for the low quality is the parents' difficulty in affording the cost of child care. If we are to expand public support of child care, this support should certainly be extended to this large group of families.

James Heckman, an eminent labor economist, calls for a major realignment of national educational priorities to reallocate scarce public funds from adult training programs directed toward the unskilled to investment in the education of the very young.[20] This change is a necessary response to the new labor market that demands new skills and lifetime learning. Heckman shows that early investments are less costly to society and more effective than attempts to remedy deficits in school-aged youth or to adapt unskilled workers to the modern economy. He argues that the emphasis on subsidies to higher education, which now represent 80 percent of the cost at major public universities, at the expense of early education may also be misplaced. The same level of investment in the very young has a higher yield because learning begets learning, so that skills learned earlier make later learning easier. Also, there is a bigger payoff to the public because young children have a longer time to make productive contributions to society than adults already well into their working lives. Heckman emphasizes that investing in the very young improves basic learning and socialization skills that can have positive long-run effects on their success as adults, and that the conservative preoccupation with cognitive gains is misplaced.

Conservative analysts downplay the importance of external benefits of child care, partly out of skepticism about the benefits to society, partly because they consider child care a poor substitute for mother care and potentially damaging to children. They recognize that some members of society consider child care a merit good, but they argue that charitable giving provides the private means for satisfying these third-party desires to help finance services for poor children. This is a misleading argument. There is no guarantee that the supply of charitable contributions will meet the needs of worthy recipients as perceived by the body politic. The amount of charitable contributions supplied depends on the number and generosity of altruistic providers and donors; this has no necessary relation to the needs of children. There is no mechanism that automatically creates a flow of voluntary charitable donations equal to that perceived need. If there is a gap between publicly perceived need and charitable contributions, and we believe there is, then government must step up to the plate to fill it. We would not leave the provision of elementary and secondary education to parent provision, supplemented by charitable contributions. The argument for public participation in financing child care is analogous.

CHILD CARE INDUSTRY ORGANIZATION

As we have seen, the child care industry includes a highly diverse group of providers. They range from grandmothers who take in one child for little or no money to large corporate chains of child care centers with stock traded on Wall Street. Some are run as charities, others operate as profit makers. Some are home-based, and others must pay rent for commercial space. Some providers are regulated, others are exempt from regulation, and some are in the underground economy—escaping whatever regulation might apply to them and paying no taxes.

The unregulated and home-based providers are in the majority. Our best guess is that about only 37 percent of the children in nonparental care are in regulated centers and regulated family child care.[21] Only centers, serving about 30 percent of children, operate in facilities that ordinarily involve rental and other facilities costs that are not incurred when children are cared for in someone's home.

Child care centers operate in a "mixed industry" composed of for-profit, nonprofit, and some publicly operated centers. Nonprofit and public suppliers help correct market deficiencies in supply to groups under-served by centers operated for profit, and different nonprofit subsectors have developed to serve specific needs. Some cater to parents who are concerned about high quality services and who believe that nonprofit centers are more trustworthy because they are not in business to make profit.[22] Some nonprofits and public centers provide high quality programs to help at-risk children prepare for school. Church-operated centers increase the availability of affordable care for their congregations and communities. Others, like centers operated by community agencies, provide child care subsidized by government and charitable contributions for low-income working parents living in poor communities.

Competition that Penalizes Quality in Centers

Competitive pressures within the center sector of the child care industry contribute to reducing child care quality in some subsectors. The diversity of providers in the child care industry creates a special situation that makes it difficult for high-quality services to be provided by centers. The source of the problem is the substantial cost advantage that home-based care has over center care. These providers use their own home, furnishings, and car, cutting down on out-of-pocket costs. They are often willing to work for less than paid center staff because they combine child care with housework and their daily personal life. They benefit from business expense tax deductions that include depreciation allowances on their own home, and from savings on their own child care. Many family child care providers are married, and so they are often covered under their husband's health insurance and retirement benefits, and not dependent on their own earnings as a sole source of family income. Those among them who evade Social Security and income taxes on their child care earnings have an additional sizeable cost saving.

In most other industries, home-based production has long since been driven out of the market by larger operators, who used machinery and equipment to lower their costs and who enjoyed economies of scale. But child care centers cannot drive small family child care competitors out of business. In child care, there are few economies of scale. The child care industry cannot make much use of technological innovation to lower costs by substituting equipment for labor. Television can occupy children, substituting for human caring to some extent, but it induces passivity in the children. It is an unreliable substitute for adult human supervision and using it reduces interactions among children and adults at a time when important language and social skills are developed.

The substantially lower prices of home-based care tempt parents and make it harder for centers to get customers. If few parents can judge or monitor quality, then a center has the best chance of attracting customers if it keeps down the costs associated with quality. They do this mainly by employing cheaper, less-qualified workers and as few workers per child as the law permits. So few good centers come into existence unless they are subsidized to improve quality or serve parents demanding it.

In the case of most other industries, especially those where customers are good judges of quality, a large cost advantage for the cheapest variety of the product would not be a problem for public policy, even if the quality was not of the best. Indeed, it would be a boon to consumers. Fast food is perhaps a good example. Conservatives say that the diversity of providers in child care means that the market works and all families can be accommodated, including those who cannot afford regular fees. For children, however, there is a public interest in seeing that they have care that is considerably above minimal quality, even if it is more than minimally expensive.

Unregulated and Illegal Care

Legally exempt and illegally operating nonparental caregivers may care for one-third of children under the age of five and possibly an even larger percent of young school-aged children.[23] They represent a steady flow of new providers with no start-up costs who can afford to charge low fees. They do not pay for licensing or criminal checks, and they do not have to conform to safety and health standards, which often involve an investment in the provider's home. Often they do not pay income taxes, or Social Security taxes that soaks up about 14 percent of a regulated provider's income, giving them a cost advantage over regulated family child care providers that can be reflected in lower fees. One study found that on average, unregulated providers' fees averaged about 75 percent and relatives' fees 58 percent of fees charged by licensed providers.[24]

As reported in chapter 5, unlicensed providers are more likely than regulated providers to give an unacceptably low quality of care. They are much less likely to consider themselves professionals and to therefore participate in professional organizations and meetings or to avail themselves of training. Unfortunately, we have little way to know how predominant the neglectful or minimal-quality care is.

These providers are hard to detect, so they are essentially impossible to regulate. But the idea that anybody, with no training and no credentials, can provide care anyplace or anywhere, without paying taxes, is disheartening, to say the least. Unfortunately, current welfare policy in some states may actually be encouraging the growth of the unregulated sector, draining potential customers and public dollars out of the formal sector.

SPECIAL COMPETITIVE PRESSURES ON FOR-PROFIT CENTERS

Nonprofit centers receive a quarter of their revenue in the form of cash or in-kind donations from private contributors and from government. There is a good case to be made that charitable donations to nonprofit centers, while financing higher quality in the nonprofit sector, may have the effect of lowering quality in the for-profit sector. Charitable contributions permit nonprofits to charge lower fees than they would if fee revenues had to cover the full cost of producing their services. This puts for-profit centers, with little access to donations or charitable contributions, at a disadvantage. This point is illustrated in table 7.1, which gives average costs and revenue sources for nonprofit and for-profit centers in the CQO study. The study found that on average for-profit centers spent more than twice as much on occupancy costs as did nonprofits, which often operate in donated or low-rent space. For-profits keep hourly fees in line with nonprofit fees by spending a lower percentage of their budgets on labor—62 percent of total cost compared to 79 percent of cash costs in nonprofit centers—and this tends to lower quality. Profit rates as a percent of sales were low, averaging 5 percent and not significantly different from the surplus of revenue over costs in nonprofit centers.[25]

In a market with poorly informed buyers, for-profit centers trying to keep costs in line have an incentive to skimp on quality characteristics parents do not know about or cannot easily monitor.[26] These centers have to meet parent expectations. Since parents tend to evaluate quality based on visible features of the physical setting, as well as rapport with the provider, for-profit centers keep up appearances that reassure parents about the quality of their center.[27] They are also quick to introduce the latest fads that purport to contribute to children's

TABLE 7.1.
Monthly costs and revenues per child in a typical child care center, 1993-4.

ITEM	NONPROFIT		FOR-PROFIT	
	DOLLARS	PERCENT OF TOTAL	DOLLARS	PERCENT OF TOTAL
COSTS				
LABOR	$331	79 %	$239	62 %
OCCUPANCY	31	7	78	20
FOOD	21	5	16	4
OTHER OPERAT-ING EXPENSES	28	7	40	10
OVERHEAD	9	2	11	3
TOTAL COST	$420	100 %	$384	100 %
REVENUES				
FEES	$332	77 %	$395	97 %
GOVERNMENT-DONATED FOOD	13	3	3	1
OTHER PUBLIC FUNDS	46	11	0	0
OTHER PRIVATE FUNDS	41	9	7	2
TOTAL REVENUE	$432	100%	$405	100%
SURPLUS OR PROFIT	$13	3%	$21	5%

Source: Suzanne W. Helburn, ed., *Cost, Quality, and Child Outcomes in Child Care Centers, Technical Report* (Denver, CO: University of Colorado, 1995), table 8.1.
Columns may not add to totals because of rounding.

development. However, they can shave quality on other characteristics related to program and staff-child interactions that are expensive to provide but that parents are not present to observe. Indeed, they must if they are to maximize profits (or, in this business, to survive). For-profit chains, the subsector most committed to profit maximization and with the most sophisticated management, seem to engage in this opportunistic behavior, and more so in states with low licensing standards.[28]

Substantial increases in public subsidies through vouchers would probably reduce the perceived need for private philanthropic giving in the child care market. That would even the playing field between the for-profits and the nonprofits. Subsidies to parents through vouchers that give adequate reimbursement to good quality providers, whether for-profit or nonprofit, would enable parents to choose better quality providers and pay their fees. Fees would more nearly reflect cost and would be a better indicator of quality, and market performance would be improved thereby.

Lower Quality in Parts of the Nonprofit Sector

CQO data indicates that church-operated centers also produce relatively low quality, particularly for characteristics that are hard to observe, a disturbing fact since this is a large and rapidly growing subsector. Churches may be partially motivated by a desire to help defray building or other costs, a motive bordering on turning a profit. Or, lower quality may reflect the desire to provide affordable services and/or the failure to hire professional directors and delegate responsibility for the center to them. Whatever the reason for the relatively low quality, the poorer performance in this subsector tends to disadvantage middle-income working families who may think they are using a trustworthy provider.[29]

That the CQO found relatively low quality among centers operated by community agencies, particularly on hard-to-observe quality characteristics, is alarming since these centers are major suppliers of child care for the subsidized children who most need good quality services. More research is needed to corroborate these findings. Centers operated by nonprofits have an ideal of voluntarism and service that often leads to paying their staff and directors an inadequate wage. This may contribute to lower quality. If it is a center that traditionally serves subsidized low-income children through a contract with the local social service agency, management may have become lax or may have to live within a budget constrained by low reimbursement rates. Some centers are run by community action program agencies, which have other priorities. To overcome these problems, local public authorities need to set reimbursement rates at levels that can finance quality services and require child care providers with whom they contract to conform to standards of good quality.

The Problem of Provider Turnover

High rates of provider turnover exist in the child care industry, particularly in family child care, but also in centers. This frequent turnover further erodes quality for families whose children are subjected to frequent changes in child care arrangements, potentially reducing their ability to form strong attachments with their caregivers.

Turnover is probably highest among unregulated family child care providers. These providers can enter and leave the industry almost at will since they do not have to conform to state licensing requirements or local zoning regulations and therefore incur essentially zero costs for starting up child care services. As we have seen, their presence in the industry holds down fees, which, in turn, makes it hard for licensed child care providers to earn a reasonable living, discouraging some of them from making a more long-term commitment to the field.[30] Furthermore, about half of family child care providers take in other children to be home with their own young children, and many go back to regular employment when their children go to school. The high turnover comes during the first two years, due to people wandering into the field and finding that the work does not suit them or that it does not pay enough.

Centers go out of business less frequently than family child care providers; however, there is considerable entry and exit of centers into and from the market, much of which is related to general economic conditions or changes in demographics and real estate values in given localities. Since competition produces low profit margins in the center sector, centers have to operate close to full capacity. Changes in local demographics causing loss of clientele or unemployment in the economy at large can push a center into the red and out of business.

Supply Gaps

As we pointed out in chapter 2, there are gaps in the supply of child care services in situations where demand for child care of a special type, at a certain time, or in certain locations is thin. Shortages exist in low-income and rural communities, for infants, sick children, children with special needs, and children needing care at night-time and on weekends.[31] Under these circumstances centers, which cannot run without a critical mass of customers, cannot survive. Family child care may not take up the slack. These are forms of care that have unusually high costs or create serious inconvenience for potential providers.

In addition, parents can face shortages and difficulties in finding a space for their child in their neighborhood because many of the centers and family child care providers are already operating at full capacity. Although there may be enough slots for all children in the region, finding them is difficult, and the available places may not fit the needs of the families needing services.[32]

Low-income parents are doubly disadvantaged by their limited earnings and the jobs they hold, which often require them to work unusual hours or rotating shifts. One-fourth of low-income mothers and as many as one-third of working-poor mothers work weekends, and half of working-poor parents work on a rotating or changing schedule. However, relatively few centers and regulated family child care providers offer services at night or on weekends.[33]

Creating licensed child care for evenings and weekends often requires employer or public provision. In rare instances, that is forthcoming. For instance, in the 1980s the city of Leadville, Colorado, converted an old schoolhouse into a 24-hour child care center when many residents lost their jobs in mining and had to find new ones in the surrounding ski areas. In western New York United Auto Workers and General Motors formed a consortium of employers to provide "Just Like Home," an extended-hours child care center for school-aged children, to accommodate shift workers and to induce workers to work overtime.[34] The Communications Workers of America, the International Brotherhood of Electrical Workers, and Verizon have set up a work/family program that includes an on-site child care program for school-aged children on school holidays.[35] In Canada, the province of Quebec, which provides care to all for $5 per day, is contracting with some nonprofit centers to stay open 24 hours a day.[36]

There are dramatic differences in the geographic distribution of services, based mainly on differences in family income, density of population, and to a lesser extent on family characteristics.[37] Centers are disproportionately located in communities with a high percent of young, high-wage families.[38]

There is less availability of licensed services in poor communities and rural areas.[39] In an area northwest of Boston, for instance, researchers found the higher the "distress level" of a community (measured by poverty levels, proportion of single parents, dependence on public assistance, and recent immigration) the fewer the licensed child care slots. Communities with high poverty and public assistance levels were more than twice as likely to have no center care compared to more affluent communities.[40]

Poor communities also have less licensed family child care than exists in more affluent communities, partly because poor family child care providers are less likely to seek licensing or know about professional opportunities in child care. For-profit centers have been reluctant to move into potentially unprofitable poor neighborhoods, so that nonprofit centers, Head Start, and public school preschools supply most of the center care in these neighborhoods. Investment by charitable organizations or government is insufficient to satisfy the need in these communities.

In rural areas the population is not large enough to support a center, and poor parents cannot find much transportation. Parents have to rely mainly on spouses, relatives, or family child care providers.

Some conservative critics claim that availability problems are caused by state licensing that outlaws low-cost providers who charge lower fees. However, regulatory restrictions do not explain supply gaps in poverty-stricken and rural areas where there are too few people to support centers regardless of regulation. Nor do they explain gaps in the availability of weekend, sick, and overnight care. Low minimum standards may make it somewhat more economically feasible to serve low-income urban communities, but these children are the ones who would benefit most from good, educationally oriented programs that require better staffing.

Capital Shortages

The expansion of center care, particularly in poor neighborhoods, is also hampered by financing problems. Nonprofit centers traditionally have had trouble raising capital to expand. If the center is part of a larger organization, their center's growth depends on the parent organization's priorities and access to capital. If the center is highly subsidized through grants and donations, it is difficult to get financing from normal lenders who want assurance of a predictable revenue stream over time. Investors consider subsidies less reliable than fees as a way of covering the center's cost. If the center operates in donated space, it has zero occupancy costs, which is reflected in lower fees. This means that its revenue stream, based on these fees, cannot cover the annualized costs of loan payments required to expand its facilities.

New centers, whether organized for nonprofit or for-profit, face problems as well. Banks consider loans to child care borrowers a bad risk, even though their delinquency rates are quite low. In general, banks shy away from lending to nonprofit organizations when underwriting does not include personal guarantees, when there may not be enough financial history to convince lenders of the safety of the loan, or when there are heavy transaction costs in completing the loan arrangement because of the inexperience of the child care center administration.[41]

For-profit chains do have the internal resources and experience to expand quickly, but they have not generally invested in poor communities. They grow by making substantial investments in facilities that they build, then normally sell and lease back, thus reducing the amount of capital tied up in real estate. For this strategy to be profitable, they must locate in neighborhoods where demand will hold during the lease period, usually 15 years. Given an expanded voucher program, for-profit chains would be more willing to move into low-income communities, but there would still be many localities that they would not be willing to serve because of low demand or for other reasons.

Family child care providers have somewhat different problems. If they are home owners they can finance renovation or dedicated space for child care through home equity loans; however, they are often not in a position to take on the debt. Family child care in rented space is even more problematic. Some community development agencies building low-income housing units are experimenting with dedicating a unit to a family child care provider, but such experiments are rare.

Some states and local communities have created financial intermediaries that facilitate financing for child care centers and family child care providers. These agencies provide much-needed technical assistance to identify potential sites, negotiate with landlords or landowners, locate architects specializing in child care facilities, qualify the borrower for loans, and put together a loan package. Some of these agencies grant loans themselves since they can borrow at lower rates than their customers can and, as nonprofits, they can tap into existing funding opportunities, for instance by cooperating with community development corporations.[42]

Generally, two types of programs exist: direct grants to providers for whom it is difficult to carry debt, and loan or loan guarantee programs for providers who can carry debt but have difficulty getting loans. Minnesota, for instance, finances grants to build or renovate child care facilities through issuing bonds that are repaid out of state appropriations. New York supports grants out of state general funds. Maryland guarantees loans and supports a loan program. Ohio and North Carolina have appropriated funds for loans that are administered through a local community development corporation. A program in San Francisco arranges for home equity loans for family child care home owners in which part of the loan repayment is forgiven for each year the provider stays in business.

These programs are needed today throughout the country, and in the event of a substantially larger voucher program they will have to be widely in place to encourage the expansion of services, particularly in the nonprofit sector.[43] Without them, the main growth in the industry will undoubtedly come in the for-profit chain subsector. While this growth would be welcome, quality and availability concerns suggest that it would be unwise to depend on these corporations as the major source of new facilities. We therefore recommend some public investment to create these financial intermediary services in all parts of the country. We have not estimated the cost systematically, but assuming an average of two such programs in each state with budgets of $500,000 per year to support a staff of five, a $50 million per year investment would suffice. In addition, initial capitalization would be necessary to establish a guarantee fund for each.

MARKET COORDINATION:
THE ROLE OF RESOURCE AND REFERRAL AGENCIES

Like residential real estate markets, where brokers act as intermediaries, child care markets need agencies that help match buyers and sellers. Parents need information and help in locating services. Providers, many of them with little experience and limited financial resources, need technical advice. Family child care providers must continually be recruited and trained. Communities and businesses need a reliable source of information about the market.

Prototypes of resource and referral agencies appeared in the early 1970s at a time when the concept of networking was taking hold, and local community organizers embraced this strategy to connect people to share information and resources. R&Rs now operate in every state in the country (although there are still many unserved communities). In many states they have formed state-wide networks, and the National Association of Child Care Resource and Referral Agencies (NACCRRA), incorporated in 1987, provides technical support for state and local initiatives. In part the system has grown because of its value to state governments and to the business community.

R&R Core Functions and Services

R&Rs are mainly nonprofit grassroots agencies that sprung up to fulfill specific local community needs. They provide services to families, providers, employers, and government agencies, combining the services of a broker, trade association, and lobbyist. They are also catalysts for change, providing a permanent, local organization to foster collaboration among public and private groups to improve the early care and education system in their locality and state. NACCRRA identifies four core R&R functions:

- *Data Collection, Management, and Analysis.* R&R databases are the main source of information about local demand and supply conditions. R&Rs maintain computerized systems listing current services available in the community and documenting their daily contacts with clients—families, employers, and public agencies. This information is used to provide referrals to parents, record consumer preferences and needs, and provide and record requests for technical assistance. These databases are also used to develop market rate studies, wage surveys, marketing projections, and other specialized analyses for program development efforts of municipal governments, employers, philanthropic organizations, and providers.

- *Consumer Education and Referral Services.* The primary function of many R&Rs is to assist parents in selecting child care services that suit their needs. R&Rs provide both regular and enhanced referrals. All clients get consumer education and a minimum of three referrals. Regular referral services involve telephone counseling to provide a list of possible providers that fit the criteria specified by the parent. Enhanced services are often provided through employer contracts with the R&R and involve more personalized services from a referral counselor assigned to work with the family throughout the child care search. R&Rs are serving an increasing number of low-income families; over a third contract with state agencies to help subsidized families locate child care, and many are providing enhanced services to these clients.

  Parents using R&R services are more likely than the average parent to make a wider search and to visit more than one potential provider.[44] They have not, however, replaced commonly used informal sources of referrals, partly because parents are not aware of their existence, and partly because they do not do what friends and neighbors do— recommend a "good" provider.[45] Most R&Rs now supply available information on accreditation and licensing violations, but the industry lacks a *Consumer's Report* for child care programs that R&Rs could use in their referral services.

- *Supply Building and Quality Initiatives.* Through their day-to-day contacts, R&Rs learn about child care needs in the community and try to find ways to satisfy them. They have been particularly important in developing a supply of licensed family child care providers. They recruit potential providers, organize training for new recruits, and provide technical support and services through the Child and Adult Care Food Program (CACFP) that almost half of R&Rs sponsor. They provide referrals for substitute care or sick care, crisis counseling, and toy and resource libraries. R&Rs also give technical assistance to centers, providing individualized consulting services, for instance, to help locate new centers, and find architects, builders, and equipment suppliers. They can also coordinate loan and loan guarantee programs for centers and family child care providers.

Training is an important function for most R&Rs. They publicize training opportunities and design training programs for workers who need convenient and affordable programs. Some R&Rs have special programs for unlicensed relatives receiving child care subsidies, nannies, and teachers of children with special needs. Many organize parent support groups. They play a central role in projects to improve quality, for instance, in facilitating accreditation, and in the statewide administration of scholarship programs like T.E.A.C.H. Early Childhood® Project (Teacher Education and Compensation Help, to be described in chapter 8).

- *Community Planning and Advocacy.* R&Rs network in their communities to facilitate community action to improve early childhood services. Effective R&R directors have the vision, energy, and contacts to create new sources of support for special projects, soliciting corporate grants and fostering public/private partnerships. Since R&R staff sit on most child and family related boards, committees, and task forces, they understand the political landscape and can bring people together for planning, public policy discussions, and special projects.

Organization and Funding

Organizational structure, functions, and funding vary considerably among R&R agencies. Twenty states now have enabling legislation to support R&Rs, subsidizing data collection, management, and analysis.[46] Some states have been instrumental in creating statewide systems. R&Rs have formed 37 state networks that provide varying degrees of support to local agencies.[47] State governments that finance local R&Rs normally finance network offices, delegating specific responsibilities to them. Some states allocate state revenue, but more often the money comes from the federal Child Care and Development Fund block grant. In many states, however, the state network is a poorly financed voluntary organization. Even well-funded state network offices differ considerably in function and in their relation to local R&Rs, depending on how the state finances R&Rs and what administrative functions it delegates to the state network office.

As a grassroots movement, R&R leaders have had to find financing wherever they can, and funding agents have influenced the mix of services provided. Most R&Rs (72 percent) are part of larger agencies where the R&R is a minor budget item and where R&R services are often peripheral to the sponsoring agency's major goal. About half of the umbrella organizations are either family service or community action agencies that came into existence in the 1960s to serve low-income families as part of the War on Poverty, whereas R&Rs serve families from all socioeconomic strata, child care providers, and community organizations. Unfortunately, this lack of autonomy of so many R&Rs limits the development of stronger state network offices, and state funding for such offices has sometimes been opposed by R&R sponsoring agencies.

R&Rs have a national presence in NACCRRA, a membership organization of local R&Rs and state networks not unlike a national trade association. Maintaining state-of-the-art technology is crucial in the field of information acquisition and dissemination, and NACCRRA provides services and activities that support the information mission of R&Rs. NACCRRA partners with other national organizations to increase the capacity and effectiveness of child care resource and referral organizations.

Needed: A Nationwide R&R Network

As relatively young organizations—30 percent have come on the scene since 1990—R&R networks are unevenly developed, both at local and state levels. Effective, well-established local agencies and state networks coexist with underserved regions with little statewide coordination. R&R services are still not available in all communities, and only 31 states have complete state-wide coverage.

To effectively serve child care consumers, the R&R network needs to be completed, adequately funded, and its services must be effectively marketed. This will require more public investment, although other sources of financial support should continue to be tapped. To facilitate expansion, local R&Rs need to be run as independent agencies coordinated through a state network office.

State network offices can also serve the important function of building a system of local agencies in states that are underserved.

We estimate that about 500 million dollars per year is needed to operate a complete R&R network that can provide basic services to most communities across the nation. This is roughly 400 million dollars more per year than the cost of operating the system in the 1990s. This would fund 870 local R&Rs (compared to the current 600 NACCRRA members), state network offices in every state, and an expansion of NACCRRA services to provide technical assistance and training and to maintain the national database.[48]

PUBLIC POLICY RECOMMENDATIONS

Analysis in this chapter points to a number of policies that could increase quality, with or without an expanded voucher system:

- Reimbursement rates must cover the cost of adequate quality in the region, including rates to cover the cost of good quality services, infant care, care for sick children, and care at nonstandard hours.
- Public contracting with centers may continue to be necessary to provide services for subsidized children in communities with serious supply gaps, but quality performance standards for these centers should be established.
- The federal government should provide ongoing funding to establish and maintain a nationwide R&R system of the magnitude suggested in this chapter. We estimate a cost of about $500 million.
- State or federal loan and loan guarantee programs need to be established for centers and family child care providers. We suggest federal funding at about $150 million per year.
- Parents need reliable, well-publicized information about provider quality. This could be supplied by state licensing agencies or R&Rs, through periodic publication of ratings and serious violations of licensing regulations, or public posting of this information by the provider. Ideally, a *Consumer's Report* on child care cost and quality should be created, subsidized, at least initially, by federal funding. A relatively small expenditure of $25 million per year could get such a program going.[49]

We do not favor policies that discriminate against for-profit centers. An advantage of an expanded voucher system is that it creates a level playing field open to all licensed providers, provided that government establishes adequate enforcement and creates quality improvement incentives and a comprehensive R&R system. For-profit centers have important advantages. They respond quickly to increases in demand and have an easier time raising capital for expansion. They provide some economies of scale through equipment purchases and facilities construction. Potentially, with the proper incentives, they could raise quality through the development of innovative curricula and effective staff training programs. They are a potentially potent political adversary or ally. As an ally they could provide political muscle in advocating an enlarged voucher system. As an adversary, which they sometimes are today, they can successfully stall public child care initiatives for improved quality at the state and national level.

The Caregivers:
How Could We Improve
Their Lot?

Andrea Anderson, 26, always wanted to work with children. When
she effuses about her role as a music therapist at Small Faces Child
Development Center, it sounds like ideal work for her. But when you
ask if she wants to make a career out of this, her sweet patient voice
takes on an inflection of irritation. "I don't see how I could. People
think I'm crazy for staying at a job that pays $8.54 an hour when I
have my master's degree and student loans to pay off. My job has no
pension and doesn't pay for all of my health insurance."

—The *Seattle Stranger,* 22 October 1998

Rene Talenti who has been in the field 10 years earns $9.01 per hour.
"I turned in my resignation last week," Talenti said, "because I can't
afford to work in this field any more. It was an incredibly difficult
decision to make. Some of the children drew pictures of themselves
for me with tears in their eyes, or with pictures of their house, with
the address on it so I'd know where to find them. But I have $26,000

in college loans to pay back, and I simply have to get a better paying
job if I'm ever going to get out of debt."

—Labor Day Dispatch—Seattle Press
special section, 26 August–8 September 1998

Child care workers earn low wages and have low status and high turnover.
Producing higher quality services requires using better trained and educated staff
and retaining them through wage and benefit packages that are competitive vis-
à-vis other jobs that require comparable training and experience. Perhaps the
most difficult problem to overcome in creating a system of good-quality,
affordable, accessible early education and care is making working in child care
attractive enough so that women and men with a talent for the work will want to
train for the occupation and enter and stay in it. Although there has been
increasing public concern and attention, and even some modest public funding
devoted to improving the training and pay of child care workers, a solution to the
problem is not really in sight. Traditional personnel practices within the industry,
the competitive conditions we have described in the last chapter, and the expense
involved in raising child care pay all make this a daunting task.

The desirability of raising the pay and status of child care workers
(including family child care providers) has become a major theme in the child
care policy debate, mainly due to the efforts of the Center for the Child Care
Workforce (CCW), which has created a voice for child care teachers and home
providers through leadership training, grassroots organization, public awareness
campaigns, research, and public policy formation.[1] Its National Child Care
Staffing Study was crucial in establishing the link between better quality child
care and higher levels of training and compensation for child care workers.[2] Its
Worthy Wage campaigns in localities around the country have raised public
awareness of low pay in the industry and created a cadre of local leaders and
advocates. It has played a major role in developing compensation and training
initiatives in California and is providing national leadership to design initiatives
to secure public federal, state, and local funds to increase the wages and status
of child care workers.

The higher pay that most people in the field believe is needed will only come
to pass if two conditions are met. The first condition is that the personnel policies
of the employers of child care labor change—that they begin to demand higher
qualifications in the people they employ and pay enough to hire and retain such

people. The second condition is an additional major flow of funds to the industry to finance the higher pay. Both of these conditions pose formidable difficulties. Employers will not, and indeed, probably cannot, change their personnel policies voluntarily, in response to well-meaning exhortations. They would have to be required by law to do it, otherwise forced to do it, or somehow induced to do it.

As to the funding requirement, there are only two possible sources for the money—parents and government. Most parents, we have argued, should be paying less, not more for child care. Leaving them to come up with the money for higher pay for child care workers would make child care still less affordable than it is now. That leaves government as the source of the necessary funds. But the government subsidies required to make child care affordable to all families, *assuming no change in the wages of child care workers at all,* would require that tens of billions of additional dollars of public money be spent each year. Raising wages would raise the government's bill for getting affordable care to families by billions more.

This chapter describes the current condition of child care workers. It explains why the wages and status of such workers are low. It discusses measures that would, if they could be implemented, raise the wages and promote the professionalization of child care workers.

No easy or promising strategy to bring about this transformation emerges from our analysis. While some political initiatives are occurring at the local, state, and federal level, and some unions are making efforts to organize child care workers, we believe the best and most realistic hope for significant, nation-wide progress would be an expanded, adequately financed federal voucher system that contained incentives for better training and pay of child care workers. Nevertheless, some measures could and should be taken to finance training and to increase incentives for workers to come into and stay in the field.

CHILD CARE LABOR MARKET CONDITIONS

The Bureau of Labor Statistics (BLS) estimated that the median wage was $8.41 per hour for preschool teachers in 1999 and $6.91 per hour for child care workers (defined to include entry-level positions in child care centers and other such facilities). These wage levels are among the lowest of any occupations. Of the 215 professional, paraprofessional, and technical occupations, only 3 of these occupations earn less than child care teachers. Among the 64 service occupations, only 5 earn less than child care workers: ticket takers, amusement park attendants, fast food cooks, food preparation workers, and ushers and lobby attendants—all entry-level jobs often filled by teenagers. Occupations with no big responsibilities, like parking lot attendants, nursing aides and orderlies, crossing guards, maids and housekeeping cleaners, and other cleaning and building service attendants, all earn more than child care workers.[3]

Along with low wages, child care workers also suffer from a good deal of economic insecurity due to inadequate health and retirement benefits. Less than half of center teaching staff have fully covered health insurance for themselves, and only 16 percent of those with full coverage received fully paid coverage for their dependents.[4] Pension programs for employees are even rarer. Fewer than 30 percent of teaching staff have retirement benefits. Sick leave, paid vacations, and pay for meetings and training are far from universal; less than two-thirds of assistant teachers and aides receive these benefits.[5] Health insurance and retirement plans for family child care providers, considered self-employed, are mostly nonexistent, except for those few providers organized in local networks. Only in a few states is progress being made to provide insurance.[6]

Many teachers in child care centers have minimal education. Forty percent have only a high school degree or less. An additional 10 percent have a two-year college degree.[7] Thirty to 40 percent of center staff have B.A. degrees.[8] The child care workers who are well educated get meager returns for their education or experience, as compared with other workers in the economy. Child care teachers earn only about a 5 percent rate of return on their education, and aides earn half that. Education has no impact on wages of family child care providers. A year of experience yields only a 1 percent rate of return for teachers and none for aides. Specialized training seems to have some influence on teacher wages; it does not affect wages of aides.[9]

Even relative to other women's occupations with similar levels of education, wages for child care workers are low. The Cost, Quality, and Child Outcomes (CQO) study estimated that child care teachers earned $5200 per year less than women of the same age and education in their regional labor market. Family child care providers, on average, also earn less a year than job-holding women with the same characteristics.[10]

Low pay results in very high turnover. The CQO study found that annual turnover rates averaged 36 percent for all teaching staff, and a whopping 52 percent among assistant teachers and aides. The centers that paid the least had the highest turnover.[11] Turnover rates were particularly high in for-profit centers, averaging around 45 percent.[12] They have increased dramatically in the whole industry since 1977, when the annual rate was only 15 percent. These rates in child care are high, whether compared to allied professional occupations such as public school teachers and social workers, with annual turnover rates of 6.6 percent and 11 percent, respectively, or to low-skilled occupations such as home heath aides and parking attendants, with turnover rates of 21 percent and 15 percent, respectively.[13]

Workers, even those who like the work, leave because they cannot continue to make the economic sacrifices necessary to stay in the field.[14] The better educated move on to jobs in the public schools or elsewhere as they become concerned about the needs of their own family for health care, saving to buy a house, or planning for retirement. During the rapid expansion of the late 1990s a real staffing crisis developed in the industry.[15]

Neither the economic expansion nor the rapid growth in the demand for child care and child care workers since 1970 has caused real wages in the industry to rise.[16] Employment growth in child care has been much higher than in most industries, about 250 percent from the early 1970s to the early 1990s. Nevertheless, real wages in child care, like wages in other occupations that accept people of limited education, were nearly constant, even in the period of rapid expansion in the late 1990s.[17]

THE DEPRESSING EFFECT OF LOW WAGES ON QUALITY

Unfortunately, low wages discourage entry into the field of many talented people who might want to work with children but expect to earn a normal return on their education and experience. They also discourage child care workers and family child care providers from investing in advanced training since it has so little effect on their earnings.

The high rates of labor turnover resulting from low wages and little reward for education or seniority directly affect service quality. High rates of turnover at a center siphon off the director's time to recruiting and orienting new staff, distracting him or her from program management. They lower staff morale and initiative. They add to the chaos that characterizes a low-quality program, particularly if replacement staff do not work out or have trouble fitting in or performing their job. High staff turnover robs children of opportunities to form trusting relations with their caregivers. Strong teacher-child attachments promote children's social competencies, but children require time to develop these relationships.[18]

High turnover reduces the benefit a center gets from on-the-job training it provides. Good quality centers are effective communities of like-minded, skilled staff members who work together effectively in achieving agreed-upon goals. Creating an effective team requires considerable on-the-job training through special workshops, regular staff meetings, mentoring by the senior staff, and the provision of time on the job to work with other staff and prepare activities. Constant turnover makes it next to impossible for a director to create an effective, stable team that can build such an environment. It makes it difficult to introduce curriculum reforms in centers because staff trained in the new approach leave and new hires have to be brought up to grade, creating problems for the whole team. It discourages centers from investing in training staff members who may quit at any time.

Continual exit from the field of trained and talented people wastes much of the investment in professional preparation and requires continual training just to maintain skill levels of the existing workforce. Similarly, family child care providers have little incentive to invest in their own training if they consider their work a temporary interlude while their children are small or if their customers are content with their services.

Centers pursuing a low-cost strategy to provide services to cost-conscious customers necessarily hire low-wage workers who produce, at best, mediocre quality services. More sophisticated management operating for-profit chains often design jobs and work routines specifically for this work force. They create a work system involving a relatively strict daily schedule, standard routines and procedures, and reliance on large group activities like listening to stories, singing, and coloring, where children can be easily managed. Staff members can learn their jobs quickly, within a day or two on the job, and so can be easily replaced. In these centers, more-qualified staff tend to be in supervisory jobs.

It is only centers that compete for clientele demanding good quality services that must hire staff who have more skill and knowledge. In these centers staff have considerable job autonomy, because of the variability and complexity of the tasks they are expected to carry out and the discretion they must exercise in deciding how to satisfy specific needs of individual children. In these centers staff members and directors have a long-term commitment to the job and management invests in training, benefits, and higher salaries to retain staff.

JOB DIFFERENTIATION AND TRAINING REQUIREMENTS

There is no generally accepted career path in early care and education that ties advancement of workers to training and experience. State licensing regulations define the occupational differentiation that does exist. Most states specify minimum qualifications and ongoing training requirements for at most four job categories: center teachers, center directors, large group family child care providers, and small group family child care providers. Only 12 states identify "master teachers" as another occupational category with special training requirements, and most states do not mention aides or assistant teacher classifications, since these positions usually have no legal entry requirements.[19]

There are no generally accepted education or training prerequisites that qualify a person for a job, including that of director, in child care centers.[20] The contrast between the legal requirements for child care teachers/providers and public school teachers is instructive. State certification restricts entry into public school teaching by requiring college degrees and completion of a specialized curriculum but little prior experience. Child care licensing encourages easy entry into child care employment with no preservice training required of aides and assistants. In many states, assistants with no formal training are allowed to become teachers and even directors, just on the strength of their experience. State regulation of school teachers restricts the workforce to individuals willing to invest in the necessary education, whereas center and family child care licensing regulation places little restrictions on the supply of child care workers.

Workers in the industry can fulfill state requirements with courses carrying college credits or continuing education units. However, child care workers and providers commonly choose noncredit courses and workshops because they are more convenient and cheaper and because workers are uninformed about college opportunities and scholarships. Most noncredit offerings are entry-level and repetitive. Generally, they do not go beyond what new practitioners need and do not provide college credit that could contribute to career advancement.

Current state training requirements are partly a response to existing industry conditions. People already employed in child care find it difficult to take college courses or work toward degrees, since those programs are organized for full-time undergraduates. Training is not a high priority for many centers, and most do not actively encourage staff to work toward professional degrees, much less give them practical help in doing so.

WHY THESE CONDITIONS EXIST AND PERSIST

The wages in child care, like the wages in any occupation, depend on the qualifications of the workers that employers seek to recruit for those jobs. As we have seen, most center directors and most of the parents who put their children in family child care or hire nannies have made the decision that they are willing to entrust their children to people with little training and without much formal education. That allows them to hire workers who will take jobs at rock-bottom wages, because those workers have no more attractive alternative jobs open to them. Only a quarter of the centers surveyed in one study required teachers to have a bachelor's degree, and only 19 percent required any college course work at all for assistants.[21]

Sex and race discrimination also play a part in the low wages in child care occupations. Work in the child care industry is available to both white and minority women with little or no education beyond high school. There are jobs in other industries that pay good wages but don't require much formal education, but many of those jobs are reserved, through discriminatory hiring practices, for white men. That leaves such women with no good alternatives to low-paying work.

So the child care industry draws labor for many of its job slots from the same pool of workers who staff the fast food industry or run cash registers in the retail industry, and it doesn't need to pay higher wages to fill those jobs. The industry can draw on housewives and teenagers with low education and little or no labor market experience. The expanded availability of labor with limited education and skills, in part due to high immigration, has helped keep the wages of such people down.

Even at the low pay they offer, centers are able to hire some well-educated women (and a few men) who place a higher value on working with children than on the monetary rewards from the higher paying jobs they could hold.[22] For many women, their decision to work in the child care field is an expression of their commitment to an ethic of care. Some choose early care and education as a career, knowing full well that they will be poorly paid. Their initial commitment, however, does not make them immune to succumbing eventually to opportunities to take more highly valued jobs. In the latter half of the 1990s, as the unemployment rate fell, people with a good education found it easy to get jobs in other industries. Center directors reported that their main response to the difficulty in hiring workers was not to raise wages but to hire less capable people.[23]

If the child care industry could fill all of its slots, even at its low wages, with well-educated people, the quality problem would be somewhat alleviated (although the turnover problem, which is an important part of the quality problem, would not be). But there are not enough of such people available to the industry. So the managements of centers fill staffing vacancies with less skilled, less experienced, poorly educated women. Some of these women like working with children, and some are good at it. But the availability of such people at low wages, and the willingness of employers to hire them, keeps wages low for everybody.

Why do centers follow this low-wage strategy? One reason is the price competition in the industry between centers, family child care, and relative care discussed in chapter 7. It puts pressure on centers to keep labor costs—the major component of center costs—as low as possible. The child care centers pursuing the low-wage strategy are those choosing to serve cost-conscious customers.

Cultural attitudes also exert a powerful influence reinforcing employer decisions to keep wages down. Caring for children is not highly valued by the general public, by many parents, and by employers in the child care industry. Many equate it with the baby-sitting provided by the teenager next door who watches television with the kids while parents step out for a few hours. The idea that children in care for long stretches of the day might need caregivers with special skills in the development and education of young children probably runs counter to the assumption that almost anybody can be a good mother and that mothers do not need training. This attitude ignores the fact that a considerable proportion of parents have a good education and so are equipped to foster their child's development. Their children get developmental care when they are at home with their parents and deserve the same kinds of skills from their caretakers when they are away from their parents. For the children of those parents who are not so equipped, having caregivers with a good education or with special training in aiding children's development is crucial to providing those children with an equal opportunity to thrive in school and later in the economy.

Raising child care wages permanently on an industry-wide basis across the country would require some kind of action that led, induced, or forced the employers of child care workers to make different decisions concerning the pay they offer and the kinds of workers they hire.

WHAT TRAINING AND EDUCATION GOALS?

A group of child care experts drawn together under the auspices of the National Research Council of the National Academy of Sciences recommends far higher standards of education and training preparation than is common in the industry. Based on research evidence about the effect of staff education on the quality of services and children's achievement, they recommend that "each group of children [over two years old] in an early childhood education and care program should be assigned a teacher who has a bachelor's degree with specialized education related to early childhood." The teacher should attain a mastery of information on effective teaching strategies and methods to provide "rich conceptual experiences" that promote the children's growth in language ability and reasoning.[24] They also recommend that states create a career ladder for early childhood teaching staff that specifies education requirements and pay levels for different job classifications. In addition, they recommend that teaching assistants have a Child Development Associate (CDA) certificate.[25]

To be effective in improving quality, colleges and universities would have to offer high quality degrees in early education. Such programs are rare at present, but some very good models exist.[26] The National Association for the Education of Young Children (NAEYC) has created guidelines outlining performance standards for baccalaureate degrees specializing in early care and education.[27]

The NAEYC does not require a specific model of staffing. Their staff training recommendations for accreditation represent realistic expectations, given present circumstances, rather than long-run goals. They do provide a suggested differential staffing structure based on levels of education in which both teachers and assistant teachers have at least a CDA credential and progress to at least a bachelor's degree, and in which each center/program has an early childhood specialist with at least a bachelor's degree in early childhood education and three years full-time teaching experience.

The Wheelock College Institute for Leadership and Career Initiatives advocates training requirements for various positions, but the requirements it advocates for the short term, particularly for teachers, are less stringent than those of the National Academy of Sciences group.[28] In the long term, it aims toward at least the standards recommended by the National Academy group but is reluctant to endorse them as an immediate requirement because they are unrealistic, given the current labor supply for child care workers.

The Wheelock group objects to adopting in early care and education the system of preparation of elementary school teachers. While college graduates may enter child care work directly from college, the Wheelock model also incorporates an adult education/apprenticeship approach to advancement in the field. This strategy helps avoid creating a two-class system of professionals. Requiring that college-based professional credentials be obtained before the person enters the child care field can preclude drawing into the profession an adequate pool of child care teachers and licensed family child care providers that reflect the demographics of the children receiving the services. The career development system encourages able people representative of the ethnic and racial communities being served to enter the field but requires them to move into a career path that involves working toward college degrees.

Wheelock has developed a model that requires a well-articulated career "lattice" consisting of: aide, assistant, teacher, lead teacher, mentor teacher, educational coordinator, director 1, and director 2. The lattice also includes classifications for people in family child care, school-age care, and in other sectors such as those in the public schools.[29] Passage from one job classification to a higher one is based on educational qualifications met through college courses and degrees ranging from the A.A. (Associate of Arts) to the masters or doctorate degrees. Salary scales are based on the amount of training completed. Course work is articulated from vocational high school courses to the doctorate, so that courses required to qualify for lower job classifications also fulfill degree requirements. Workers are individually licensed or certified by state licensing authorities based on their higher education records. States maintain a personnel registry and career record for each person in the field. There is some form of approval of training programs to ensure that they meet licensing requirements.

For the Wheelock model to work for low-income women it would need considerable financial support. Some of this support is starting to become available, for instance, in the T.E.A.C.H. Early Childhood® Project described later in the chapter, in registered apprenticeship programs,[30] and in federal higher education Pell grants. Nevertheless, progress toward a degree for these employed individuals is likely to be slow, and funding is still inadequate.

The suggestions for training and licensing schemes we have reviewed would create a more effective training system, provide a career path within the industry, and justify higher wages for those with higher credentials. But justifying higher wages doesn't necessarily mean achieving them. Unless there is explicit, detailed, and effective regulation of the qualifications required to perform particular functions, the industry will contrive to continue to hire and use the same proportion of poorly trained people they have on board now. Wages would continue to be low for those both with and without training. In grade schools, the simple requirement that every room have a teacher with a bachelor's degree prevents children from being taught by uncredentialed people. The National Academy recommendations, which would extend that requirement to early care and education, would achieve that for young children if there were funding to pay salaries to attract enough B.A.'s.[31]

WHAT MIGHT BE EFFECTIVE IN RAISING WAGES AND THE STATUS OF CHILD CARE WORK?

Effective measures to significantly raise wages and/or raise qualifications for child care workers nationwide would have to involve such means as regulation or unionization and the appropriation of public money for the added cost. It might be possible to raise pay in the child care industry in the absence of new legal requirements for training and education. This would probably not have as beneficial an effect on the quality of care as would the mandating of training requirements, but it could be expected to have some positive effect. Higher pay should raise morale and it should reduce turnover; both of these effects should increase quality. In addition, higher wages would make it easier for employers to attract more qualified workers. However, any governmental action to raise the pay for child care workers would undoubtedly have to be justified politically by new requirements for training and education on the part of workers in the industry.

Most schemes to raise child care wages and/or worker qualifications focus on centers, where there is an employer-employee relationship. However, family care providers, who are paid directly by parents, are in competition with centers. Their pay and qualifications are also of concern, and both need to be raised.

Federal funding standards concerning educational levels of caregivers would allow uniformly high standards to be maintained throughout the country. They would be difficult to pass, but working for such regulations on the national level might economize on the political energy required to achieve the goal of better training throughout the industry. The alternative is enacting such regulations on a state-by-state basis, perhaps with federal funding as an incentive.

Requiring Credentials and Lengthy Training

The most direct way to raise the qualifications of child care workers would be through new state government regulations mandating educational qualifications for each grade of worker in the career ladder, together with specifications of the role in actual day-to-day care each grade would play. Such regulations would obviously be most effective if they were tied in some way to governmental pay subsidies. An alternative approach to mandating higher qualifications and/or pay would be an incentive scheme. The vouchers that parents receive could pay more to providers with better qualifications and/or pay. Voucher programs in 24 states now give higher reimbursement rates to centers with higher quality (and some give them to accredited family child care), so there is ample precedent.

Even if higher pay were not mandated, higher qualification requirements would lead to a tendency for wages to rise. The industry would have to use more workers with the required qualifications and eliminate workers without them from some jobs. To get those additional qualified workers, and to motivate them to get the required education, the wages offered would have to rise. If the new regulations were to mandate the hiring of many more people with bachelor degrees, as the National Academy model would require, people with bachelor degrees would have to be drawn from other occupations where they are currently earning more.

If the law were to require an educational credential as a condition for working at a particular job in the industry, it would have the effect of raising wages only if the course of study required for the credential was a serious one, requiring the person taking it to master a considerable body of relevant material. Mandating trivial preparation that virtually anybody could pass in a short time without serious study would not succeed in raising quality and would not succeed in raising pay. It would just set up a minor additional hoop that the people willing to work at low wages would all be able to jump through.

Even the requirement that child care workers responsible for children have credentials requiring significant education would not necessarily raise pay in the near term. The behavior of American hospitals during the shortage of registered nurses that occurred in recent decades provides a caution concerning the firmness of the link between education requirements and higher pay and the long time lag involved to bring about substantial wage increases. Hospitals did not respond to the nurse shortage by raising pay across the board; they lived with the shortage and tried to find ways around it. They increased the number of patients per nurse and hired lesser-educated aides to do much of the work. Eventually, nurses' pay rose considerably, but it took decades. This kind of evasive employer behavior seems to occur particularly when it is women's wages that need to be raised to equate supply and demand. In the case of child care workers, we could be sure that higher education requirements would cause an increase in pay in a timely way only if the funds to finance an increase were an integral part of the package.

Professionalization of the child care labor force and the higher pay that would presumably in time accompany it would benefit the better-qualified workers currently in the industry by raising their pay. However, it would reduce the employment opportunities of the less-qualified workers whom the industry employs, who would not have or be able to get the credentials. Some of the excluded ones might be very talented in caring for children but not good at formal education and taking tests. The Wheelock model provides a way for those in the field to meet the new training requirements. Even so, some will be excluded, and this would be part of the price paid for professionalization.

Public Funding to Supplement Pay for
Child Care Workers, with Training Conditions

Public money can be used to supplement the pay and benefits of child care workers. ECE advocates see this as the most promising approach. Because families cannot afford to pay more for early care and education, they argue that substantial wage increases require public funding to break the link between wages and fees. This was the strategy Department of Defense officials employed when they decided to make heavy investments to upgrade the military child care system to provide good quality, affordable services to all military personnel. A key element of the strategy was to divorce provider salaries from fees paid by parents. The fee structure is based on what families can afford and the wage scale is based on earnings that reflect training, experience, and a living wage that attracts and retains competent teachers and providers. The Department of Defense subsidizes the difference between revenue and earnings.[32] Head Start also increased wages and training standards substantially in the 1990s.

Advocates for better quality child care services argue that a similar approach needs to be taken for the rest of child care provision. So far, although legislation has been introduced, federal programs to mimic the military have not been enacted by Congress.[33] However, several states have initiated programs to improve training and raise child care wages and provider income. The most successful nonfederal program is T.E.A.C.H. Early Childhood® (Teacher Education and Compensation Help) launched by North Carolina through a direct appropriation from the state Assembly and business and private foundations. T.E.A.C.H. programs are now operating in several other states. The North Carolina program makes available scholarships covering 80 to 90 percent of tuition, books, and transportation to help participants earn North Carolina child care credentials or associate or bachelor degrees in child development, or to become an early childhood model/mentor teacher. The program provides incremental compensation incentives tied to completion of specified amounts of course work. Teachers in the program average 15 completed credit hours a year and compensation increases of 10 percent per year and 41 percent over the period of four contracts. The salary increases reflect increased job performance and promotions.

The child care center must provide three to six hours per week of paid released time for each participant and a raise or bonus on completion of each year's contract, partly reimbursed by T.E.A.C.H. The participant agrees to remain with the sponsoring center for an additional year after completion of the contract. Staff turnover rates have been slashed to 10 percent for participants in the program for one year and to 4 percent after four years in the program.

North Carolina also funds a program called WAGE$ to raise earnings of center staff and family child care providers who have not enrolled in T.E.A.C.H. but have already earned degrees, if their earnings fall below a threshold. Results in Orange County indicate the success of the program. After five years operating the program, the percent of teachers with two- or four-year degrees has increased from 36 to 45 percent, and the county turnover rate for all teachers declined from 36 to 22 percent. A health insurance program has been introduced, financed by federal block grant funds, for T.E.A.C.H. participants and staff in any program where all teaching and administrative staff have two- and four-year degrees.[34]

CCW has developed a program in California, C.A.R.E.S. (Compensation and Recognition Enhances Stability), that has been implemented in San Francisco and Alameda counties with local funds and is being considered seriously in other counties. The state has passed legislation to provide matching grants to assist counties in implementing the program. C.A.R.E.S. provides monetary rewards from $500 to $6500 per year for center staff and family child care providers who commit to continuing their professional development and agree to stay in the field for a specified period of time. Funds are also provided to child care programs for differential reimbursement rates and grants to assist them in achieving accreditation and increasing staff retention.[35]

Another approach to career enhancement and increased compensation is through mentoring programs that reward experienced teachers who stay in the field by creating a new job classification of master or mentor teacher. For instance, in the California Early Childhood Mentor Program created by CCW, mentor teachers are reimbursed for training expenses, earn an annual stipend of $1000, and use their child care classroom to train student teachers.

Although these are interesting models, little headway has been made in raising compensation for child care workers outside the military and, possibly, North Carolina. One-time or temporary stipends rather than substantial wage increases will not have a significant effect on the child care labor market. To be effective, initiatives have to increase market wages enough to attract and hold better qualified people in child care and induce existing workers to get the required training.

Public funds used to raise the pay of child care workers would have the disadvantage of not being targeted to helping lower-income parents. Some of the wage subsidies would go to workers caring for the children of well-to-do parents. Those parents might well be able to afford to finance the higher wages for child care workers by paying higher fees.

Special Minimum Legal Wages for Child Care Workers

Special minimum wages applying to particular occupations are unknown in the United States but do exist elsewhere. In Australia, a large number of occupations have legal minimums, which are set by appointed review boards. As with all other methods to raise wages, to avoid a shift from center care to family child care providers, the latter would need to be included. As with regular minimum wages, an enforcement agency that would track down those not complying would be required if such a strategy is to be effective. It would not do to restrict the application of the special minimum wage to those taking special training. Employers might respond by hiring more untrained workers.

A special minimum wage might be required of all providers. Or the requirement might be restricted to providers taking part in the subsidy program under the Child Care and Development Fund (CCDF) block grants to states. This would be somewhat analogous to the Davis-Bacon Act, which regulates the wages that federal contractors must pay. The higher wages that providers would be forced to pay would mean higher costs and higher prices for care. Under a subsidy program that allowed families to pay no more than 20 percent of their over-the-poverty-line income for child care, the vast majority of families would not be affected; almost all of the extra cost would be borne by government.

In the first initiative that we know about of this kind, San Francisco has included child care workers in community child care programs serving low-income families in the city's living wage ordinance if they are not eligible for benefits and raises received by public employees. While a special legal minimum wage for child care workers would succeed in raising wages, passage of such laws at the federal level has be rated as politically unlikely. It remains to be seen if other localities follow the example of San Francisco.

A rise in the existing U.S. minimum wage applied to all workers would bring child care workers, along with other low-wage workers, a higher standard of living, and this is certainly desirable. However, that would not change the position of child care jobs on the wage totem pole. Child care jobs would continue to pay less than most other jobs. For this reason, raising the minimum wage for everybody would be unlikely to reduce turnover among child care workers, and it wouldn't bring higher quality, better educated workers into the field, either.

Shifting Child Care to the Public Sector

Wages in the public sector are sometimes higher than in the private sector. Formal or informal "pay equity" calculations by public sector personnel administrators raise the pay of some workers on the public payroll above those in the private sector. More importantly, child care workers who are in regular public sector jobs are likely to receive the same health insurance, vacations, and other benefits that workers in other public sector jobs receive, which are worth thousands of dollars a year. The public sector workers are more easily organized into unions, which are sometimes able to obtain higher wages for those workers, largely through political pressure.

The movement to provide all-day kindergarten and to provide universal prekindergarten, which currently has considerable momentum in the United States, is always presented as an educational measure. The growth of these programs provides an opportunity to move a significant share of child care activities from private to public providers. However, relocation of child care services and jobs to the public sector, especially those involving 4-year-olds, would no doubt spark grave opposition from for-profit and nonprofit providers in the private sector, weakening any chance for a successful coalition to achieve greater government subsidies for child care.

The current practice in many cases is to pay for prekindergarten services by nonpublic providers with public money. Unionization of these workplaces might well be facilitated because of the public funding source, since often federal grantees are required by law to remain neutral in worker representation elections. In California this has been the case with home care workers who help the aged and disabled and are paid for by public funds, but who work for nonpublic agencies.

Unionization

One traditional way to raise wages and improve working conditions is through unionization. Since only 5 percent of child care employees are covered by collective bargaining agreements, it might seem wishful thinking to pin hopes on unions to transform working conditions in the child care industry. This is particularly true for the child care labor force, composed as it is of easily replaced workers in many small centers with high turnover rates, more educated staff and providers who, considering themselves professionals, may be biased against unionization, and self-employed family child care workers.

Unions, however, are becoming more interested in child care, both as a collective bargaining benefit in union contracts and as a potential occupation to organize.[36] Unions have been most successful in organizing government employees or employees of government contractors (Head Start), whose employers are not supposed to use federal funds to fight unionization, and nonprofit centers in very large metropolitan areas.[37] In New York City, for instance, staff of all city-operated agencies and Head Start programs are covered by contracts with the American Federation of State, County, and Municipal Employees (AFSCME). AFSCME has close to 9,000 child care worker members in the city, in addition to membership in the region around Albany. The United Auto Workers has had collective bargaining agreements with some centers in Massachusetts for years, and the teachers' unions have organized some child care workers. Unions have been active participants in several states in political initiatives to increase child care funding and worker compensation.

An interesting organization drive in Seattle by District 925, an affiliate of the Service Employees International Union (SEIU), has resulted in the organization of several centers.[38] In 2000, the union signed a master collective bargaining agreement with 12 child care centers, along with addenda agreements with the individual centers. The union uses a nonconfrontational strategy in organizing campaigns and contract negotiations that also involves collaboration through joint political activity between unions and employers to achieve legislative goals that would benefit both workers and employers.

SEIU aims at multiple employer collective bargaining between the union and a coalition of child care centers. Initially, the organization drive targeted good quality centers interested in finding ways to increase wages to further improve quality. The union holds initial discussions with employers about mutual interests and advantages of cooperation with the union and among employers, and tries for an agreement by employers to remain neutral during the drive to organize their employees.[39] The union can provide savings on group coverage of health and pension benefits, jointly managed funds to finance staff training, and a union/employer-operated hiring hall for substitutes, in addition to political cooperation that benefits employers by seeking public financing. Long-run goals, if regional multiple-employer bargaining is successful, involve raising workplace standards for the whole industry by raising wages, standardizing labor costs, and increasing investments in training. A public education campaign seeks to build a coalition of workers, parents, directors, advocates, and community leaders that lobbies at the state and local level. The state has funded a pilot project to publicly subsidize wages based on a career ladder that reflects levels of staff education, experience, and responsibility.[40]

In Philadelphia and Delaware County, Pennsylvania, the United Child Care Union (UCCU) has been working to organize both center staff and family child care providers, mostly serving low-income families. Although the organizing strategy shares many features with that used in Seattle, it is an ambitious attempt to organize and restructure the industry in a region that is more hostile to unionization.[41] The union's parent organization, the National Union of Hospital and Health Care Employees, has committed significant resources to organizing workers and to child care political advocacy. UCCU helped establish the Philadelphia Area Jobs with Justice Coalition of unions and religious and community organizations to educate the larger community about workers' rights to organize. Jobs for Justice enlists community leaders to encourage employers to engage in fair organizing campaign practices. UCCU won a hard-fought election to represent Head Start workers in Delaware County and is negotiating a contract with the largest provider of services in Philadelphia, the Pittsburgh-based Alleghany Child Care Academy, a for-profit company that serves low-income, often subsidized, children.

UCCU has formed a collaborative partnership with other organizations to promote union-management cooperation in order to increase public investment in child care, restructure jobs, and improve the quality of child care services.[42] With a grant from the U.S. Department of Labor, the partnership will upgrade child care training, develop a career ladder, develop a state-wide apprenticeship program, and organize a demonstration project to create a worker/employer group. With other child care advocacy groups it has helped increase state reimbursement rates and roll back increases in parent copayment rates.

Unions recognize the need to organize family child care workers. One model is being adapted from the successful organization of home health care workers in California, where SEIU created a collective bargaining unit for workers paid from public funds and bargains with a county-based public authority. In Illinois SEIU has organized several hundred family child care providers and negotiates directly with the state for higher reimbursement rates and better benefits.

In New York City, the Consortium for Worker Education has organized the Satellite Child Care Program to train welfare recipients and others to provide family child care in their own home.[43] The new family child care provider is connected to a center-based child care agency, increasing the capacity of the center by essentially providing another classroom in the provider's home. The new providers become a member of AFSCME and an employee of the child care agency. Their wages and benefits, including health insurance, are determined through collective bargaining. New recruits complete a 16-week program that includes practical experience and 150 hours of classroom instruction. The model is being replicated in Milwaukee, Hartford, Connecticut, Pittsburgh, Yonkers, and in rural Alabama, but not all those locations have union involvement.

There are many reasons to be cautious about the chances of effectively attacking low pay and qualifications in child care through unionization. In addition to the difficulty of organizing workers, who have high turnover and are so easily replaced, there is the high cost of organizing them. Employers are most often hostile to unions because they erode management prerogatives and make it more difficult to do business. For instance, unionization may bring cumbersome grievance procedures that interfere with firing an incompetent worker. While small employers might gain from participation in joint union-employer provision of benefits and training that they could not afford by themselves, for-profit chains would not benefit as much and are likely to fight to keep unions out. Indeed, the unions have met a lot of employer opposition in their organizing campaigns, despite the considerable potential gains that could be achieved through cooperation.

Child care advocates need help in pushing forward their public policy agenda, and, undoubtedly, unions (many of whose members are young parents) are politically powerful allies. With the increasing importance of services in the U.S. economy and the growing disparity in incomes, there will be increasing interest on the part of unions in organizing low-wage workers who have, so far, not benefited from economic prosperity. It is possible that over time unions can help bring about a constructive transformation of the child care industry that brings about higher wages, greater investment in training, and better quality child care. If so, it will be important for child care advocates and leadership to encourage these efforts and start making appropriate alliances.

If unions are able, through political activity, to get public money for wage increases, then the chance of successful unionization is greatly enhanced. It is impossible at this time to predict how much success these organizing initiatives will have, but widespread success is by no means guaranteed. Certainly, raising

wages through unionization will take time and continuing dedi⟨
unions. In 1999, in the Quebec province of Canada, the Confe⟨
National Trade Unions finally won a 35 percent increase in the avera
the child care workforce, over 34 years after the start of a campaign t   ...⟨e
workers and win a publicly supported universal child care system.

THINKING ABOUT PRIORITIES

The early care and education field is moving forward to institute a career ladder
that defines a hierarchy of occupations with increasing responsibility requiring
increasing amounts of formal training. These career ladders will have to be
institutionalized through changes in state licensing regulations, and the appropriate training programs will have to be made available. Doing so would increase
the status of child care workers and improve their performance. They will not
have much effect on increasing wages and income unless a substantial number
of untrained workers are replaced by trained ones.

Low wages, lack of occupational differentiation, and insufficient investment in training are major impediments to improving quality in child care.
However, the kinds of initiatives we have discussed to bring wages up to levels
high enough to convert child care teaching into a profession would be expensive.
To make a child care teacher's salary comparable to that of a kindergarten
teacher's involves about an 85 percent increase in wages.[44] Doing that might
increase child care costs by 40 percent.

We believe that instituting a system of universally affordable services
should take priority over a major overhaul of child care wages and jobs.
Nevertheless, some steps toward wage parity with the public school system,
which would bring quality improvements, should be incorporated in a program
of affordable access to services. In the expanded voucher system we recommend,
reimbursement rates must be high enough to pay for adequate quality services,
and higher rates need to be set for good quality care, which would permit these
centers to compete with public education in the hiring of teachers and directors.
The reimbursement differential would have to be high enough to adequately
reward workers' investment in training and to encourage them to remain in the
field, and good quality centers would have to be required to use a significant
portion of the differential on wages.

In addition to encouraging wage increases through adequate reimbursement rates, additional public funding is needed to provide adequate training of

child care staff and family child care providers. There needs to be more federal support for scholarship and training grants than is currently provided for quality improvement through the CCDF block grants. At current tuition costs of junior and state colleges, $500 million per year would provide tuition scholarships of $1,000 per year to cover nine hours of college credit per year for 500,000 child care workers, roughly one-sixth of those employed in the field.

One step toward increasing compensation for child care workers would be federal funding to aid states in guaranteeing important fringe benefits for child care workers such as health insurance, free child care, or retirement plans. States could design benefit packages around a cafeteria-style plan to take into consideration the needs of workers.[45] Such a program could reduce turnover significantly. We recommend investing $500,000 per year in federal funds to experiment with such programs.

A plan has recently been patterned after the military model designed to improve quality and increase retention of skilled child care staff and providers. It would provide funding up to $7,000/staff person or provider for members of a local consortium. Organized through a local child care agency such as resource and referral agencies (R&Rs), member providers and their staff who would agree to a number of quality improvement stipulations and be eligible to receive a cafeteria-style plan of benefits such as: subsidized health care, low-cost training, assistance in seeking accreditation, reimbursed family leave, reimbursement of Social Security taxes for family child care providers, access to consulting services, and subsidized child care for children of staff.[46] Such a program, in providing the organizational structure for the necessary quality improvement incentives that we have recommended, fits well with the expanded voucher program we are advocating.

It must be emphasized that all of the approaches to higher wages, including higher minimum wages and unionization, would raise child care costs. But an expanded voucher program with higher reimbursement for better quality care would make it possible to pay higher wages without increasing the amount that lower-income parents would have to pay for care.

CHAPTER NINE

The Cost:
How Much Would It Take to
Provide Affordability and
Improved Quality?

"I'm not going to be swayed by people who want to accuse me of being anti-poor. I'm not going to be swayed by people who say, 'You have no compassion.' I have great compassion. I think of the unwed mother who is working as a cook in a little restaurant, working ten or eleven hours a day. She is barely making ends meet. It is wrong that people who aren't working are getting more money than she is. I think she ought to get to keep more of what she earns. I don't think it's fair that because she is working, she gets no medical coverage, or has difficulty getting it, and somebody who doesn't work gets the best in the world."

— Senator Phil Gramm (R-Texas),Quoted in D. Frum, "Righter Than Newt," *The Atlantic Monthly* (March 1995): 83-84.

❧   ❧   ❧

The "somebody who doesn't work" that Senator Gramm was talking about was, of course, a welfare mother. His idea of showing compassion for the woman working as a cook was not to help her by providing her with government-financed child care and health care benefits, but rather to even things up by forcing the welfare mother to join her in the work force.[1] Thanks to welfare reform, that has presumably happened, and now both mothers need help with child care expenses and health insurance. While the appropriations for child care subsidies have increased somewhat, they still do not suffice by a large margin to guarantee that all working parents have access to government help in getting affordable quality child care.

A realistic approach to the problem of child care in America requires recognition of the need for a reliable flow of funds that would finance on a continuing basis, year after year, the provision of improved quality services to millions of children. At the same time it would need to allow hard-pressed parents to reduce what they currently pay for care out of their own pockets to a reasonable amount that they can afford. Any reasonably comprehensive plan would require tens of billions of dollars per year. As we have seen, the federal and state government programs that currently exist give no help at all to many eligible families whose need is extreme. Those families who are covered receive, in many instances, minimal help in meeting the cost of decent care. And many families of modest means are currently ineligible for help.

We need a new national plan that would build on and enlarge our present program, increasing the number of families helped and the amount of help they receive. We present here three plans, so that their virtues, defects, coverage, and costs can be compared. The plans differ in terms of how many families would get help, the extent of the help they would get, the quality of care that each plan would offer, and, of course, how much they would cost. We anticipate that, as now, most of the financing would be federal, but that administration would be done by the states. The plans are:

1. A relatively modest "interim" plan that would provide the resources to subsidize all families who are currently eligible for help under the programs that already exist in each state.
2. A plan that would provide affordable care of improved quality for all American children, including those in the middle class. A publicly financed free full-day prekindergarten year could be integrated with the program.
3. A plan that would provide care of improved quality that was totally free for all children enrolled, regardless of their parents' income.

Movement to a more generous subsidy plan will induce some mothers to take jobs, and induce some families to switch from free care by relatives to paid care. The extent to which this will occur is uncertain, so the national cost estimates presented here are intended only as indicators of orders of magnitude.[2] If there were to be a substantial increase in the average wages of child care workers, these estimates would have to be raised considerably.

There are disadvantages to putting forth a comprehensive national plan. The magnitude of the funds needed to implement such a plan make it an easy target for attack by those who would like married mothers to stay home, by those with other priorities for government spending, and by those opposed to "big government." Those who advocate a large national program with a low chance of enactment anytime soon are in danger of looking foolishly unrealistic. There is fear that such advocacy might get in the way of obtaining more modest advances in child care funding.

However, there are important advantages to be gained in formulating such plans, estimating their cost, and trying make them part of the public discussion. First, most discussions on "affordable care" lack concreteness. Specifying the characteristics of a plan and estimating its cost forces us to define what is meant by "affordable care" and what is meant by its "lack," and to come to an understanding of what would constitute an acceptable and prudent solution. Second, it is worthwhile to get an estimate of the financial magnitude of the task, because the strategy that is adopted for dealing with the problem depends crucially on that magnitude. Voluntary, local efforts to increase children's access to affordable child care might suffice if the financial magnitude of the effort needed were relatively modest. Considerably larger magnitudes would require a sizeable program financed by the federal government in order for progress to be made on a uniform basis throughout the country. Third, the discussion of a significant new national program in child care is necessary if such a program is to have any chance of eventual enactment. Even if that discussion takes place in a period when public opinion and politicians' opinions are unsupportive of a much-enlarged program, the discussion itself may help to nudge opinion in its favor.

Would increased funding guarantee that an adequate quantity of care would be provided? The subsidies that parents would receive would increase their ability to go onto the market and buy care, and the American economy is highly responsive to such changes. The child care industry, like any other competitive industry, could be expected to respond with an increased supply of its product in response to the new demand, albeit after a lag. As we have noted, in poor neighborhoods or rural areas, and on nights and weekends, where demand might continue to be thin, special provisions would have to be made. This might be done through higher subsidies or direct government provision.[3]

Anxiety would certainly be warranted concerning the quality of the child care that would result from an enlarged subsidy program. The quality provided would depend on the size of payments that providers could receive under the program (the reimbursement rates), the quality and safety standards required of providers receiving public funds, the extent and efficacy of enforcement of those standards, and the incentives given to make quality improvements and raise wages. If the reimbursement rates were at a generous level but the required standards were low, some part of the public subsidies would surely flow to care that is unacceptably poor, just as some government subsidies and parent fees do now. But adequate standards would not produce the desired result if reimbursement rates were too low to finance the costs of such standards. Adequate standards and an adequate level of reimbursement rates are both necessary. Better informed parents would also be needed.

PLAN 1. THE INTERIM PLAN:
FULLY FUNDING EXISTING STATE PROGRAMS

The first plan we present, which we would view as a reasonable interim goal, would considerably expand funding for the child care programs we already have: programs that exist in every state and are financed by the federal Child Care and Development Fund (CCDF) and by state appropriations. Much of the funding available for these programs has been used to help single parents make the transition from welfare to work. However, all low-income families are eligible for help from this program.

As we have seen, appropriations for the CCDF programs are far below the level that would allow all eligible children to participate.[4] The interim plan would make benefits under the state CCDF programs available to all those who meet their eligibility rules and wish to participate. This plan would put the availability of the CCDF programs on a par with the availability of the child care subsidies that middle-class families can claim through tax credits, making the CCDF programs, in effect, an entitlement.

Full funding of the CCDF programs has been called for by the Children's Defense Fund as part of its "Campaign to Leave No Child Behind," which also includes among its proposals many of the quality-improving measures advocated in this book. The campaign's proposals were embodied in a bill introduced in 2001 by Senator Christopher Dodd (D-CT) and Congressman George Miller (D-CA).

TABLE 9.1.

Estimated annual cost of three plans for child care subsidies.[1]
($billions)

AGES	"INTERIM PLAN" (fully funding existing state plans)	"AFFORDABLE CHILD CARE AT IMPROVED QUALITY" (parents pay no more than 20 percent of their above-poverty-line income; higher quality providers receive a $2,000 differential)	FREE, UNIVERSAL CARE
0-1	$7.5	$16.8	$26.4
2-3	6.4	13.5	22.6
4	3.4	7.7	11.9
5	1.6	4.6	8.1
6-12	11.1	26.7	53.5
TOTAL COST	29.9	69.3	122.5
COPAYMENTS	4.1	22.9	0.0
ANNUAL NET COST TO GOVERNMENT	25.8	46.4	122.5
NEW MONEY REQUIRED OVER CURRENT SPENDING	$12.8 [2]	$26.4	$102.5

1. Estimates are for the year 2000 and assume that all eligible children currently in paid care would get subsidies, plus one-third of eligible children not now in paid care. Numbers of children needing care and family incomes determining eligibility and copayment levels based on the March 2000 Current Population Survey. Family incomes for 1999 given in the 2000 Survey were brought up to levels of the year 2000 using the Consumer Price Index. Columns may not add to totals due to rounding.

2. This assumes that the approximately $7 billion spent for Head Start and prekindergarten in 2000 would continue in those programs, and would not be available to increase coverage under the CCDF.

We estimate that a national program that would extend the benefits of each of the state plans to all of the families who would meet their eligibility rules and would want to participate would require $13 billion a year in new funds.[5] (See table 9.1.) Reimbursements to providers would total $30 billion, of which $4 billion would be covered by parents' copayments. The states might bear some of this cost, as they do under the present program, but presumably the federal government would continue to pay the lion's share. This program would give benefits to an estimated 10 million children, as compared with the approximately 2 million currently estimated to be getting benefits under the federal block grants and associated state funds. The families of new children taken onto the program would make higher copayments and thus cost the government less on average than those currently served, who are poorer on average than the currently excluded. About a third of the gross cost of this program is due to its provision of after-school care and summer and holiday care to lower-income children between 6 and 12 years old.

If there is a substantial expansion in the availability of subsidies for child care, some parents who currently do not hold jobs will decide to enter the paid labor force. Furthermore, parents already working may switch their children from unpaid care to paid-for care. The potential costs of these increases in the demand for paid-for care need to be considered.[6] We have some actual examples of parental reaction to subsidies that greatly reduce the price parents have to pay for care. Georgia's prekindergarten program, which is free to parents and provides enough places for all who wish to enroll, is attended by 70 percent of the state's children and 90-100 percent of children in urban counties.[7] France's *écoles maternelles,* which offer free public preschool to all, enroll almost 100 percent of children 3 to 5 years old and about 75 percent of toilet-trained children between 2 and 3.[8] These examples suggest that fully funding the current state programs, which would provide low-income parents with a big drop in their out-of-pocket cost for paid care, would cause a considerable expansion of the number of children whose parents would ask for subsidies. We have calculated the cost of the program on the assumption that one-third of the eligible children currently cared for on an unpaid basis (whether by parents or others) would move into paid-for care.[9]

Current state programs are in many cases poorly publicized, with very little outreach on the part of the agencies running them. Our cost estimates are based on the assumption that these programs would become well-publicized so that all parents would know of their existence and so that eligible children who need care could benefit if their parents wished.

Even if fully funded, the CCDF programs have numerous disadvantages, which the more adequate plan we recommend as an ultimate goal would eliminate. Federal rules require states to restrict their help to families whose income is below 85 percent of the state median income, and some draw the limit even lower. Those families who cross that limit by as much as a dollar stand to lose thousands of dollars in benefits. This is called a "cliff effect," because the family's resources—income plus benefits—fall precipitously. Some states limit fees severely. The interim plan would not remove any of these drawbacks. It would, however, relieve many families at the lower end of the income scale of the excessive financial burden of paying for care and allow their children to step up from unlicensed informal care to safe care of better-than-minimal quality in a licensed facility.

PLAN 2. AFFORDABLE CARE OF IMPROVED QUALITY

In this section, we describe and present estimates of the cost of a national plan that would be a worthy longer-term goal. Like the interim plan it would provide services to all families who meet its income-eligibility test. It is far from the most generous program that might be proposed. However, it would have significant improvements over the interim plan. It would allow all families, not just those with the lowest incomes, access to "affordable" care, as we have defined it. It would offer reimbursement rates to providers that would pay the cost of giving all children care at a level of quality equal to the current national average. It would also incorporate a system of giving providers higher reimbursement rates if they achieved higher quality. And as a family's income rises, the subsidies would be phased out gradually. It eliminates the "cliff effect" of current state plans under CCDF. In accordance with the discussion in chapter 2, we have defined "affordable care" as requiring a family to devote to child care costs no more than 20 percent of that part of its income that is above the poverty line. This formulation gives free care to families at or below the poverty line. For most middle-class parents with preschool children, this plan would be far more generous than the federal tax credit that it would presumably replace. (See table 2.2 on pages 30-31 for examples of benefits and copayments that this plan would entail for families at various income levels.)

What quality of care should such a program finance? Higher quality means higher costs and necessitates higher fees to providers. We should certainly be aiming for the long term at a system in which the standard of care would be characterized as "good" by standard rating techniques.[10] However, only a distinct minority of the nation's child care providers currently meet that standard. If we sent all child care providers a fee typical of providers giving care rated as "good," we would be paying for a standard that most do not achieve.

A way to reconcile current and near-term realities with the gradual improvement of the quality of the supply would be to offer a base reimbursement rate that reflects average fees (which should provide a standard about halfway between "minimally adequate" and "good") and provide a higher reimbursement to providers who demonstrate that the care they give is of good quality.

Accordingly, in simulating cost figures for this program, we have used national average fees and allowed an annual quality bonus of $2,000 per child for "good" care.[11] If such a program were actually to be set up in the United States, a method of designating those programs eligible for the quality bonus would have to be established. Allowable fees would presumably vary by locality.

Annual costs for the plan to provide affordable care of improved quality are estimated at $46 billion per year, requiring $26.4 billion in new money.[12] Our simulations indicate that this program would serve 17 million children.[13] If all 4-year old children in the United States were to have access to a year-round free prekindergarten open 9 hours per day, that would raise the estimated cost for four-year-olds from $7.7 billion to $16.4 billion.[14]

PLAN 3. FREE CARE FOR ALL

Finally, we present estimates of the cost of a plan that would provide free care to all families, regardless of income. It is calculated on the basis of the same fee structure as the plan to provide affordable care of improved quality but with zero copayments. This plan is estimated to cost $123 billion per year, requiring $102 billion in new money.[15]

THE COST OF QUALITY

The discussion of quality issues in chapters 3 through 8 suggests that the improvement of child care quality would require a better system of quality control than the one we have now and incentives for providers and child care staff to improve quality. We need more rigorous regulation and inspection by state agencies than has been the rule. Accreditation as the indicator of good quality should be more common; for that to occur, providers need financial help in undergoing that process. Improved coordination and better consumer information should be achieved through enhanced resource and referral services. The industry needs to provide evaluations of provider quality to parents. The industry also needs financial intermediaries to provide financial consulting and to facilitate financing of capital expansion. Child care teachers, their employers, and family child care providers need an incentive to invest in training. We have estimated the annual cost of improved quality control, coordination, and incentives at around $2.25 billion per year, about 5 percent of the cost of our proposed program of affordable care of improved quality. (For a summary of all of the recommendations we make, see appendix A.) As we have pointed out earlier, while these expenditures are necessary to our voucher program, they would all contribute to quality improvement of the present system and represent a rather small investment.

WHERE WOULD THE MONEY COME FROM?

As the foregoing discussion should have made clear, for the definition of "affordable care" we have adopted, and, for that matter, for any plausible one we might adopt, the expenditure that would be necessary to finance it year after year throughout the United States would be far too large to be raised from nongovernmental sources. As we have seen, business and charitable groups currently contribute a tiny portion of the costs of child care. Even if contributions from them were to increase many times over, they would not make even a small dent in the need for funds.

While states and localities could in principle fund child care as they currently fund public education, it is unlikely that they will do so. The competition that forces states to keep taxes in line with those of other states makes it difficult even for those favorably inclined to undertake big new initiatives. Even if substantial progress could be made in some states, others would inevitably lag. The goal of affordable care for every American child cannot be reached without a federal effort.

Federal funding for a $50 billion federal program—$30 billion over current spending—could be obtained through borrowing, through increased taxation, through a reallocation of federal funds currently being devoted to other uses, from a budget surplus, or through a combination of such means. Advocates for new or greatly expanded spending programs have good reason to avoid suggesting that they be financed by contracting particular existing programs that are of lower priority. Such discussions naturally tend to turn the beneficiaries of those existing programs into enemies of the new program. Nevertheless it is worthwhile to look at the costs and benefits of other substantial federal programs. Doing so puts the proposed costs into perspective and helps to sort out priorities.

As an example, we can cite one current federal program that costs each year about as much money as would be needed to fully fund affordable child care of improved quality. An editorial in the *Washington Post* on 24 July 2001 assessed, quite correctly we believe, the value of this program:

Last year, the United States spent a record $32 billion on direct payments to farmers, but it's not clear what the nation got for it. The spending is justified with rhetoric about the need to help small farms, but most of the money goes to big ones. It is excused with references to floods, low prices and other "extraordinary" disasters, but every year turns out to be extraordinary. The real purpose of the spending is to subsidize middle-class farmers, who are scarcely more deserving than hard-working folk in other trades. But the spending does not even serve this purpose well. It encourages overproduction, and so drives down prices for the farmers' harvest.[16]

Agricultural programs are far from the only example of current programs with low or negative benefits. Five other such federal programs whose costs may exceed their benefits are shown in the top half of table 9.2. The bottom half gives a list of costly "tax expenditures," which are the cost to the Treasury of tax breaks for special groups of taxpayers, most of them well-off. The question that the items in the table invite is "How does the nation's benefit from making decent child care achievable and affordable to American families compare with the nation's benefit from programs such as those listed?"

A big federal child care program may be unlikely in the near future. It has been made less likely by the federal income tax cut that took place in 2001, done with the express purpose of limiting the expansion of government spending. Yet the federal government is surely the only promising source of large-scale amounts of funds. The energy and resources of activists for child care are limited; we believe that a significantly greater share of that energy should be concentrated on the federal level, where it might have the best pay-off.

People tend to view child care as the sole responsibility of parents, much as they tended to view elementary education as the responsibility of parents in the days before public schools. The public apparently does understand that mothers who are leaving welfare need and deserve government help with child care.[17] But there is little understanding of the fact that millions of families who have never been on welfare need help for the same reasons and that such need is widespread. An adequate child care policy is an impossibility without better public understanding of the problem.

There are natural allies who need to be mobilized. Public school administrators, the teachers and their unions should be advocating full-day kindergartens, full-day preschools, and school-based before- and after-school care. The union movement contains in its membership a large pool of parents of young children, and it sees child care workers as potential members. The

TABLE 9.2.

Selected federal outlays and tax expenditures, year 2000.

FEDERAL OUTLAYS	
Department of Defense	$257.1
Energy Department expenditure on nuclear bombs	11.7
Military aid to foreign countries	6.0
Space flight	12.2
Veteran benefits and services	44.0
TAX EXPENDITURES	
Deductibility of mortgage interest on owner-occupied homes	56.5
Forgiveness at death of taxes on capital gains	9.8
Tax exemption for Social Security benefits	27.2
Nontaxation of interest on "public purpose" bonds	15.1
Tax exemption of interest on life insurance	15.0
Accelerated depreciation of machinery	29.4

Source: Outlays from Office of Management and Budget, *The Budget for Fiscal Year 2000* (Washington, DC, 1999), Table 33-2. Tax expenditure from Office of Management and Budget, *Analytic Perspective, Fiscal Year 2002* (Washington, DC, 2001), Table 5-1.

corporations that own child care centers should be lobbying for appropriations to provide them with revenues, just as defense contractors do. And just as defense contractors do, they should be asking for funds to provide high-quality merchandise, not stripped-down models. Finally, employers generally would benefit from better and more reliable child care, because their present workforce would have lower rates of absenteeism, and lower turnover. Workers less distracted by child care problems would have higher productivity. The children getting better care would in time become better workers. If mobilized in this cause, employers could be formidable allies.

Many attempts to educate the public on child care issues are eloquent about unmet needs and the difficulties families face in finding care they can afford. The public also needs to be acquainted with the shape of a program that would solve the problem, and with the magnitude of the funds involved in providing such a program. Currently, the public does not have the knowledge needed to get the politicians to act. A necessary condition for moving child care to the higher place it deserves on our national agenda is that advocates propose and push a long-range plan that is commensurate with the needs we have, whether it is the plan we advocate here, one of the other two we have outlined, or some other program.

CHILD CARE AS A NATIONAL NEED

An adequate child care program is certainly not the only desirable public program lacking in the United States. The country lacks universal access to health care, including care for mental health; well-maintained schools that would offer children in all neighborhoods a decent education; access to higher education for anyone who can profit from it; immediate help for those addicted to drugs or alcohol; affordable housing; adequate public transportation; and adequate social services to counter child abuse, homelessness, and other social pathologies. To create such programs, or bring the ones we have to adequacy, would require major expenditures of public money. The program we have outlined to provide the United States with affordable care of improved quality would also, as we have seen, entail major new public expenditures, year after year. How high is the priority of such a child care program? Does it belong in the list of major national needs?

A program that confers on all families the ability to buy decent child care might "pay for itself," in the sense that such a program would have beneficial results that could eventually save money that the government would otherwise have to spend. Better child care might be expected to promote improved performance in school, to reduce the need for special education instruction, and to reduce discipline problems. The better school performance would be expected to result in improved labor force productivity (resulting in higher tax payments) and reduced criminal behavior (reducing expenditures for the justice system and prisons, to say nothing of sparing trauma to those who would otherwise be victimized or undergo punishment).

The strongest case for a large-scale expansion of government help with child care rests not on the calculation that it will save the government money (although it might) but on the fact that it will prevent the considerable misery to children and their families that derives from low living standards and poor quality care. Making child care of decent quality affordable to all families would

result in safer, more educational, and more enjoyable care for c
would give a financial boost in a non-stigmatizing way to families pi\
of resources. If it had no other benefits, a program providing afford,
care would be amply justified by the fact that it is an indispensable pa   ⌐ie
cure for child poverty, which afflicts almost one in five American children. It
would reduce still further enrollment in welfare-type programs, and give parents
a chance to participate in the world of work and achieve the gains in resources
and status that such a participation allows.

We do not really have to decide whether the benefits of the child care
program are greater or less than the benefits from universal access to health care,
well-maintained public school buildings, and the other desirable amenities and
services that are missing in the United States. The simple truth is that we can
afford them all.

Policy Recommendations

This appendix summarizes the recommendations we make in this book. We propose a set of policies built around our current market-oriented system of child care provision, which will give parents more freedom to choose good quality services from regulated providers, encourage suppliers of services to improve their standards, and promote the development of the market intermediaries necessary to increase the efficiency of local child care markets.

THE CHILD CARE SUBSIDY PROGRAM

The proposal is built around an expanded subsidy program intended to solve the affordability problem. Much of the financing should be through vouchers, financed by the federal government and administered by state and local governments, with the following characteristics:

- Families at or below the poverty level receive a full subsidy for services.
- Families earning incomes above the poverty level pay no more than 20 percent of their family income *in excess of the poverty line* as copayments for child care services.
- Children from birth up to and including 12 years old are eligible for benefits.

- All *licensed* centers, public schools, large group homes, and family child care providers would qualify to receive reimbursement. So would nannies and relatives, if licensed. Parents can choose freely among these providers.
- Reimbursement rates are set at rates that fully compensate providers of at least average quality services.
- Higher reimbursement rates would be paid to providers of good quality services. The award could be based, for instance, on accreditation or percentage of staff with higher education/training degrees. Higher reimbursement rates should reflect the cost of providing higher quality and a more highly trained staff.
- Public contracting with centers may continue, particularly to provide services for subsidized children in communities with serious supply gaps. Quality performance standards for these centers should be established.

This subsidy program would give families a wide range of choice of child care providers at copayments they could afford. It improves the current system by expanding eligibility to more families, and eliminating the "cliff effect," which abruptly cuts off child care subsidies when parent earnings rise beyond some low arbitrary amount. It would give providers a monetary incentive to increase the quality of their services. It would prevent use of public money to fund unlicensed services that put children at risk, encouraging parents to move from informal child care arrangements to those monitored by state regulatory agencies. To help create a seamless system of services for families and to make the most efficient use of subsidies, the program should be closely coordinated with prekindergarten and full-day Head Start programs.

The total cost to the federal government would be about $50 billion a year for the expanded voucher program and higher fees, plus the $2.25 billion a year for the measures to increase quality and improve market efficiency. This expenditure represents an increase of $29 billion per year over current spending on CCDF, Title XX, the child care tax credit, Head Start, and state funding of child care/prekindergarten subsidies. It could provide subsidies to another 15 million children. An interim measure to fully fund existing state subsidy programs would reduce the cost to about $26 billion a year ($15 billion a year in new funding, including the quality improvement measures) and would provide subsidies for an estimated ten million children as compared to the approximate two million currently subsidized by federal block grants and associated state funds.

QUALITY IMPROVEMENT MEASURES

Accompanying this federally funded subsidy program, the following additional measures, some taken by the federal government, some by the states, and some by providers, would be necessary to promote the provision of more *good* quality services (as defined in chapter 4):

State Licensing

- Eliminate all center exemptions from licensing, e.g., for religiously affiliated centers, part-day preschools, and prekindergarten programs.
- Limit licensing exemption for family child care providers to those serving no more than two children or children from one family. (However, to receive federal subsidies providers would have to be licensed.)
- Raise licensing standards in those states falling seriously below the norm. e.g., raise staffing ratios to at least 4:1 for infants and 10:1 for three-year-olds; require a minimum of 6 hours preservice training and 8 hours per year of ongoing training for family child care workers; require criminal and child abuse checks of all center staff and persons living in family child care residences; outlaw smoking in all areas where children are cared for.
- Provide federal funding to insure that state licensing agencies conduct at least two unannounced monitoring visits per year, provide adequate technical assistance, and follow through on enforcement proceedings in a timely fashion—for both centers and family child care providers.

Quality Standards for Providers Receiving Federal Subsidies (Federal Funding Standards)

- Require providers receiving public funds to be licensed and in compliance with state licensing provisions.
- Introduce federal funding standards to protect children in states where licensing requirements for centers and family child care are too low to protect children from harm. With an expanded subsidy system, the major practical objection to federal funding standards, that they raise market prices, would be overcome since the majority of families would be eligible for subsidies and all families would be able to afford good quality care and pay the higher fees.

- Set federal funding quality standards at levels that are in line with licensing standards that have become commonly agreed to in most states.
- Set adequate training requirements for staff and providers at facilities receiving public funds. Require a B.A. or equivalent for lead teachers in centers.
- Through federal initiatives create more public information about child care quality conditions, for instance, by supporting and publishing research on appropriate standards and quality rating systems, collecting and disseminating information on state licensing/enforcement practices and monitoring procedures, and identifying states with inadequate licensing and funding standards.

Professional Accreditation

- If accreditation status is used as a funding standard in a differential reimbursement system, require accrediting agencies to move toward standardization of accreditation requirements and evaluation procedures. This would require a comparison of current accreditation standards and practices among agencies and an evaluation of their effectiveness in screening for good quality.
- Introduce annual monitoring that involves cost-effective on-site program evaluations and quality control measures to assure reliability of the accreditation process.
- Provide federal subsidies to help centers and family child care providers defray the investment costs required to meet accreditation standards and costs of more extensive monitoring.

Child Care Workforce Training and Compensation

- Through state licensing reforms, establish a professional career path for ECE personnel that defines a hierarchy of occupations with increasing responsibility, and requiring increasing amounts of formal training.
- Overhaul the system of training for early childhood education to emphasize the acquisition of college-level credentials.
- Provide federal subsidies for training.
- Require good-quality centers receiving higher reimbursement rates to pay wages commensurate with training.

- Use federal incentives to encourage states to guarantee fringe benefits for child care center staff and family child care providers.

MEASURES TO IMPROVE MARKET EFFICIENCY

These measures would support the growth of institutions that provide technical support services for both buyers and sellers, services that normally exist in well-functioning markets.

- Provide reliable information about the location and quality of child care providers in every community.
- Provide federal funding to create a comprehensive, nationwide resource and referral network that provides core services to most communities. (Supply-building functions of R&Rs will be particularly crucial to the expansion of licensed child care services that will be required to meet the increased demand created by a more generous subsidy program.)
- Encourage the expansion of family child care networks, possibly organized through R&Rs, that give technical assistance to providers preparing for licensing and provide important member services such as training, lending libraries, access to the Department of Agriculture food program (CACFP), licensing and accreditation consulting, health insurance, and provision of substitutes.
- Through federal financing establish a system of local financial intermediaries, possibly connected to existing community development agencies and/or coordinated through resource and referral agencies, that give technical assistance to child care providers to help them expand services and gain access to credit or grants for capital expansion. This may involve the creation of capital investment funds to provide loans, loan guarantees, and grants to providers.

COSTS OF IMPROVING QUALITY AND EFFICIENCY

Improving the quality of child care depends to a great degree on improving the pay of child care workers. The $50 billion program we propose for subsidies includes funds for higher reimbursement rates to good quality providers, sufficient to pay wages competitive with worker pay in other occupations. We estimate the cost of other programs to improve quality and market operation we recommend as follows:

	(in $ millions)
improved state enforcement of regulations	$335
aid to providers seeking accreditation	250
core services from a nationwide resource and referral system	500
system of financial intermediaries	150
staff/provider training subsidies	500
subsidy of staff/provider benefit programs	500
child care evaluation program	25
TOTAL	$2,260

Checklist for Parents Trying to Evaluate Caregivers[1]

Good things to look for in a center or family child care home:

- is licensed and, preferably, has professional accreditation
- no more than 4 infants or 8 preschoolers per adult
- if a center, has a low staff turnover rate (e.g., less than 20 percent of staff left in the last year)
- a safe, clean environment for children indoors and outdoors with appropriate equipment adequately maintained (e.g., no broken parts, peeling paint, sharp corners)
- books, toys for fine motor coordination, art supplies are plentiful, appropriate to the age of the children, and easily available to them
- areas for both quiet activities and for louder, more active playing
- children spend much of their time in small groups or in individual work
- the children seem happy, secure, and stimulated
- parents are welcome to visit at any time

---

1. Items on this checklist were adapted from quality evaluation instruments and "Choosing Child Care," a brochure developed by Children, Youth and Families Services of Boulder, Colorado.

Good things to look for in a caregiver/teacher

- she/he has training in early childhood care and education, preferably a bachelors degree
- speaks frequently and warmly to the children, on a level they can understand
- seems relaxed, patient, warm and cheerful toward children, enjoys the children
- listens attentively when children speak to her/him, and shows respect for *each* child
- encourages children to talk and explore ideas
- plays on the floor with the children
- uses positive and nonpunitive discipline methods
- when the children misbehave, explains the reason for the rule they are breaking
- encourages children to try new experiences
- seems enthusiastic about the children's activities and efforts
- encourages children to share
- is involved in local professional early care and education organizations

Bad things to watch out for in a caregiver:

- speaks with irritation or hostility to the children
- threatens children in trying to control them
- punishes children without explanation
- finds fault easily with children
- seems unnecessarily harsh when scolding
- seems distant or detached from the children
- spends considerable time in activity not involving interaction with the children
- doesn't supervise the children very closely
- doesn't intercede when children misbehave
- doesn't wash hands after diapering each child
- doesn't wash children's hands before snacks and meals
- doesn't sit, eat, and talk with children at mealtime
- doesn't teach children self-help skills

NOTES

CHAPTER 1.
THE PROBLEM: WHAT'S WRONG WITH CHILD CARE IN AMERICA?

1. The source of these data are the U. S. Bureau of Labor Statistics web page. We refrain from giving exact web addresses, as they are likely to change through time.
2. Lynne M. Casper, "What Does It Cost to Mind Our Preschoolers?" *Current Population Reports* P70-52 (Washington DC: U.S. Bureau of the Census, September 1995).
3. Elizabeth Rose, *A Mother's Job: The History of Day Care, 1890-1960.* (New York: Oxford University Press, 1999); Sonia Michel, *Children's Interests/Mothers' Rights: The Shaping of America's Child Care Policy.* (New Haven, CT: Yale University Press, 1999).
4. The original name of the program was Aid to Dependent Children.
5. For a more extended treatment of the history of child care legislation, see Sandra L. Hofferth, "The 101st Congress: An Emerging Agenda for Children in Poverty," in *Child Poverty and Public Policy,* edited by Judith A. Chafel (Washington, DC: Urban Institute Press, 1993).
6. Sonia Michel, *Children's Interests/Mothers' Rights,* 255.
7. This poll was done by Princeton Survey Research Associates in January 1998.

CHAPTER 2.
THE QUESTION: HOW COULD WE MAKE CHILD CARE
AFFORDABLE TO ALL?

1. Darcy Olsen, *The Advancing Nanny State: Why the Government Should Stay Out of Child Care* (Washington: Cato Institute, 1997), 13.
2. See Magaly Queralt and Ann Dryden Witte, "Estimating the Unmet Need for Services: A Middling Approach" *Social Service Review* 73, no. 4 (December 1999): 524-559.
3. Louise Stoney, *Looking into New Mirrors: Lessons for Early Childhood Finance and System-Building* (Boston: Horizons Initiative, 1998).
4. Weighted national average of state-level fees given in Karen Schulman, *The High Cost of Child Care Puts Quality Care Out of Reach for Many Families* (Washington, DC: Children's Defense Fund, 2000). School-age care cost an average of $3,470 in a center and $2,778 in family care. The Children's Defense Fund's data are based on prices listed with the state resource and referral agencies.
5. Suzanne W. Helburn, *Cost, Quality, and Child Outcomes in Child Care Centers, Technical Report* (Center for Research in Economic and Social Policy, Department of Economics, University of Colorado, Denver, 1995). See table 7.1 below.
6. Ibid.

7. The source of this information is the Bureau of Labor Statistics consumer price index for all items and the consumer price index component for child care and nursery school.

8. U. S. Department of Health and Human Services, Administration for Children and Families, "New Statistics Show Only Small Percentage of Eligible Families Receive Child Care Help" *HHS News* (December 6, 2000). Federal data for 2000 from the 2000 Green Book, p. 600. Estimates of prekindergarten spending ($1.7 billion) are from Karen Schulman, Helen Blank and Daniele Ewen, *Seeds of Success: State Prekindergarten Initiatives, 1998-1999.* Children's Defense Fund, 1999.

9. Other sources of funds include TANF monies freed up because of the reductions in the welfare rolls, monies from the Title XX program, and the Agricultural Department Child and Adult Care Food program that provides meals and snacks.

10. Part of the federal funds sent to the states to pay for living expenses for welfare families could, if not used for that purpose because of the drop in the welfare case load, be used for child care subsidies also.

11. U. S. Department of Health and Human Services, Administration for Children and Families, "New Statistics Show Only Small Percentage of Eligible Families Receive Child Care Help" *HHS News* (December 6, 2000). HHS reported that only 12 percent of eligible children are covered. However, the parents of some of the 15 million children reported as eligible for the program would not want them enrolled, so the under-coverage is less than 88 percent.

12. See Barbara R. Bergmann, *Saving Our Children from Poverty: What the United States Can Learn from France* (New York: Russell Sage Foundation, 1996).

13. See Harriet B. Presser, "Some Economic Complexities of Child Care Provided by Grandmothers," *Journal of Marriage and the Family* 51 (August 1989): 581-591.

14. A panel of experts, charged by the National Academy of Sciences with suggesting an improved methodology for setting the poverty line, worked out a detailed budget that provides a more realistic and detailed accounting for minimal needs for food, clothing, shelter, transportation, services, and taxes. The panel came to the conclusion that almost $2,000 more would be needed (exclusive of child care and health care costs) than would be provided by the current official poverty line income. See Constance F. Citro and Robert T. Michael, eds., *Measuring Poverty: A New Approach* (Washington, DC: National Academy Press, 1995). See also Trudy J. Renwick and Barbara R. Bergmann, "A Budget-Based Definition of Poverty, With an Application to Single-Parent Families," *Journal of Human Resources* 28:1 (Winter 1993): 1-24.

15. This figure assumes they receive a dependent care federal tax credit which relieves them of the tax liability of $717 they would otherwise have.

16. When the family computes their dependent care credit according to Internal Revenue instructions, the amount turns out to be $1033, but they can only take advantage of part of it. Without the credit, they would owe $717 in taxes, and that is their maximum benefit from the credit, since it is not refundable.

17. Ingrid Peritz, "Tired of the Kids? Try 24 Hour Day Care; Quebec Tests Program Aimed at Shift Workers," *The Globe and Mail,* 31 August 2000.

18. The two schemes extract equal copayments when .10 * income = .20 * (income–poverty line). This equation holds when income = 2 * poverty line.

CHAPTER 3. THE DESIGN: WHAT SHOULD A NEW CHILD CARE SYSTEM LOOK LIKE?

1. Rebecca M. Blank, *It Takes a Nation: A New Agenda for Fighting Poverty* (Princeton, NJ: Princeton University Press, 1997), p. 191.

2. This statement was part of the 1995 State of the Union Address of President Bill Clinton.

3. Anne Mitchell, Louise Stoney and Harriet Dichter, *Financing Child Care in the United States: An Illustrative Catalog of Current Strategies.* (Kansas City, MO: The Ewing Marion Kauffman Foundation and the Pew Charitable Trusts, 1997), 3.

4. In an address at Rice University, May 4, 2000, former President Bush said, "When I was privileged to serve as President, I often talked about a concept I called being "one of a thousand

points of light." Simply put, Points of Light are caring citizens who volunteer their time and effort to help make the world a better place than they found it — whether through public service, or working through their church or synagogue, or a local club or organization."

5.   Lisa Bell, Lea Grundy, and Netsy Firestein, *Union Child Care Initiatives* (Berkeley, CA: Labor Project for Working Families, 1999).

6.   See Suzanne W. Helburn, ed., *Cost, Quality and Child Outcomes in Child Care Centers: Technical Report* (Denver, CO: University of Colorado at Denver, 1995), 229-30.

7.   To preserve fairness and to recognize different needs over the life cycle, large companies are using "cafeteria plans" which allow employees to choose the benefits most appropriate to them.

8.   Lisa Belkin, "Your Kids Are Their Problem," *New York Times* 23 July 2000, Sunday Magazine.

9.   U.S. Bureau of the Census, *Statistical Abstract of the United States, 1994* (Washington, DC: U.S. Department of Commerce, 1994), 546, table 843.

10.   See Mitchell, Stoney and Dichter, *Financing Child Care.*

11.   "Marriott Cautions Congress: Corporate Child Care Not the Primary Answer," *National Report on Work and Family* (5 May 1998), 91.

12.   Ibid.

13.   See Teresa Vast, *Higher Education as a Model for Financing Early Care and Education* (Minneapolis, MN: The Minnesota Early Care and Education Financing Partnership, 1998).

14.   Child care finance figures are from Vast, *Higher Education.* Higher education finance figures include both public and private institutions and were derived from material in U.S. Department of Education, National Center for Education Statistics, *Digest of Education Statistics, 1998,* NCES 1999-036, 1999.

15.   Teresa Vast, *Higher Education..*

16.   Barbara R. Bergmann, *Saving Our Children from Poverty: What the United States Can Learn From France* (New York: Russell Sage Foundation, 1996).

17.   Edward F. Zigler and Matia Finn-Stevenson, "Funding Child Care and Public Education," *The Future of Children* 6, no. 2 (summer-fall 1996): 104-121.

18.   See Douglas J. Besharov and Nazanin Samari, "Child Care Vouchers and Cash Payments," in C. Eugene Steuerle, Van Doorn Ooms, George Peterson, and Robert D. Reischauer, eds., *Vouchers and the Provision of Public Services* (Washington, DC: Brookings Institution Press, 2000), 195-223.

19.   Mother-care using three times the labor at an average wage 33 percent higher than that paid child care workers would cost four times as much as paid child care.

20.   Sumner Rosen, "Public Employment and the Welfare State in Sweden," *Journal of Economic Literature* 14 (June 1996): 729-740.

21.   While Rosen complains that child care subsidies tend inordinately to increase quality, economists David M. Blau and Alison P. Hagy have the opposite complaint. They claim that child care subsidies have the effect of reducing the quality of care that parents purchase. Their conclusions are not based on any actual observations of parents who were initially without subsidies, were subsequently given subsidies, and as a result put their children into lower-quality care. Rather, they are based on comparisons of parental behavior in different cities. Decreased prices usually lead people to buy both a higher quantity and better quality of the good. Moreover, child care subsidies enable parents to purchase care of better quality, care which would be out of their reach without subsidies. See David M. Blau and Alison P. Hagy, "The Demand for Quality in Child Care," *Journal of Political Economy* 106, no. 1 (1998): 104-146.

CHAPTER 4: THE YARDSTICK: WHAT CHILD CARE DESERVES TO BE CALLED "GOOD"?

1.   Dr. Spock's change of heart came in the 1976 edition. See Maxine L. Margolis, *Mothers and Such: Views of American Women and Why They Changed* (Berkeley, CA: University of California Press, 1984), 79.

2.   Penelope Leach, *Children First: What Our Society Must Do—and Is Not Doing—for Our Children Today* (New York: Alfred A. Knopf, 1994), 88-92.

234   AMERICA'S CHILD CARE PROBLEM

3. Jay Belsky, "Infant Day Care: A Cause for Concern?" *Zero to Three* 6 (1986):1-7. Jay Belsky and Michael J. Rovine, "Nonmaternal Care in the First Year of Life and the Security of Infant-Parent Attachment," *Child Development* 59 (1988): 929-949. Deborah Phillips, Kathleen McCartney, Sandra Scarr and Carollee Howes, "Selective Review of Infant Day Care Research: A Cause for Concern," *Zero to Three* 7 (1987):18-21.

4. The detailed study design takes into account many variables, such as characteristics of child care and the family environment. Children's development has been assessed at frequent intervals using several methods (testing, observations by trained observers, interviews, questionnaires) and measuring many facets of their development (cognitive, social, emotional, linguistic, behavioral, and physical). See *The NICHD Study of Early Child Care,* prepared by Robin Peth-Pierce, Public Information and Communications Branch, NICHD (Washington, DC: National Institute of Child Health and Human Development, National Institutes of Health, U.S. Department of Health and Human Services, April 1998).

5. The special cases where the mother/child attachment was affected were for those children who had less sensitive or less responsive mothers and who also had poor quality care. NICHD Early Child Care Research Network, "The Effects of Infant Child Care on Infant-Mother Attachment Security: Results of the NICHD Study of Early Child Care," *Child Development,* 68 no. 5 (October 1997): 860-879; NICHD Early Child Care Research Network, "Child Care and Child-Mother Attachment Security at 36 Months," manuscript under review. For an extensive summary of this research, see also Margaret Burchinal, "Child Care Experiences and Developmental Outcomes," *Annals of the American Academy of Political and Social Sciences* 563 (1999).

6. The NICHD Early Child Care Research Network, "Parenting and Family Influences When Children Are in Child Care: Results from the NICHD Study of Early Child Care," in J. Borkowski, S. Ramey and M. Bristol-Power, eds., *Parenting and the Child's World: Influences on Intellectual, Academic, and Social-Emotional Development* (Mahwah, NJ: Erlbaum, forthcoming).

7. This study, using data from the National Longitudinal Survey of Youth (NLSY), and the Children of the NLSY, did not take into consideration the quality of child care provided. Enrollment in a child care center, of whatever quality, substantially offset the negative effects of the mother's employment on reading and math scores. Mothers' employment in years two and three, combined with the children's enrollment in center programs, appears to have *increased* verbal abilities at three years old. Christopher J. Ruhm, "Parental Employment and Child Cognitive Development," Working Paper W7666 (Washington DC: National Bureau of Economic Research, April 2000).

8. Margolis, 91-92.

9. Margaret Talbot, "Attachment Theory: the Ultimate Experiment," *The New York Times Magazine* (24 May 1998): 22-30, 38, 46, 50, 54.

10. Script from the "ketchup" segment on "A Prairie Home Companion" the broadcast of May 5, 2001. Available at <www.pmc.mpr.org>.

11. Sandra Hofferth, April Brayfield, Sharon Deich and Pamela Holcomb, *National Child Care Survey, 1990* (Washington, DC: Urban Institute, 1991), 203, 207.

12. Cheryl Hayes, John L. Palmer and Martha Zaslow, eds., *Who Cares for America's Children?: Child Care Policy for the 1990s* (Washington, DC: National Academy Press, 1990), 241.

13. Darcy Olsen, "The Advancing Nanny State: Why the Government Should Stay Out of Child Care," Cato Policy Analysis #285 (Washington DC: Cato Institute, 1997). Available at *www/cato/org/pubs/pas/pa.htm*).

14. Barbara Bowman, M. Suzanne Donovan and M. Susan Burns, eds., *Eager to Learn: Educating Our Preschoolers, Executive Summary,* Committee on Early Childhood Pedagogy, Commission on Behavioral and Social Sciences and Education, National Research Council (Washington, DC: National Academy Press, 2000), 2.

15. For a review see L. M. Dunn and Susan S. Kontos, "What Have We Learned About Developmentally Appropriate Practice?" *Young Children* 52, no. 5 (July 1997): 4-13.

16. Research indicates that children, particularly little boys, in more academically oriented, teacher controlled environments exhibit more stress than children who are freer to choose their own activities. Children in more child-centered classrooms appear to have more self-confidence. M. C. Hyson, K. Hirsh-Pasek and L. Rescorla, "The Classroom Practices Inventory: An Observation Instrument Based on NAEYC's Guidelines for Developmentally Appropriate Practices for 4- and

5-Year-Old Children," *Early Childhood Research Quarterly* 5 (1990): 475-494; D. C. Burts, C. H. Hart, R. Charlesworth and L. Kirk, "A Comparison of Frequency of Stress Behaviors Observed in Kindergarten Children in Classrooms with Developmentally Appropriate Versus Developmentally Inappropriate Instructional Practices," *Early Childhood Research Quarterly* 5 (1992): 407-23. Some research indicates that academically oriented preschools do not even promote better grades and achievement test scores when the children go to school. C. W. Sherman and D. P. Mueller, "Developmentally Appropriate Practice and Student Achievement in Inner-city Elementary Schools," paper presented at Head Start's Third National Research Conference, Washington, DC, June 1996; R. A. Marcon, "Differential Effects of Three Preschool Models on Inner-City 4-Year-Olds," *Early Childhood Research Quarterly* 7, no. 4 (1992): 517-530.

17. Thelma Harms, Richard Clifford and Debby Cryer, *Early Childhood Environment Rating Scale: Revised Edition* (New York and London: Teachers College Press, Columbia University, 1998); Thelma Harms, Debby Cryer and Richard Clifford, *Infant/Toddler Environment Rating Scale* (New York and London: Teachers College Press, Columbia University, 1990); Thelma Harms and Richard Clifford, *Family Day Care Rating Scale* (New York: Teachers College Press, Columbia University, 1989).

18. Harms, Cryer, and Clifford, *Infant/Toddler Environment Rating Scale.*

19. See Harms and Clifford, *Family Day Care Rating Scale.*

20. The National Association for Family Child Care has developed a self-study manual as part of their accreditation system that describes exemplary practices and opportunities available to family child care providers as compared to centers. The Family Child Care Accreditation Project, *Quality Standards for NAFCC Accreditation: Provider's Self-Study Workbook* (Des Moines, IA: The National Association for Family Child Care, 1999).

21. Deborah Lowe Vandell and Barbara Wolfe, *Child Care Quality: Does It Matter and Does It Need to Be Improved?* (Madison, WI: Institute for Research on Poverty, University of Wisconsin-Madison, 2000). Available at *aspe.hhs.gov/hsp/ccquality00/ccqual.htm*

22. Lyda Beardsley, in her touching book, *Good Day, Bad Day,* contrasting children's days in excellent and horrific child care conditions, illustrates the danger to children due to staff irritability and bad judgement from inadequate staffing. Lyda Beardsley, *Good Day, Bad Day: The Child's Experience of Child Care* (New York: Teachers College Press, Columbia University, 1990).

23. Patricia Divine-Hawkins, *Family Day Care in the United States: National Day Care Home Study Final Report, Executive Summary* (Washington, DC: Day Care Division, Administration for Children, Youth and Families, U.S. Department of Health and Human Services, 1981); Susan Kontos, Carollee Howes, Marybeth Shinn and Ellen Galinsky, *Quality in Family Child Care and Relative Care* (New York and London: Teachers College Press, Columbia University, 1995); NICHD Early Child Care Research Network, "Characteristics and Quality of Child Care for Toddlers and Preschoolers," *Journal of Applied Developmental Science* 4, no. 3 (1999): 116-135.

24. Kontos et al., *Quality in Family Child Care and Relative Care.*

25. C. Coelen, R. Glantz and D. Calore, *Day Care Centers in the U.S.: A National Profile* (Cambridge, MA: Abt Associates, 1977); Marcy Whitebook, Carollee Howes and Deborah Phillips, *Who Cares? Child Care Teachers and the Quality of Care in America: Executive Summary, National Child Care Staffing Study* (Oakland, CA: Child Care Employee Project, now Center for the Child Care Workforce in Washington, DC, 1990). Suzanne W. Helburn, *Cost, Quality, and Child Outcomes in Child Care Centers, Technical Report* (Denver, CO: Center for Research in Economic and Social Policy, Economics Department, University of Colorado at Denver, 1995).

26. Carollee Howes, "Children's Experiences in Center Based Child Care as a Function of Teacher Background and Adult:Child Ratio," *Merrill-Palmer Quarterly* 43, no. 3 (1997): 404-425.

27. Whitebook, Howes and Phillips, *Who Cares? Child Care Teachers and the Quality of Care in America;* Helburn, *Cost, Quality, and Child Outcomes,* NICHD Early Child Care Research Network, "Characteristics and Quality of Child Care for Toddlers and Preschoolers."

28. NICHD Early Child Care Research Network, "Child Outcomes When Child Care Centers Meet Recommended Standards for Quality," *American Journal of Public Health* 89, no. 7 (1999): 1072-1077.

29. These factors only account for about half of the difference in quality among providers. Helburn, *Cost, Quality, and Child Outcomes*. Studies by David Blau suggest that individual structural quality characteristics may be less important to quality than the distinctive, nonobserved features of the center, such as the quality of center management and leadership. David M. Blau, "The Production of Quality in Child Care Centers," *The Journal of Human Resources* 32, no.2 (1997): 354-387; David M. Blau, "The Production of Quality in Child Care Centers: Another Look," *Applied Developmental Sciences,* forthcoming. See Vandell and Wolfe, *Child Care Quality* for a critique of Blau's conclusions.

30. Louise Derman-Sparks and the A.B.C. Task Force, *Anti-Bias Curriculum: Tools for Empowering Young Children* (Washington, DC: National Association for the Education of Young Children, 1989).

31. In 1995 *The Education Reporter,* published by Phyllis Schlafly's Eagle Forum, included an influential article criticizing the NAEYC, accusing it of promoting anti-Christian curricula in *The Anti-Bias Curriculum: Tools for Empowering Young Children* by Louise Derman-Sparks, published by NAEYC.

32. Ruth Sheehan, "Day-Care Reform Advocates Under Fire: Group Galvanizes Critics of N. C. Rules," *The News Observer,* Saturday, 29 November 1997.

33. *1998 ACSI Manual of School Accreditation Evaluative Criteria: Preschool Accreditation Program (PK) of the Association of Christian Schools International* (Colorado Springs, CO: Association of Christian Schools International, 1998). This group does not speak for all Christian congregations. The Ecumenical Child Care Network has been promoting better quality child care in churches and religious organizations for centers for many years. They advocate anti-bias, anti-racist principles in their work.

34. Bruce Mallory and Rebecca New, eds., *Diversity and Developmentally Appropriate Practice: Challenges for Early Childhood Education* (New York: Teachers College Press, Columbia University,1994); Susan D. Holloway and Bruce Fuller, "Families and Child Care: Divergent Viewpoints," in *The Silent Crisis in U.S. Child Care,* a special volume edited by Suzanne W. Helburn, of *The Annals of the American Academy of Political and Social Science* 563 (May 1999): 98-115.

35. Lynn Okagaki and Karen E. Diamond, "Responding to Cultural and Linguistic Differences in the Beliefs and Practices of Families with Young Children," *Young Children* 55, no. 3 (May 2000): 74-80.

36. See Sue Bredekamp and Carol Copple, *Developmentally Appropriate Practice in Early Childhood Programs,* rev. ed. (Washington DC: National Association for the Education of Young Children, 1997); National Academy of Early Childhood Programs, *Accreditation Criteria & Procedures of the National Association for the Education of Young Children,* 1998 edition (Washington DC: National Association for the Education of Young Children, 1998).

37. L. L. Hestenes, S. Kontos and Y. Bryan, "Children's Emotional Expression in Child Care Centers Varying in Quality," *Early Childhood Research Quarterly* 8 (1993): 295-307.

38. Betty Hart and Todd R. Risley, *Meaningful Differences in the Everyday Experience of Young American Children* (Baltimore: Paul H. Brookes Publishing Co., 1995).

39. Many other studies have found that the frequent verbal interactions between caregivers and very young children in good quality child care contribute to their language and cognitive development. Disadvantaged preschoolers who experience higher quality care during infancy have been reported to show more progress on tests of language and cognitive functioning than children who did not attend such programs. See Kathleen McCartney, "Effect of Quality of Day Care Environment on Children's Language Development," *Developmental Psychology* 20, no.2, (1984): 244-260; Margaret R. Burchinal, Joanne E. Roberts, Laura A. Nabors and Donna Bryant, "Quality of Center Child Care and Infant Cognitive and Language Development," *Child Development* 67, no.6 (1996): 606-620; Margaret R. Burchinal, M. W. Lee and C. T. Ramey, "Type of Day Care and Preschool Intellectual Development in Disadvantaged Children," *Child Development* 60 (1989):128-137; J. E. Roberts, S. Rabinowitch, D. M. Bryant, M. R. Burchinal, M. A. Koch and C. T. Ramey, "Language Skills of Children with Different Preschool Experiences," *Journal of Speech and Hearing Research* 32 (1989): 773-786. In one study, children who attended poorer quality centers in infancy continued to score lower on academic outcomes assessments through middle childhood. D. L. Vandell and M. A. Corasaniti, "Child

Care and the Family: Complex Contributors to Child Development," in Kathleen McCartney ed., *New Directions in Child Development* (San Francisco: Jossey-Bass, 1990).

40. NICHD Early Child Care Research Network, "The Relation of Child Care to Cognitive and Language Development," *Child Development* 71, no. 4 (July-August 2000): 960-980; NICHD Early Child Care Research Network, "The NICHD Study of Early Child Care: Contexts of Development and Developmental Outcomes over the First Seven Years of Life," in J. Brooks-Gunn and L. J. Berlin, eds., *Young Children's Education, Health, and Development: Profile and Synthesis Project Report* (Washington, DC: Department of Education, in press). NICHD Early Child Care Research Network, "Early Child Care and Children's Development Prior to School Entry," paper delivered at the Society for Research in Child Development meetings in Minneapolis, MN, 19 April 2001.

41. In the NICHD study a larger percent of children who had spent over 30 hours a week in child care were rated by their teachers to exhibit more problem behaviors—aggressiveness toward other children, disobedience and defiance toward teachers—than children in care for fewer hours per week. Good quality of care did not offset these negative effects of time in care. One possibility is that the NICHD quality measure, based exclusively on "positive caregiving" behaviors of the provider, does not pick up other aspects of good quality that help children overcome behavior problems The positive caregiving measure was based on observations by a trained observer of the caregiver's interaction with the target child. Observations varied to some extent depending on the age of the child. At the end of the observation period specific caregiver behaviors were rated on a four point scale from "not at all characteristic" to "highly characteristic." For caregivers of 24-month-old children the "positive caregiving" rating is the mean of five ratings of caregiver behavior: sensitivity to the child's nondistress signals, stimulation of child's development, positive regard toward child, detachment, and flatness of affect. See NICHD Early Child Care Research Network, "Characteristics and Quality of Child Care for Toddlers and Preschoolers," *Journal of Applied Developmental Science* 4, no.3 (2000): 116-135.

42. CQO evaluated the quality of 400 typical child care centers and a sample of over 800 four-year-old children from these centers who had been enrolled at least a year and then followed these children as they entered school. Helburn, *Cost, Quality, and Child Outcomes in Child Care Centers, Technical Report.*

43. These results held after controlling for family and child characteristics. Ellen S. Peisner-Feinberg, Margaret. R. Burchinal, Richard M. Clifford, Mary L. Culkin, Carollee Howes, Sharon L. Kagan, Noreen Yazejian, Patricia Byler, Jean Rustici and Janice Zelazo, *The Children of the Cost, Quality, and Outcomes Study Go to School: Technical Report* (Chapel Hill: University of North Carolina at Chapel Hill, Frank Porter Graham Child Development Center, 2000).

44. Recent Studies report similar results. In the NICHD study children in single-parent households had lower levels of social competence and school readiness and more problem behavior unless they received full-time nonparental care. NICHD Early Childhood Research Network, "Parenting and Family Influences When Children Are in Child Care." See also NICHD Early Child Care Research Network, "The Relation of Child Care to Cognitive and Language Development." In the CQO study, higher child care quality for children of mothers with lower levels of education appeared to improve the children's math skills and reduce behavior problems in second grade. Peisner-Feinberg, "Children of the Cost, Quality, and Child Outcomes Study Go to School."

45. A review of 15 high-quality model programs and 5 large-scale public school programs indicates that for most of these programs children in the third grade or later had higher scores than control groups on achievement tests. They also made IQ gains, but the effects tended to decline over time. In two experimental studies that studied children enrolled as infants in full-day programs and in two other model programs the IQ gains persisted into adolescence. Steven W. Barnett, "Long-term Effects of Early Childhood Programs on Cognitive and School Outcomes," in "Long-Term Outcomes of Early Childhood Programs," *The Future of Children* 5, no. 3 (1995): 25-50; Hirokazu Yoshikawa, "Long-Term Effects of Early Childhood Programs on Social Outcomes and Delinquency," *Future of Children* 5, no.3 (1995): 51-75. Barnett argues that methodological flaws in most of the studies may contribute to the fade-out of effects on cognitive achievement.

46. C. T. Ramey, F. A. Campbell, M. Burchinal, M. L. Skinner, D. M. Garner and S. L. Ramey, "Persistent Effects of Early Intervention on High-Risk Children and Their Mothers," *Applied Developmental Science* (forthcoming); Lynn Karoly, Peter Greenwood, Susan Everingham, Jill Hoube, M. Rebecca Kilburn, Peter Rydell, Matthew Sanders and James Chiesa, *Investing in Our*

Children: What We Know and Don't Know about the Costs and Benefits of Early Childhood Interventions (Santa Monica, CA: Rand, 1998).

47. Arthur J. Reynolds, "Alterable Predictors of Educational Attainment in the Chicago Longitudinal Study: A Symposium," papers presented at the Biennial Meetings of the Society for Research on Adolescence, Chicago, IL, 30 March 2000. Two others projects found that early interventions help reduce chronic juvenile delinquency and the risk factors associated with delinquency, namely, antisocial behavior in childhood and low verbal ability. S. R. Andrews, J. B. Blumenthal, D. L. Johnson et al., "The Skills of Mothering: A Study of Parent Child Development Centers (New Orleans, Birmingham, Houston)," *Monographs of the Society for Research in Child Development,* Serial No. 198 (1982) 46,6; D. L. Johnson and T. A. Walker, "Follow-up Evaluation of the Houston Parent Child Development Center: School Performance," *Journal of Early Intervention* 15, no.3 (1991): 226-36. J. R. Lally, P. Mangione and A. Honig, "The Syracuse University Family Development Program: Long-Range Impact of an Early Intervention with Low-Income Children and Their Families," in D. Powell, ed., *Parent Education as Early Childhood Intervention: Emerging Directions Theory Research and Practice* (Norwood, NJ: Ablex, 1998).

48. Rima Shore, *Rethinking the Brain: New Insights into Early Development* (New York: Families and Work Institute, 1997). For a thorough and balanced review of the literature, see Jack P. Shonkoff and Deborah A. Phillips, eds., Committee on Integrating the Science of Early Childhood Development, Board of Children, Youth, and Families, *From Neurons to Neighborhoods: The Science of Early Childhood Development* (Washington, DC: National Academy Press, 2000).

49. In the publicity about brain development, much has been made of the fact that a very rapid expansion of synapses is followed by a process of elimination that brings the number down to adult levels.This has inspired misleading claims that individuals are hardwired for life in their first three years because there are critical periods appropriate for learning certain skills and children are vulnerable to the absence of essential experiences during these periods. In fact, while brain development is affected by experience, except in a few instances timing is not that important. Individuals continue to learn and develop throughout their lives. John T. Bruer, in *The Myth of the First Three Years* (New York: The Free Press, 1999), is highly critical of the campaign carried out by some leaders in the early care and education community who he argues helped create these erroneous impressions.

50. See Gwen Morgan, "Licensing and Accreditation: How Much Quality is *Quality?*," in Sue Bredekamp and Barbara A. Willer, eds., *Accreditation: A Decade of Learning and the Years Ahead* (Washington DC: National Association for the Education of Young Children, 1996): 130.

51. Olsen, "The Advancing Nanny State."

52. Sandra Scarr, "New Research on Day Care Should Spur Scholars to Reconsider Old Ideas," *The Chronicle of Higher Education,* 8 August 1997: A48.

53. EDK Associates, *Choosing Quality Child Care: A Qualitative Study Conducted in Houston, Hartford, West Palm Beach, Charlotte, Alameda, Los Angeles, Salem and Minneapolis* (Prepared for the Child Care Action Campaign, New York, NY, 1992: 9.

54. "French and Italian Preschool: Models for U.S.?" *The New York Times,* 25 April 2001, A3.

CHAPTER 5: THE REPORT CARD:
HOW MUCH OF AMERICA'S CHILD CARE IS GOOD?

1. U.S. Department of Health and Human Services, Administration for Children and Families, Child Care Bureau, *Child Care Bulletin,* issue 17 (Vienna, VA: National Child Care Information Center, September–October 1997): 14-15; Sandra L. Hofferth, April Brayfield, Sharon Deich, and Pamela Holcomb, *National Child Care Survey, 1990* (Washington, DC: Urban Institute, 1991), 28.

2. Hofferth, et al., *National Child Care Survey,* 412-413.

3. J. West, D. Wright and E. G. Hausken, *Child Care and Early Education Program Participation of Infants, Toddlers, and Preschoolers* (Washington, DC: U.S. Department of Education, 1995), 410-411.

4. Additional supporting information concerning children's health, child care for children with special needs and comparisons of studies of quality in centers, Head Start, and family child care is available at *www.ffcd.org. Link to America's Child Care Problem: The Way Out.*

5. Lynn M. Casper, *Who's Minding Our Preschoolers? Current Population Reports: Household Economic Studies,* series P70-53 (Washington, DC: U.S. Census Bureau, Economics and Statistics Administration, U.S. Department of Commerce, 1997); Lynne M. Casper, *Who's Minding Our Preschoolers? Fall 1994 update, Current Population Reports: Household Economic Studies,* series P70-62 (Washington, DC: U.S. Census Bureau, Economics and Statistics Administration, U.S. Department of Commerce, January 14, 1998). Many children are in more than one child care arrangement. These figures are for primary care, the arrangement in which the child spends the most time in child care.

6. Kristin Smith, "Who's Minding the Kids? Child Care Arrangements, Fall 1995," Current Population Reports P70-70 (Washington, DC: U. S. Census Bureau, 2000), table 1.

7. Smith, "Who's Minding the Kids?"; Jeffrey Capizzano, Gina Adams and Freya Sonenstein, "Child Care Arrangements for Children Under Five: Variation Across States," a product of *Assessing the New Federalism,* series B, #B-7 (Washington DC: The Urban Institute, 2000).

8. Hofferth et al., *National Child Care Survey,* 2; Capizzano et al., "Child Care Arrangements for Children Under Five."

9. Casper, *Who's Minding Our Preschoolers? Fall 1994,* summary of findings, 4-5.

10. News item released October 8, 1997, "Economic Conditions Can Influence Married Fathers' Caring for Preschoolers" (Washington, DC: U.S. Census Bureau, Economics and Statistics Administration, U.S. Department of Commerce, 1997).

11. Harriet B. Presser and Virginia S. Cain, "Shift Work among Dual-Earner Couples with Children," *Science* 219 (February 18, 1983): 876-79.

12. Harriet B. Presser, "Some Economic Complexities of Child Care Provided by Grandmothers, "*Journal of Marriage and the Family* 51 (August 1989): 581-591.

13. Bruce Fuller, Susan D. Holloway, and Xiaoyan Liang, "Family Selection of Child-Care Centers: The Influence of Household Support, Ethnicity, and Parental Practices," *Child Development* 67, no. 6 (1996): 3320-3337. Also, Casper, "Who's Minding Our Preschoolers?," 70-53.

14. In 1994 care in someone else's home accounted for about 31 percent of the care for children aged zero to five, roughly half provided by relatives and half by nonrelatives. A 1990 study estimated that there were 118,000 regulated family child care providers with a capacity to serve 860,000 children, and the number of regulated family child care homes has been declining since 1990; Ellen E. Kisker, Sandra L. Hofferth, Deborah A. Phillips and Elizabeth Farquhar, *A Profile of Child Care Settings: Early Education and Care in 1990,* prepared under contract with the U. S. Department of Education by Mathematica Policy Research, Inc. (Washington, DC: U.S. Government Printing Office, 1991), 5. Thus, of the roughly 1.6 million children in nonrelative family child care, possibly 750,000 are in unregulated care. Another 1.6 million children are in relative care outside their homes, so that a total of about 2.3 million children are in legally exempt or illegal family child care arrangements. This represents more than a fifth of the children of working mothers in this age group.

15. Kristin Smith, "Who's Minding the Kids? Child Care Arrangements Fall 1995," *Current Population Reports,* series P70-70, table 10.

16. Ibid., table 2, and page 23.

17. Roger Neugebauer, "Who Provides Child Care in the USA?" in *Inside Child Care: Trend Report 2000: "The Best of the Exchange"* Reprint Collection #12 from *Child Care Information Exchange* (Redmond, WA: Child Care Information Exchange 1999): 40-41.

18. Roger Neugebauer, "Religious Organizations Taking Proactive Role in Child Care," *Child Care Information Exchange* 133 (May-June 2000): 18-20.

19. Rachel Y. Moon, M.D., Kantilal M. Patel and Sarah J. McDermott Shaefer, "Sudden Infant Death Syndrome in Child Care Settings," *Pediatrics* 106, no. 2 (August 2000): 295-300.

20. For a good reference and literature review on health and safety practice in child care see *Pediatrics* 94 no.8 supplement: *Proceedings of the International Conference on Child Day Care and Health: Science, Prevention, and Practice* (December 1994)

21. Ibid.
22. Kisker et al., *A Profile of Child Care Settings,* 7; Suzanne W. Helburn, ed., *Cost, Quality, and Outcomes in Child Care Centers, Technical Report* (Denver: Center for Research and Economic and Social Policy, Economics Department, University of Colorado at Denver, 1995), table 4.4.
23. Marcy Whitebook, Carollee Howes and Deborah Phillips, *Who Cares? Child Care Teachers and the Quality of Care in America,* the National Child Care Staffing Study (Oakland: Child Care Employee Project, now The Center for the Child Care Workforce, 1990); Kathleen McCartney, Sandra Scarr, Anne Rocheleau, Deborah Phillips, Martha Abbott-Shim, Marleen Eisenberg, Nancy Keefe, Saul Rosenthal, and Jennifer Ruh, "Teacher-Child Interaction and Child-Care Auspices as Predictors of Social Outcomes in Infants, Toddlers, and Preschoolers," *Merrill-Palmer Quarterly* 43, no.4 (July 1997): 426-450; Helburn (ed), *Cost, Quality, and Child Outcomes in Child Care Centers;* Carollee Howes, Ellen Galinsky, Marybeth Shinn, Leyla Gulcur, Margaret Clements, Annet Sibley, Martha Abbott-Shim and Jan McCarthy, *The Florida Child Care Quality Improvement Study: 1996 Report* (New York: Families and Work Institute, 1998).
24. From tape-recorded sessions with the Colorado observers in July, 1993.
25. Observers evaluate 26 aspects of the caregiver's behavior on a four point scale from "behavior not observed at all" to "behavior observed very much." Items include: listens attentively when children speak to her; seems to enjoy the children; when the children misbehave, explains the reason for the rule they are breaking; exercises firmness when necessary; encourages children to try new experiences; places high value on obedience; seems to prohibit many of the things that children want to do; expects children to exercise self-control; doesn't correct children when they misbehave. See Jeffrey Arnett, "Caregivers in Day-Care Centers: Does Training Matter?" *Journal of Applied Developmental Psychology* 10, no. 4 (1989): 541-552.
26. Carollee Howes, Deborah A. Phillips and Marcy Whitebook, "Thresholds of Quality: Implications for the Social Development of Children in Center-based Child Care," *Child Development* 63 (1992): 449-460.
27. NICHD Early Child Care Research Network, "Characteristics and Quality of Child Care for Toddlers and Preschoolers," *Journal of Applied Developmental Science* 4, no. 3 (2000): 116-135.
28. Ibid, 24 and table 5.
29. John R. Morris and Suzanne W. Helburn, "Child Care Center Quality Differences: The Role of Profit Status, Client Preferences, and Trust," *Nonprofit and Voluntary Sector Quarterly* 9, no. 3 (September 2000): 377-399.
30. Differences in subsector quality existed in statistical analyses after controlling for state, so they do not merely reflect state regulatory standards.
31. Not enough centers in private schools and colleges fell into the sample to include them in the analysis of variance test for significant differences.
32. *Child Care Information Exchange,* an industry magazine for center directors, is the best source of information on employer-sponsored centers. They publish an annual status report, the latest of which is Roger Neugebauer, "Status Report #10 on Employer Child Care: Employer Child Care Continues Rapid Expansion," *Child Care Information Exchange* 134 (July-August 2000): 35-38.
33. Helburn, *Cost, Quality, and Child Outcomes,* Table 11.14b.
34. Roger Brown, "How We Built a Strong Company in a Weak Industry," *Harvard Business Review* (February 2001) R0102B, 3-8.
35. For more information on the Military Child Development program contact the National Clearinghouse for the Military Child Development Program, Office of the Secretary of Defense, Office of Family Policy, Arlington, VA at 1-888-CDP-3040 or online at *http://military-childrenandyouth.calib.com.* Also see G. L. Zellman and A. S. Johansen, *The Implementation of the Military Child Care Act of 1989* (Santa Monica, CA: RAND, 1998); N. D. Campbell, J. C. Appelbaum, K. Martinson, and E. Martin, *Be All That We Can Be: Lessons From the Military for Improving Our Nation's Child Care System* (Washington, DC: National Women's Law Center, April, 2000).
36. U.S. General Accounting Office, *Child Care: How Do Military and civilian Center Costs Compare?* GAO/HHS-00-7 (Washington, DC: U.S. General Accounting Office, 1999).
37. Patricia Divine-Hawkins, *Family Day Care in the United States: National Day Care Home Study Final Report Executive Summary* (Washington, DC: Day Care Division, Administration for Children, Youth and Families, Office of Human Development Services, U.S. Department of

Health and Human Services, 1981); Ellen Eliason Kisker, Sandra L. Hofferth, Deborah A. Phillips and Elizabeth Farquhar, *A Profile of Child Care Settings; Early Education and Care in 1990,* prepared under contract to the U. S. Department of Education by Mathematica Policy Research, Inc. (Princeton, NJ, Washington, DC: U. S. Department of Education, 1991); Susan Kontos, Carollee Howes, Marybeth Shinn, and Ellen Galinsky, *Quality in Family Child Care and Relative Care* (New York and London: Teachers College Press, Columbia University, 1995); Susan Kontos, *Family Day Care: Out of the Shadows and Into the Limelight* (Washington, DC: National Association for the Education of Young Children, 1992).

38. Kontos, et al., *Quality in Family Child Care and Relative Care,* 194.
39. Divine Hawkins, *Family Day Care in the United States;* Mary Tuominen, "Redefining the 'Working Mother': The Synthesis of Paid and Unpaid Caregiving Labor among Culturally Diverse Home-Based Child Care Workers," paper presented at the Race, Gender, and Work Roundtable, ASA meeting, Toronto, Ontario, 1997.
40. Caroline Zinsser, *Raised in East Urban: Child Care Changes in a Working Class Community* (New York and London: Teachers College Press, Columbia University, 1991).
41. Kontos, *Family Day Care: Out of the Shadows and into the Limelight,* 63-64.
42. Kontos et al., *Quality in Family Child Care and Relative Care,* 192.
43. Divine-Hawkins, *Family Day Care in the United States.*
44. Kontos, et al., *Quality in Family Child Care and Relative Care;* Carollee Howes and Deborah J. Norris, "Adding Two School Aged Children: Does It Change Quality in Family Child Care? *Early Childhood Research Quarterly* 12 (1997): 327-342.
45. Kontos, et al., *Quality in Family Child Care and Relative Care.*
46. Several smaller studies report average overall FDCRS ratings ranging from 2.9 to 3.7. In the two studies that included regulated and unregulated providers, average scores for unregulated providers were less than 3 and a full point lower than those for the regulated caregivers. See A. R. Pence and H. Goelman, "Who Cares for the Child in Day Care? An Examination of Caregivers from Three Types of Care," *Early Childhood Research Quarterly* 23, no.4 (1987): 315-334; Carollee Howes, K. Keeling, and J. Sale, "The Home Visitor: Improving Quality in Family Day Care Homes" (unpublished Manuscript,1988); Susan Kontos, "Predictors of Job Satisfaction and Child Care Quality in Family Day Care," paper presented at the annual meeting of the American Educational Research Association, San Francisco, CA, 1989; H. Goelman, E. Shapiro and A. R. Pence, "Family Environment and Family Day Care," *Family Relations* 39 (1990): 14-19; Carollee Howes and P. Stewart, "Child's Play with Adults, Toys, and Peers: An Examination of Family and Child-Care Influences," *Developmental Psychology* 23, no.3 (1987): 423-430.
47. Howes and Norris, "Adding Two School Aged Children."
48. Kontos, et al., *Quality in Family Child Care and Relative Care*
49. Kontos, et al., *Quality in Family Child Care and Relative Care.*
50. Howes and Morris, "Adding Two School Aged Children."
51. Lynn Casper, *Child Care Costs and Arrangements: Fall 1993,* PPL-34, U.S. Bureau of the Census, Population Division. See also Kontos et al., *Quality in Family Child Care and Relative Care,* Chapter 11.
52. Kontos et.al., *Quality in Family Child Care and Relative Care,* 86-87.
53. Casper, *Who's Minding Our Preschoolers? Fall 1994 update,* table A, "Primary Child Care Arrangements Used for Preschoolers by Families with Employed Mothers: Selected Years, 1977 to 1994".
54. Julia Wrigley, *Other People's Children: An Intimate Account of the Dilemmas Facing Middle-Class Parents and the Women They Hire to Raise Their Children* (New York: Basic Books, 1995).
55. For more information contact Au Pair Programme USA from their web site, www.aupairprogrammeusa.com.
56. Sonia Michel, *Children's Interests/Mother' Rights: The Shaping of America's Child Care Policy* (New Haven, CT:Yale University Press, 1999).
57. Nicholas Zill, Gary Resnick, Ruth H. McKey, Cheryl Clark, David Connell, Janet Swartz, Robert O'Brien and Mary Ann D'Elio, *Head Start Program Performance Measures, Second Progress Report* (Washington, DC: Research, Demonstration and Evaluation Branch and the Head Start Bureau, Administration on Children, Youth and Families, U.S. Department of Health and Human Services, 1998), 2. Statistical information on Head Start can be accessed through the Head Start fact sheets on the web at www2.acf.dhhs.gov.

58. 2000 Head Start Fact Sheet, www2.acf.dhhs.gov/programs/hsb.htm

59. See note 32, chapter 6 for a description of the CDA certificate.

60. U.S. General Accounting Office, *Early Childhood Programs: Local Perspectives on Barriers to Providing Head Start Services,* GAO/HHS-95-8 (Washington, DC: U.S. General Accounting Office, December 1994).

61. Marcy Whitebook and Andrew Gaidurgis, *Salary Improvements in Head Start: Lessons for the Early Care and Education Field* (Washington, DC: The National Center for the Early Childhood Work Force (now the Center for the Child Care Workforce), 1995).

62. Zill et al., *Head Start Program Performance Measures,* 16-18, 21-23; Gary Resnick and Nicholas Zill, "Is Head Start Providing High-Quality Educational Services. 'Unpacking' Classroom Processes." Available from the Head Start web site at www2.acf.dhhs.gov/programs/hsb/hsreac/quality.2pdf

63. Steven W. Barnett, "Long-Term Effects of Early Childhood Programs on Cognitive and School Outcomes," in "Long-Term Outcomes of Early Childhood Programs," *The Future of Children* 5, no.3 (1995): 25-50. More recently, see Sherri Oden, Lawrence J. Schweinhart and David P. Weikart, *Into Adulthood: A Study of the Effects of Head Start* (Ypsilanti, MI: High/Scope Press 2000).

64. Oden et al., *Into Adulthood: A Study of the Effects of Head Start.* The authors believe that data limitations create biases that mask other positive effects.

65. Ibid., Resnick et al., "Is Head Start Providing High-Quality Educational Services." 36, 39-42; Nicholas Zill, Gary Resnick, and Ruth Hubbell McKey, "What Children Know and Can Do at the End of Head Start and What It Tells Us About the Program's Performance." Available from the Head Start web site at www2.acf.dhhs.gov/programs/hsb/hsreac/faces/albqfin12.pdf

66. V. E. Lee and S. Loeb, "Where Do Head Start Attendees End Up? One Reason Why Preschool Effects Fade Out," *Educational Evaluation and Policy Analysis* 17, no. 1 (spring 1995): 62-82.

67. For instance, Darcy and Eric Olsen conclude, "The naked truth is that one to two years after entering public school, children from Head Start programs score no differently on tests of academic achievement, social behavior, emotional adjustment and other measurable outcomes than do their non-Head Start peers." They rely on a General Accounting Office (GAO) study that they say found no evidence that Head Start provides lasting benefits. In fact, the report concludes that the research did not allow the GAO to draw conclusions about the effectiveness of Head Start because there are not enough studies, most of those that exist focus on cognitive outcomes alone and have serious methodological weaknesses, and none are based on a nationally representative sample. Darcy Olsen and Eric Olsen, "Don't Cry for Me, Head Start," CATO Today's Commentary, April 15, 1999 available at *www/cato.org.,*); U.S. General Accounting Office, *Head Start: Research Provides Little Information on Impact of Current Program,* Report to the Chairman, Committee on the Budget, House of Representatives, GAO/HHS, (April 1997), 97-59.

68. Anthony Raden, *Universal Prekindergarten in Georgia* (New York: Foundation for Child Development, 1999).

69. Many of these preschool programs are funded with federal funds made available through the public schools through the Individuals with Disabilities Education Act (IDEA) and Title I of the Elementary and Secondary Education Act. Most school districts offered some type of prekindergarten program. One report estimates that one in nine children in prekindergarten public school programs were supported through Title I funds. Less is known about how many children with disabilities are served in public school preschools and the contribution of IDEA funds to these efforts. See Richard M. Clifford, Diane M. Early and Tynette W. Hills, "Almost a Million Children in School Before Kindergarten: Who Is Responsible for Early Childhood Services?" *Young Children* (September 1999): 48-51.

70. Karen Schulman, Helen Blank, and Danielle Ewen, *Seeds of Success: State Prekindergarten Initiatives, 1998-1999* (Washington, DC: Children's Defense Fund, 1999), 16.

71. A considerable part of current spending for prekindergarten is done in the state of Georgia, which does have a program that is free to all children, but which probably has relatively low labor costs. Using the ratio of U.S. children age 4 to Georgia children age 4 and assuming that costs in other states were equal to Georgia's per-child costs produces a cost estimate for applying the Georgia program to the whole country of $7.3 billion. Actual U.S. spending is 23 percent of that.

72. Raden, *Universal Prekindergarten in Georgia.*

73. This assumes that the number of days of service would rise to 250 from 180, and the hours per
    day from 6.5 to 9. The child care and nursery school component of the Consumer Price Index
    was used to put the cost into dollars of the year 2000. In all likelihood, the cost of the extra hours
    are lower, so that this is likely to be an overestimate.
74. Raden, *Universal Prekindergarten in Georgia,* 51.
75. Ibid, 49.
76. "After-school time" *CDF Reports* 18, no. 12 (November 1997): 5.
77. Fight Crime: Invest in Kids, *Quality Child Care and After-school Programs: Powerful Weapons
    Against Crime* (Washington DC: Action Against Crime and Violence Education Fund, February
    1998), 1.
78. DeeAnn W. Brimhall and Lizabeth M. Reaney, "Statistics in Brief: Participation of Kindergart-
    ners Through Third-Graders in Before-and After-School Care," NCES 1999-013 (Washington
    DC: Office of Educational Research and Improvement, National Center for Education Statistics,
    U.S. Office of Education, 1999).
79. Patricia S. Seppanen, Dianne Kaplan deVries and Michelle Seligson, *National Study of Before-
    and-After-School Programs: Executive Summary* (Portsmouth, NY: Final Report of the Office of
    Policy and Planning, RMC Research Corp., 1993), 5.
80. Gregory S. Pettit, Robert D. Laird, John E. Bates and Kenneth A. Dodge, "Patterns of After-
    school Care in Middle Childhood: Risk Factors and Developmental Outcomes," *Merrill-Palmer
    Quarterly* 43, no.3 (1997): 532; Deborah Lowe Vandell, and Lee Shumow, "After-School Child
    Care Programs," in "When School Is Out," *Future of Children* 9, no. 2 (1999): 64-80; Robert
    Halpern, "After-School Programs for Low-Income Children: Promises and Challenges," in
    "When School Is Out," *Future of Children* 9, no.2 (1999):81-95.
81. Deborah Lowe Vandell and Lee Shumow, "After-School Child Care Programs."
82. Beth M. Miller, Susan O'Connor, Sylvia W. Sirigano and Pamela Joshi, *Out-of-School Time in
    Three Low Income Communities,* Executive Summary (Wellesley, MA: Wellesley College,
    1996), 5; Smith, "Who's Minding the Kids?" 22.
83. Janette Roman, ed., *The NSACA Standards for Quality School-Age Care* (Boston: The National
    School-Age Care Alliance, 1998).
84. Robert Halpern, "After -School Programs for Low-Income Children,"81-95.
85. NICHD Early Child Care Research Network, "Parenting and Family Influences When Children
    Are in Child Care: Results from the NICHD Study of Early Child Care," in J. Burkowski, S.
    Ramey, and M. Bristol-Power, eds., *Parenting and the Child's World: Influences on Intellectual,
    Academic, and Social-Emotional Development* (Mahwah, NJ: Erlbaum, forthcoming).
86. Susan Kontos, Carollee Howes, Margaret Shinn, and Ellen Galinsky, "Children's Experiences in
    Family Child Care and Relative Care as a Function of Family Income and Ethnicity," *Merrill-
    Palmer Quarterly* 43, no. 2 (1997): 386-403.
87. NICHD Early Child Care Research Network, "Parenting and Family Influences When Children
    Are in Child Care: Results from the NICHD Study of Early Child Care," manuscript, contact
    NICHD Study of Early Child Care at the National Institute of Child Health and Human
    Development.

CHAPTER 6: THE REGULATIONS:
HOW MUCH QUALITY CONTROL IN CHILD CARE?

1. North Carolina has since raised its minimum staffing requirements for infants to 1:5.
2. Carollee Howes, Deborah A. Phillips and Marcy Whitebook, "Thresholds of Quality: Implications for the Social Development of Children in Center-based Child Care," *Child Development*
   63 (1992): 449-460.
3. Gwen Morgan and Sheri Azer, *Trends in Child Care Licensing and Regulation, 1999,* and *2000*
   (Boston, MA: The Center for Career Development in Early Care and Education (now Institute
   for Leadership and Career Initiatives, Wheelock College, 1999); Also see Kathryn T. Young,
   Katherine W. Marsland and Edward Zigler, "The Regulatory Status of Center-Based Infant and
   Toddler Care," *American Journal of Orthopsychiatry* 67, no. 4 (October 1997): 535-544. The

Young article traces changes from 1982 to 1990, reporting improvements in ratios in group size but actual declines in staff training requirements.

4. Most of the information in this section comes from The Children's Foundation, *2000 Child Care Center Licensing Study* (Washington, DC: The Children's Foundation, February 2000), supplemented by information from Sheri L. Azer and Darnae Eldred, *Training Requirements in Child Care Licensing Regulations* (Boston, MA, The Center for Career Development in Early Care and Education, now Institute for Leadership and Career Initiatives, Wheelock College, 1997) and correspondence with Azer.

5. Staff with bachelor degrees are only required to be in ongoing training for an equivalent of 1 percent of their annual hours working in child care.

6. This is true despite significant increases in staffing in at least 22 states at the end of the 1990s. See Morgan and Azer, "Trends in Child Care Licensing and Regulation, 2000."

7. The Children's Foundation, *2000 Family Child Care Licensing Study;* The Children's Foundation, *2000 Child Care Center Licensing Study.*

8. William Gormley Jr., *Everybody's Children: Child Care as a Public Problem* (Washington, DC: The Brookings Institution, 1995).

9. NICHD Early Child Care Research Network, "Child Outcomes When Child Care Center Classes Meet Recommended Standards of Quality," *American Journal of Public Health* 89, no. 7 (July 1999): 1072-1077.

10. This argument is made in William Gormley Jr., "Regulatory Enforcement Styles," *Political Research Quarterly* 51, no. 2 (June 1998):363-384.

11. William Gormley Jr., "Regulating Mister Rogers' Neighbourhood: The Dilemmas of Day Care Regulation," *Brookings Review* 8, no. 4 (1990): 21-28.

12. Darcy Olsen, *The Advancing Nanny State: Why Government Should Stay Our of Child Care* (Washington, DC: Cato Institute, 1997).

13. Suzanne W. Helburn, ed., *Cost, Quality, and Child Outcomes in Child Care Centers: Technical Report* (Denver, CO: Center for Research in Economic and Social Policy, Economics Department, University of Colorado at Denver, 1995); Marcy Whitebook, Carollee Howes, and Deborah Phillips, *Who Cares? Child Care Teachers and the Quality of Care in America, The National Child Care Staffing Study* (Oakland, CA: Child Care Employee Project, now Center for the Child Care Workforce in Washington, DC, 1990).

14. Susan Kontos, Carollee Howes, Marybeth Shinn, and Ellen Galinsky, *Quality in Family Child Care and Relative Care* (New York and London: Teachers College Press Columbia University, 1995), 111-112.

15. Three early studies used state level data to examine the effect of different aspects of regulation on service usage: Anton D. Lowenberg and Thomas D. Tinnon, "Professional Versus Consumer Interests in Regulation: The Case of the U.S. Child Care Industry," *Applied Economics* 24 (1992): 571-580; S. Rose-Ackerman, "Unintended Consequences: Regulating the Quality of Subsidized Day Care," *Journal of Policy Analysis and Management* 3, no. 1 (1983): 14-30; William T. Gormley Jr., "State Regulations and the Availability of Child Care Services," *Journal of Policy Analysis and Management* 10 (winter 1991): 78-95.

    One study used county level data to examine the effects of training and ratios on the availability of centers: Bruce Fuller and Ziaoyan Lian, *The Unfair Search for Child Care, Preschool and Family Choice Project* (Cambridge, MA: Harvard University, 1993).

    One study used family-level data from the fifth follow-up to the National Longitudinal Survey of the High School Class of 1972. V. J. Hotz and M. R. Kilburn, *Regulating Child Care: The Effects of State Regulations on Child Care Demand and Its Cost,* paper presented at the annual meeting of the Population Association of America,1995.

    The two remaining studies used the National Child Care Survey of 1990, involving family-level data: Sandra L. Hofferth and Duncan D. Chaplin, "State Regulations and Child Care Choice," *Population Research and Policy Review* 00 (1997): 1-30; Tasneem Chipty, "Economic Effects of Quality Regulations in the Day-Care Industry," *American Economic Review* 85, no.2 (May 1995): 419-424.

16. Annette Sibley, Martha Abbott-Shim, and Ellen Galinsky, *Child Care Licensing: Georgia Impact Study* (Atlanta, GA: Quality Assist, Inc., 1994).

17. However, one study found that the existence of licensing or registration reduced use of family child care. Hofferth and Chaplin, "State Regulations and Child Care Choice."

18. Hofferth and Chaplin, "State Regulations and Child Care Choice"; Chipty, "Economic Effects of Quality Regulations."

19. Gormley, "State Regulations and the Availability of Child Care Services."

20. Chipty, "Economic Effects of Quality Regulations." Two other studies found higher licensing standards related to higher prices: Hotz and Kilborn, *Regulating Child Care;* Hofferth and Chaplin, "State Regulations and Child Care Choice."

21. Chipty, "Economic Effects of Child Care Choice."

22. Harold Gazan, *Regulation: An Imperative for Ensuring Quality Child Care,* Working Paper Series (New York: The Foundation for Child Development, 1998)

23. Ibid.

24. The calculation of the cost, nationally, of increasing licensing staff to correct current inadequacies and to meet the needs created by voucher expansion involved estimating: (1) the number of licensed centers and family child care providers that would exist under an expanded voucher system where only licensed providers are eligible to accept vouchers; (2) the number of required inspectors and field supervisors, given caseloads that permit inspectors to provide effective enforcement. The extra cost is the difference in wages and compensation between employing the number of licensing specialists and field supervisors needed and the number actually employed in 1999, summed over all states plus an allowance of 15 percent overhead, and an allowance for a 33 percent increase in wages.

    We assume caseloads of 60:1 for centers based on calculations using the National Association for Regulatory Administration, *Licensing Workload Assessment,* Technical Assistance Bulletin #99-01 (Saint Paul MN: The National Association for Regulatory Administration) and on the advice of state licensing administrators. Caseload for family child care of 80:1 is not much higher than for centers even though inspections of family child care homes should take less time, because inspectors handle a much larger number of new applications for family child care. Data on the current number of regulated centers and family child care providers is from the Children's Foundation *1999 Child Care Center Licensing Study* and *1998 Family Child Care Licensing Study.* State licensing offices supplied the number of full time equivalent (FTE) licensing specialists, the number of FTE field supervisors, and the salary ranges of the two job classifications.

    The following adjustments were made to estimate the number of centers and family child care establishments used in the analysis: (1) For the 11 states that exempt church centers, our center count was increased by either the number of such centers reported by the state administrator or a number equal to the average percent such centers represent of licensed centers in the states where information was available. For 20 states that exempt part-day programs operating less than four hours a day, our center count was increased to allow for the fact that about 27 percent of centers operate part day according to the Census Bureau. For states where we learned there is more than one licensing agency, we included the number of licensed centers or family child care homes serving children up to five years old from these other agencies (e.g., Departments of Education preschool programs). (2) The number of regulated family child care providers was increased by 10 percent, assuming that the subsidy program would expand supply and induce more existing providers to seek licensing. (3) For states exempting family child care providers caring for less than 4, 5, or 6 children, the number was adjusted to approximate the number there would be with no exemptions.

25. Telephone conversation with Judy Collins of Judy Collins Consulting, Norman, OK, March 1999.

26. Most of this summary comes from Deborah Phillips and Edward Zigler, "The Checkered History of Federal Child Care Regulation," *Review of Research in Education* 14 (Washington, DC: American Educational Research Association, 1987).

27. American Public Health Association, American Academy of Pediatrics, *Caring for Our Children: The National Health and Safety Performance Standards—Guidelines for Out of Home Child Care Programs* (Washington, DC: American Public Health Association, American Academy of Pediatrics. 1992). The most important standards are included in U.S. Department of Health and Human Services Public Health Services, Health Resource and Services Administration, Maternal and Child Health Bureau, *Stepping Stones to Using "Caring for Our Children": National Health and Safety Performance Standards Guidelines for Out-of-Home Child Care Programs* (Denver, CO: National Resource Center for Health and Safety in Child Care, University of Colorado Health Sciences Center, 1997).

28. Gail. L. Zellman and Anne S. Johansen, "The Effects of Accreditation on Care in Military Child Development Centers," in Sue Bredekamp and Barbara Willer, eds., *NAEYC Accreditation: A Decade of Learning and the Years Ahead* (Washington, DC: National Association for the Education of Young Children, 1996).

29. Paula Jorde-Bloom, "The Quality of Work Life in Early Childhood Programs: Does Accreditation Make a Difference?" In Sue Bredekamp and Barbara Willer, eds., *NAEYC Accreditation: A Decade of Learning and the Years Ahead* (Washington, DC: National Association for the Education of Young Children, 1996).

30. Sue Bredekamp and Stephanie Glowacki, "The First Decade of NAEYC Accreditation: Growth and Impact on the Field," in Bredekamp and Willer, *NAEYC Accreditation: A Decade of Learning and the Years Ahead,* p. 3. However, the process takes much longer for centers that start the process from a low level of quality.

31. There is considerable overlap between NAEYC accreditation standards and the APHA/AAP *Caring for our Children . . . Guidelines.* The NAEYC standards came first but have been revised after publication of *Guidelines.*

32. Instituted in 1971 and administered by the Council for Early Childhood Professional Recognition, the CDA was initially designed as an alternative college training fro Head Start staff. CDA candidates must meet competency standards in six areas, complete 120 clock hours of formal child care education and 480 clock hours of experience in a group setting. The candidate compiles a portfolio that includes parent evaluations and results of a formal observation by an ECE professional of the candidate working as a lead teacher in a state-approved child care setting. The Council then arranges a visit from a trained ECE professional who gives the candidate a written examination and an oral interview.

33. *Accreditation Criteria and Procedures of the National Association for the Education of Young Children, 1998 edition* (Washington, DC.: National Association for the Education of Young Children, 1998), 14. Normally, there is a high rate of agreement, upwards of 95 percent, among commissioners reviewing the same program.

34. Based on a telephone conversation with Pat Muchi, NAEYC accreditation office, December 17, 2000.

35. The accreditation programs are briefly summarized in the text. A more complete summary and comparison of the programs is available at *www.ffcd.org,* link to America's Child Care Problem: The Way Out.

36. For a thorough review of accreditation programs see Philadelphia Citizens for Children and Youth, *Assuring Quality in Early Childhood Settings: A Report on Accreditation Processes and Quality Standards* (Philadelphia, PA: Philadelphia Citizens for Children and Youth, 1999). Our conclusions, independently arrived at, about program differences and relative merit are quite similar. However, the Philadelphia report does not include the accrediting program of the Association of Christian Schools International in their analysis.

37. Richard Fiene, "Using a Statistical-Indicator Methodology for Accreditation," in Bredekamp and Willer, *NAEYC Accreditation: A Decade of Learning.* For documents on the accreditation system see National Early Childhood Program Accreditation Commission, *National Early Childhood Program Accreditation, NECPA* (Conyers, GA: The National Early Childhood Program Accreditation Commission, Inc., 1996); also *National Early Childhood Program Accreditation Standards: A Guide for Programs Seeking Accreditation* (Conyers, GA: The National Early Childhood Program Accreditation Commission, Inc., 1998).

38. *1998 ACSI Manual of School Accreditation, Preschool Accreditation Program of the Association of Christian Schools International* (Colorado Springs, CO: Association of Christian Schools International), 12-13.

39. Council on Accreditation of Services for Families and Children, *Self-Study Manual for Behavioral Health Care Services and Community Support and Education Services,* Volumes 1 and 2, United States Edition (New York: Council on Accreditation of Services for Families and Children, Inc., 1997).

40. National Association for Family Child Care, *Quality Standards for NAFCC Accreditation: Provider's Self-Study Workbook* (Des Moines, IA: National Association for Family Child Care Foundation, 1997); Janette Roman, ed., *The NSACA Standards for Quality School Age Care* (Boston, MA: The National School-Age Care Alliance, 1998).

41. Marcy Whitebook, Carollee Howes, and Deborah Phillips, *The National Child Care Staffing Study Final Report: Who Cares? Child Care Teachers and the Quality of Care in America* (Oakland CA: Child Care Employee Project, now The Center for the Child Care Workforce in Washington, DC, 1990).

42. Cost, Quality and Child Outcomes Team, *Cost, Quality, and Child Outcomes in Child Care Centers Public Report* (Denver, CO: Center for Research in Economic and Social Policy, Economics Department, University of Colorado at Denver, 1995), 40-41.

43. Marcy Whitebook, Laura Sakai and Carollee Howes, *NAEYC Accreditation as a Strategy for Improving Child Care Quality* (Washington, DC: National Center for the Early Childhood Work Force [now the Center for the Child Care Workforce], 1997).

44. Telephone conversations with Pat Muchi, of the NAEYC accreditation office, December, 2000, and with Suzanne Grace, NECPA program director, March 2000.

45. This estimate is based on the number of regulated family child care and large family child care centers reported in *The 2000 Family Child Care Licensing Study,* and the percent of good quality regulated family child care programs reported in Susan Kontos, Carollee Howes, Marybeth Shinn and Ellen Galinsky, *Quality in Family Child Care and Relative Care* (New York and London: Teachers College Press, Columbia University, 1995).

46. William T. Gormley, Jr., "Differential Reimbursement and Child Care Accreditation," draft of a paper presented at Georgetown University, Washington DC, June 9, 2000.

47. The DHS Ad Hoc Early Childhood Accreditation Work Group, *Final Report to the Department of Human Services* (New Jersey, April 1998).

48. *The Robert R. McCormick Tribune Foundation 1999 Annual Report* (Chicago, IL: The Robert R. McCormick Tribune Foundation, 1999).

CHAPTER 7: THE MARKETPLACE: WHAT IS PECULIAR ABOUT THE CHILD CARE INDUSTRY?

1. Darcy Olsen, *The Advancing Nanny State: Why the Government Should Stay Out of Child Care,* Cato Policy Analysis No. 285 (Washington, DC: Cato Institute, October 1997). Available online at www.cato.org/pubs.

2. Cheryl D. Hayes, John L. Palmer and Martha J. Zaslow, eds., *Who Cares for America's Children? Child Care Policy in the 1990s* (Washington, DC: National Research Council, National Academy Press, 1990), 241; Susan Kontos, Carollee Howes, Marybeth Shin, and Ellen Galinsky, *Quality in Family Child Care and Relative Care* (New York and London: Teachers College Press, Columbia University, 1995), 241.

3. Arthur Emlen, "Quality of Care From a Parent's Point of View: A Place at the Policy Table for Child Care Consumers," prepared for Innovations in Child Care Education leadership forum, Child Care Bureau, Washington, DC, February 19, 1997.

4. Karen Gullo, "One-Third of Households Make Multiple Child-care Stops," *The Denver Post,* 8 March 2000, 4A. Reporting on a U.S. Department of Health and Human Service's Child Care Bureau report available online www.acf.dhhs.gov.

5. EDK Associates, *Choosing Quality Child Care: A Qualitative Study Conducted in Houston, Hartford, West Palm Beach, Charlotte, Alameda, Los Angeles, Salem and Minneapolis* prepared for Child Care Action Campaign (New York: EDK Associates, 1992).

6. Philip K. Robins and R. G. Spiegelman, "An Economic Model of the Demand for Child Care," *Economic Inquiry* 16 (1978): 83-94.

7. EDK Associates, *Choosing Quality Child Care.*

8. Sandra L. Hofferth, Kimberlee A. Shauman, Robin R. Henke and Jerry West, *Characteristics of Children's Early Care and Education Programs: Data from the 1995 National Household Education Survey,* National Center for Education Statistics Statistical Analysis Report, NCES 98-128 (Washington, DC: U.S. Department of Education, Office of Educational Research and Improvement, Government Printing Office, 1998), viii, 89; Hayes et al., *Who Cares for America's Children?,* 241.

9. Linda J. Waite, Arleen Leibowitz and Christina Witsberger, "What Parents Pay For: Child Care Characteristics, Quality and Costs," *Journal of Social Issues* 47, no. 2 (1991):33-48; Cost, Quality, and Child Outcomes Team, *Cost, Quality and Child Outcomes in Child Care Centers, Executive Summary* (Denver, CO: Center for Research in Economic and social Policy, Economics Department, University of Colorado at Denver, 1995), 9; David M. Blau and Alison P. Hagy, "The Demand for Quality in Child Care," *Journal of Political Economy* 106, no. 1 (February 1998): 104-146. Blau and Hagy found that when center fees decline parents substitute more hours of care for quality. This conclusion is overstated, given our reading of the results. (They study the relation between price and inputs to quality, and these conclusions are apparently based on their finding that one quality input, group size, is inversely related to price). Nevertheless, the study reinforces other findings that price and quality demanded are not highly related.

10. The finding in Blau and Hagy, "The Demand for Quality in Child Care," that parents do substitute formal for informal care when the price drops to zero, suggests that when not constrained by cost considerations, parents want their child in a good quality situation.

11. Angela Miller Browne, *The Day Care Dilemma: Critical Concerns for American Families* (New York: Insight Books, 1990); Debby Cryer, *The Day Care Dilemma: Critical Concerns for American Families* (New York: Plenum, 1994); Debby Cryer and Margaret Burchinal, "Parents as Child Care Consumers," *Early Childhood Research Quarterly* 12 (1997): 35-58.

12. Cost, Quality, and Child Outcomes Team, *Cost, Quality, and Child Outcomes in Child Care Centers: Public Report* (Denver, CO: Center for Research and Economic and Social Policy, Economics Department, University of Colorado, Denver, 1995), 68-69.

13. Susan Chira, "Hispanic Families Use Alternatives to Day Care, Study Finds," *New York Times National,* Wednesday, 6 April 1994.

14. EDK Associates, *Choosing Quality Child Care,* 4.

15. Richard N. Brandon, "Public Attitudes About Early Childhood Care and Education (ECE)," in S. Bales and R. N. Brandon, eds., *Effective Language for Discussing Early Childhood Education and Policy* (Washington, DC and Seattle, WA: Benton Foundation and University of Washington, Human Services Policy Center, 1998).

16. Lynn A. Karoly, Peter W. Greenwood, Susan S. Everingham, Jill Hoube, M. Rebecca Kilburn, C. Peter Rydell, Matthew Sanders and James Chiesa, *Investing in Our Children: What We Know and Don't Know about the Costs and Benefits of Early Childhood Interventions* (Santa Monica, CA: Rand, 1998); Steven W. Barnett, "Benefit-Cost Analysis of Preschool Education: Findings from a 25-Year Follow-Up," *American Journal of Orthopsychiatry* 63, no. 4 (1993): 500-508.

17. Arthur J. Reynolds, "Alterable Predictors of Educational Attainment in the Chicago Longitudinal Study: Overview"; Arthur J. Reynolds, Judy A. Temple, Dylan L. Robertson and Emily A. Mann, "Long-term Benefits of Participation in the Title I Chicago Child-Parent Centers," paper presented at a symposium on the Chicago Longitudinal Study at the Biennial Meeting of the Society for Research on Adolescence in Chicago on March 30, 2000. For more information, contact Arthur Reynolds, Waisman Center, Madison, WI.

18. Sanford Newman, T. Berry Brazelton, Edward Zigler, Lawrence Sherman, William Bratton, Jerry Sanders and William Christeson, *America's Child Care Crisis: A Crime Prevention Tragedy* (Washington, DC: Fight Crime: Invest in Kids, 2000) 18.

19. This argument has been made by Nancy Folbre, *Who Pays for the Kids?* (London & New York: Routledge, 1994); Nancy Folbre, "Children as Public Goods," *American Economic Review* 84, no. 2 (1994): 86-90.

20. James J. Heckman, *Policies to Foster Human Capital,* Working paper 7288 (Cambridge MA: National Bureau of Economic Research, 1999). Available online at www.nber.org/papers/W7288.

21. This is a guess based on Census data reported in chapter 5 that 30 percent of children are in center programs and 15 percent in nonrelative family child care. We do not know how much of the latter category is unlicensed, we have assumed that about half is licensed.

22. See Burton A. Weisbrod, *The Nonprofit Economy* (Cambridge, MA: Harvard University Press, 1988).

23. It is hard to estimate the size of this underground economy, but the Census Bureau data given in chapter 5 on the number of children in different types of care allows a rough approximation. That data indicate that about 25 percent of preschool-aged children are cared for by relatives (9.4 percent in their own home and 15.9 percent in the relative's home), and that another 15.4 percent

are in nonrelative family child care. We do not know what percent of the children in the latter category are cared for in unregulated and illegal family child care homes, but if half of them are, then about one-third of children under the age of five receive child care outside the formal market sector of regulated family child care and preschools/centers.

24. Kontos et al., *Quality in Family Child Care and Relative Care.*

25. It is the rate of return on investment, not the rate of return on sales, that is crucial in comparing profit rates, but data were not available from CQO to estimate investment returns. There is not much reason to believe that there is much variation by profit sector in real capital investment since nonprofit centers usually rent space or own space that was depreciated out long ago. In the case of for-profit centers, there is probably variation in capital investment by proprietors of for-profit independent centers, depending on the age of the center. Common practice for chains is to build a center, sell it, and lease it back.

26. Weisbrod, *The Nonprofit Economy.*

27. Roger Neugebauer, "To Profit or Not to Profit: That Is the Question," *Child Care Information Exchange* 128 (July-August 1999): 76-81.

28. John R. Morris and Suzanne W. Helburn, "Child Care Center Quality Differences: The Role of Profit Status, Client Preferences, and Trust," *Nonprofit and Voluntary Quarterly* 9, no. 3 (September 2000). This study used CQO data to test the hypothesis that to produce quality, profit-maximizing firms emphasize ECERS quality characteristics that are easier for parents to observe rather than those that are harder to observe but more important in the promotion of children's development or to their health. Easy-to-observe items include furnishings, greeting and departing, space for active play, gross motor equipment, and provisions for parents. Hard-to-observe characteristics include nap time, diaper changing, learning to reason, informal use of language, supervision of creative play, staff opportunities for professional growth. Results showed that for given ratings of easy-to-observe qualities, scores on hard-to-observe qualities were lower for for-profit chains compared to nonprofit independent centers in all states, but particularly in North Carolina, and also for for-profit independent centers in North Carolina.

29. Child care professionals working in church-operated centers are aware of the quality problem and are working to surmount it. To foster better quality they consider it essential for the church and its leadership to develop clear lines of communication and cooperation with its child care center administration. To this end the Ecumenical Child Care Network (ECCN) has developed a self-study procedure so churches can create the mechanisms that enable the two organizations to work together effectively. Often this is a first step in moving toward NAEYC accreditation.

30. A 1993 study found that family child care providers (both licensed and unlicensed) caring for three or more children averaged a net cash income of about $10,000 in 1993 ($13,000 in year 2000 dollars). Suzanne W. Helburn and Carollee Howes, "Child Care Cost and Quality," *The Future of Children: Financing Child Care* 6, no. 2 (summer/fall 1996): 76.

31. Ellen E. Kisker, Sandra L. Hofferth, Deborah A. Phillips and Elizabeth Farquhar, *A Profile of Child Care Settings: Early Education and Care in 1990, Volume I,* prepared under contract for the U.S. Department of Education by Mathematica Policy Research, Inc. Washington, DC: U.S. Government Printing Office, 1990); Sandra Hofferth, "Child Care in the United States Today" in *Financing Child Care, The Future of Children* 6, no. 2 (1996): 41-61.

32. Kisker, et al., *A Profile of Child Care Settings,* p. 75-77; Helburn, *Cost, Quality and Child Outcomes Technical Report,* table 4-1.2.

33. Sandra L. Hofferth, "Caring for Children at the Poverty Level," *Children and Youth Services Review* 27, no. 1-2 (1995): 61-90.

34. U.S. Department of Treasury, *Investing in Child Care: Challenges Facing Working Parents and the Private Sector Response* (Vienna, VA: National Child Care Information Center, 1998).

35. For information on the CWA-Verizon-IBEW Dependent Care Reimbursement Fund, contact Donna Dolan, Work/Family Issues, CWA District 1 at 212-344-7332.

36. Ingrid Peritz, "Tired of the Kids? Try 24 Hour Day Care; Quebec Tests Program Aimed at Shift Workers," *The Globe and Mail,* 31 August 2000.

37. Magaly Queralt and Ann Dryden Witte, "Influences on Neighborhood Supply of Child Care in Massachusetts," *Social Services Review* 72, no. 1 (March 1998): 17-46; Bruce Fuller and Xiaoyan Liang, "Market Failure? Estimating Inequality in Preschool Availability," *Educational Evaluation and Policy Analysis* 18 (1996): 31-49; Bruce Fuller, Casey Coonerty, Fran Kipnis and Yvonne Choong, "An Unfair Head Start: California Families Face Gaps in Preschool and Child

Care Availability," working paper, Berkeley, CA: University of California, Berkeley,1997; G. L. Siegel and L. A. Loman, *Child Care and AFDC Recipients in Illinois: Patterns, Problems and Needs* (St. Louis, MO: Institute of Applied Research, 1991).

38. Fuller and Liang, "Market Failure?"

39. Ibid.

40. Queralt and Witte, "Influences on Neighborhood Supply."

41. In this section we rely in part on information from conversations with Carl Sussman, Sussman Associates, Newton, MA, the last of which took place in February 2001.

42. For a thorough review of these programs see Anne Mitchell, Louise Stoney and Harriet Dichter, *Financing Child Care in the United States: An Expanded Catalog of Current Strategies: 2001 Edition* (Kansas City, MO: The Ewing Marion Kauffman Foundation, 2001).

43. The National Children's Facilities Network of 18 local community development agencies has been formed, and community development agencies are increasingly concerned about helping to finance child care facilities. The Local Initiatives Support Corporation, the largest community development agency in the country, is mounting an effort specially designed for the child care industry.

44. Cheryl D. Hayes, John L. Palmer and Martha J. Zaslow, eds., *Who Cares for America's Children: Child Care Policy for the 1990s* (Washington, DC: National Academy Press, 1990), 241.

45. Sandra L. Hofferth, April Brayfield, Sharon Deich and Pamela Holcomb, *National Child Care Survey, 1990* (Washington, DC: The Urban Institute Press, 1991), reported that only 9 percent of parents located care by following up on referrals from R&Rs. Also see Ellen B. Magenheim, "Information, Prices, and Competition in the Child-Care Market: What Role Should Government Play?" in J. M. Pogodzinski, ed., *Readings in Public Policy* (Cambridge, MA: Blackwell Publishers, 1995).

46. The 20 states are: Arizona, California, Colorado, Florida, Iowa, Illinois, Kentucky, Maine, Minnesota, Montana, New Hampshire, New York, North Dakota, Ohio, Oklahoma, Oregon, Rhode Island, Texas, Washington, and Wisconsin. NACCRRA, *Draft Child Care Resource and Referral State Networks 2000* (Washington, DC: National Association of Child Care Resource and Referral Agencies, 2000).

47. These counts were provided by the NACCRRA membership director. The oldest agencies, organized before 1980, are in California, New York, and Hawaii.

48. For each state we estimated the number and size of R&R agencies needed. For a given state we based the need on the state population in urban and rural areas using 1996 Census Bureau population estimates for each metropolitan statistical area (MSA). The rural population was estimated as the state population minus the population in its MSAs. We estimated the number of R&Rs needed for four different sizes: very large, serving a population greater than 800,000; large, serving 500,000–800,000; medium, serving 100,000–500,000; and small, serving less than 100,000. Rural areas were assigned a local R&R agency based on one R&R per 200,000 population, except in the great plains and intermountain regions, where one R&R was assigned per 100 square miles. State totals were summed to arrive at a national total number of local R&Rs needed in each of the four size groups, adjusted by 5 percent to account for population increases to 2001.

    Separate budgets were estimated for small (including rural), medium, large, and very large R&Rs based on data from Maryland, where R&Rs are reasonably well funded and corrected by a multiplier of 1.4 to allow for higher salaries and for additional costs for marketing and Internet access. The 1.4 multiplier was based on a comparison of salaries in Maryland with those for the Boulder, Colorado R&R that is a municipal agency with salary scales comparable to other salaries in the city government. These salaries more nearly reflect market rates for individuals with comparable training, experience, and responsibility.

    The budget for very large R&Rs (serving more than an 800,000 population) was interpolated from the budget for large R&Rs. These budgets were then reviewed and corrected by a panel of R&R directors from across the country. The total cost of this system summed across the nation was $473 million dollars.

    Funding of state network offices in each state (except Rhode Island and Delaware) added $24 million. States were categorized as needing a very small, small, medium, or large network office based on number of R&Rs in the state and the number of R&Rs that could be serviced by one technical assistant/trainer, 15-20 R&Rs, according to our informant. Budget estimates were based mainly on network budgets for Maryland and Colorado with additions suggested by our panel of informants and represent estimates of public expenditures for basic services (larger state network offices have far larger budgets than this suggested federal contribution). Adding a basic budget for NACCRRA of $3 million brings the total estimate to $500 million per year.

49. Participation in such a program would have to be voluntary on the part of providers. The suggested $25 million could, for instance, finance initial organizational and administrative costs, evaluator training, and rating of 40,000 centers at $500 per center.

CHAPTER 8: THE CAREGIVERS:
HOW COULD WE IMPROVE THEIR LOT?

1. The Center for the Child Care Workforce is located in Washington, DC. Call 202-737-7700 or reach them on the Internet at www.ccw.org.

2. Marcy Whitebook, Carollee Howes and Deborah Phillips, *Who Cares? Child Care Teachers and the Quality of Care in America. The National Child Care Staffing Study* (Oakland, CA: Child Care Employee Project, now the Center For the Child Care Workforce in Washington, DC, 1990). See also, Marcy Whitebook, Carollee Howes and Deborah Phillips, *Worthy Work, Unlivable Wages: The National Child Care Staffing Study, 1988-1997* (Washington DC: The Center for the Child Care Workforce 1998).

3. U.S. Bureau of Labor Statistics, Occupational Employment Statistics, *Table 1 National Employment and Wage Data from the Occupational Employment Statistics Survey by Occupation, 1999 stats.bls.gov/news.release/ocwage.t01.htm* 2000. BLS collects wage data on two child care classifications that do not mirror actual practice in the industry. They define preschool teachers as those who "instruct children (normally up to 5 years of age) in activities designed to promote social, physical and intellectual growth needed for primary school in preschool, day care center, or other child development facility." Child care workers are defined as people who dress, feed, bath, and oversee play of children in child care centers, schools, and businesses and institutions, excluding preschool teachers and aides.

4. Whitebook et al., *Worthy Work, Unlivable Wages,* 20.

5. Suzanne W. Helburn, ed., *Cost, Quality, and Child Outcomes in Child Care Centers: Technical Report* (Denver, CO: Center for Research in Economic and Social Policy, Economics Department, University of Colorado at Denver, 1995), table 5.16.

6. In 1997, Rhode Island made medical and dental benefits available to family child care providers and their dependents through its Rite Care health insurance program for the uninsured, and in 1999 extended coverage to pay for 50 percent of the cost to center-based staff who care for children receiving state subsidies. New Hampshire is considering similar legislation and in North Carolina private insurers are considering a plan. *Rights, Raises, Respect: News and Issues for the Child Care Workforce,* Washington, DC: Center for the Child Care workforce 13, no.1 (winter 1999).

7. Barbara Willer, Sandra L. Hofferth, Ellen Kisker, Patricia Divine-Hawkins, Ellen Farquhar and Frederic B. Glantz, *The Demand and Supply of Child Care in 1990: Joint Findings from the National Child Care Survey 1990 and A profile of Child Care Settings* (Washington, DC: National Association for the Education of Young Children, 1991).

8. Estimates vary in the different studies. Helburn, *Cost, Quality, and Child Outcomes,* table 6.15, 7.1; Whitebook, et al., *Who Cares?;* Whitebook, et al., *Worthy Work, Unlivable Wages;* Ellen Eliason Kisker, Sandra L. Hofferth, Deborah A. Phillips, and Elizabeth Farquhar, *A Profile of Child Care Settings; Early Education and Care in 1990,* prepared under contract to the U.S. Department of Education by Mathematica Policy Research, Inc. (Washington, DC: U.S. Department of Education, 1991).

9. David Blau, "The Child Care Labor Market," *The Journal of Human Resources* 27, no. 1 (1992): 9-39; Naci Mocan and Deborah Viola, *The Determinants of Child Care Workers' Wages and Compensation: Sectoral Difference, Human Capital, Race, Insiders and Outsiders* (New York: National Bureau of Economic Research Working Paper 6328, 1997).

10. Reported in Suzanne W. Helburn and Carollee Howes "Child Care Cost and Quality," *The Future of Children: Financing Child Care* 6, no. 2 (Summer-Fall 1996), 78.

11. Helburn, *Cost, Quality, and Child Outcomes,* table 5.11, 5.12.

12. Cost, Quality, and Child Outcomes in Child Care Centers Team, *Cost, Quality, and Child Outcomes in Child Care Centers, Public Report* (Denver, CO: Center for Research on Economic and Social Policy, Department of Economics, University of Colorado, Denver, 1995) 54; Whitebook, Howes and Phillips, *Worthy Work, Unlivable Wages.*

13. Marcy Whitebook and Dan Bellm, *Taking on Turnover: An Action Guide for Child Care Center Teachers and Directors* (Washington, DC: Center for the Child Care Workforce, 1999), 32. High turnover rates in child care do not approach the high turnover rates in some industries. For instance, turnover rates of 100 percent per year have been reported in nursing home care. See Stephen A. Herzenberg, John A. Alic and Howard Wial, *New Rules for a New Economy: Employment and Opportunity in Postindustrial America* (Ithaca, NY and London: IRL Press, an imprint of Cornell University Press, 1998), 54.

14. In the CQO study 92 percent of staff said they chose to work in the field either because of the job environment or the importance of the work. However, 33 percent of those responding said they were likely to quit within the year: 32 percent for higher wages, and 40 percent for a career change or to return to school. Helburn, *Cost, Quality, and Child Outcomes,* table 5.15.

15. "Shortage of Child Care Providers," *Denver Rocky Mountain News,* 21 July 1999: 5A.

16. Whitebook, et al., *Worthy Work, Unlivable Wages,* 12.

17. William Goodman, "Boom in Day Care Industry the Result of Many Social Changes," *Monthly Labor Review* (August 1995); Blau, "The Child Care Labor Market"; Whitebook et al., *Who Cares?;* Marcy Whitebook and Deborah Phillips, *Child Care Employment: Implications for Women's Self Sufficiency and for Child Development* (New York: Foundation for Child Development, 1999), 9.

18. Marcy Whitebook and Dan Bellm, *Taking on Turnover: An Action Guide for Child Care Center Teachers and Directors;* Carollee Howes and C. Hamilton, "Children's Relationships with Caregivers: Mothers and Child Care Teachers," *Child Development* 63 (1992): 859-866; Carollee Howes and C. Hamilton, "Children's Relationships with Child Care Teachers: Stability and Concordance With Parental Attachments," *Child Development* 63 (1992): 867-868; Carollee Howes and C. Hamilton, "The Changing Experience Of Child Care: Changes in Teachers and in Teacher-Child Relationships and Children's Social Competence with Peers," *Early Childhood Research Quarterly* 8 (1993): 15-32.

19. Massachusetts specifies qualifications and ongoing training requirements for two classes of directors, two classes of teachers, apprentices, and different levels of family child care providers in both small and large group homes. Sheri L. Azer and Darnae Eldred, *Training Requirements in Child Care Licensing Regulations* (Boston, MA: The Center for Career Development in Early Care and Education, now the Institute for Leadership and Career Initiatives, Wheelock College, 1997).

20. Gwen Morgan, Sheri Azer, Joan Costley, Andrea Genser, Irene Goodman, Joan Lombardi, and Bettina McGimsey, *Making a Career of It: The State of the States Report on Career Development in Early Care and Education, Executive Summary* (Boston, MA: The Center for Career Development in Early Care and Education, now the Institute for Leadership and Career Initiatives, Wheelock College, 1993).

21. Whitebook, Howes, and Phillips, *Worthy Work, Unlivable Wages,* 20.

22. Participation of educated and committed women who are not in early childhood care and education for the money goes back to the beginning of the day nursery in the latter half of the nineteenth century. Dorothy Hewes, a historian of the U.S. preschool education movement, argues that the expansion of charity day nurseries for immigrant children provided a popular, almost faddish, outlet for wealthy young women seeking meaningful work. Elizabeth Peabody, one of its leaders, ardently promoted the view that these teachers should be saintly women "above merely pecuniary motive" working, with God, "to set the feet of little children in the paths of righteousness." Dorothy W. Hewes, *It's the Camaraderie: A History of Parent Cooperative Preschools* (Davis, CA: Center for Cooperatives, University of California, 1998), 11 and 14.

23. "Rights Raises Respect: News and Issues for the Child Care Workforce," Center for the Child Care Workforce (winter-spring 1998). Exceptions exist, of course. Bright Horizons, the corporate

chain that operates employer-based centers, was able to convince its corporate clients to finance wage increases.

24. Barbara Bowman, M. Suzanne Donovan, and M. Susan Burns, eds., *Eager to Learn: Educating Our Preschoolers,* Executive Summary (Washington, DC: National Academy Press, 2000), 10,11.

25. A slightly lower set of training standards have been recommended in Sharon L. Kagan and Nancy E. Cohen, *Not By Chance: Creating an Early Care and Education System for America's Children* (New Haven, CT: The Bush Center at Yale University, 1997).

26. One is the Bachelor of Science in Early Childhood Development and Education at the University of Delaware. For information, contact the Department of Individual and Family Studies, College of Human Resources, Education and Public Policy, University of Delaware, Newark, DE, 17716.

27. National Association for the Education of Young Children, *Guidelines for Preparation of Early Childhood Professionals* (Washington, DC.: National Association for the Education of Young Children, 1996). This document also includes standards for the Associate, Masters, and Doctoral degrees.

28. In part, this is due to their recognition of more than one category of "teacher," depending on the level of responsibility.

29. Sheri L. Azer, Karen L. Capraro and Kimberly A. Elliott, *Working toward Making a Career of It: A Profile of Career Development Initiatives in 1996* (Boston, MA: The Center for Career Development in Early Care and Education, now the Institute for Leadership and Career Initiatives, Wheelock College, 1996).

30. The U.S. Department of Labor Bureau of Apprenticeship collaborates with state and local agencies to operate the Apprenticeship for Child Development Specialist (ACDS) program. Fourteen states had been funded by 2001. For instance, the West Virginia program is built around the CDA competency goals, and graduates can apply 33 credits toward an associates degree at state junior colleges.

31. For descriptions of some exemplary higher education and training programs for early care and education professionals, go to www.ffcd.org. Link to America's Child Care Problem: The Way Out.

32. *Making a Difference in Child Care: Lessons Learned While Building the Military Child Development System* (Arlington, VA: The National Clearinghouse for the Military Child Development Program, The Office of the Secretary of Defense, The Office of Family); Linda Smith and Laura Colker, "Making It a Reality: An Infrastructure to Attain High-Quality Child Care," *Young Children* 56, no.1 (May 2001): 78-85.

33. In 2000, the National Council of Women's Organizations created a Child Care Legislative Working Group that collaborated with the Center for the Child Care Workforce and other child advocacy groups to draft a national child care compensation bill to reward and retain child care workers.

34. For more information on these programs contact Child Care Services Association, P.O. Box 901, Chapel Hill, North Carolina, 27514.

35. Marcy Whitebook, "Child Care Workers: High Demand, Low Wages," in Suzanne W. Helburn, ed., *The Silent Crisis in U.S. Child Care, the Annals of the American Academy of Political and Social Science* 563 (1999): 146-161.

36. Lisa Bell, Lea Grundy and Netsy Firestein, *Union Child Care Initiatives* (Berkeley, CA: Labor Project for Working Families, 1999).

37. Although the Head Start statute forbids such expenditures, enforcement has been uneven, even lax, and many drives to organize Head Start workers have been fought by contractors. Nevertheless, successful organization of Head Start programs is proceeding, particularly by District 925 of the Service Employees International Union (SEIU) and the American Federation of State, County, and Municipal Employees (AFSCME). AFSCME is providing extra support for district councils that decide to organize these workers.

38. This organization drive benefited from a strong Worthy Wage movement in the region. District 925 is a women-run union serving mainly working women. It grew out of the Nine to Five office workers actions in the 1970s and has members in Cleveland, Cincinnati, Dayton, Boston, Seattle, and New Haven. Information on the District 925 Seattle campaign is based on telephone conversations in July 1999 and April 2000 with Kim Cook, Seattle District 925 local president, and Debby Schneider, President of District 925 headquartered in Cincinnati.

39. District 925 uses a "union without election" strategy to bypass the National Labor Relations Board (NLRB) election process that employers can use against the union. If employers do not object, if the union gets a majority of workers to sign a union card, the employer agrees to union representation of the employees. By contrast, the NLRB election procedure is often a more adversarial and costly approach to organization and creates a climate of distrust and antagonism.
40. The union collaborates with an independent consulting group, the Economic Opportunity Institute (EOI), for policy development and media work. EOI developed the career ladder.
41. Information is based on several telephone and e-mail conversations (May through November 1999 and February 2001) and materials supplied by Denise Dowell at the United Child Care Union.
42. Partners include the Keystone Research Center; the Training and Upgrading Fund of NUHHCE, the union's parent union; and the Philadelphia Area Jobs with Justice Coalition.
43. The Consortium for Worker Education was organized in 1985 as a consortium of labor unions to provide job training services for union workers and dislocated workers in order to help them maintain self-sufficiency. For more information contact the Consortium for Worker Education Satellite Child Care Program, New York City, 212-647-1900.
44. U.S. Bureau of Labor Statistics, Occupational Employment Statistics, *Table 1: National Employment and Wage Data.*
45. Note 6 above describes a plan instituted in Rhode Island for providing health insurance through an already existing program in the state for the uninsured. Federal funds could help leverage state funds to create new programs or expand existing ones.
46. Linda Smith and Laura Colker, "Making It a Reality: An Infrastructure to Attain High-Quality Child Care."

CHAPTER 9. THE COST: HOW MUCH WOULD IT TAKE TO PROVIDE AFFORDABILITY AND IMPROVED QUALITY?

1. Senator Gramm seems to advocate lowering the taxes of the restaurant cook. Unfortunately, the Republican-sponsored tax cut passed in 2001 provided large reductions for the rich but no relief at all for the lowest-paid workers.
2. The simulations were based on the reimbursement rates and copayment rules of each plan, and on data in the Current Population Survey (CPS) for 2000 for 48,000 sample households giving the number and ages of children, which adults in the family were in the labor force, the number of hours per week the mother worked, and the family income and poverty line. Children deemed to need nonmaternal care were assigned a mode of care, including free care by a relative, based on Census data on child care modes from the year 1994. Children were assigned to full-day care or half-day care depending on the hours their mother worked. More detailed information on the methodology used in arriving at these estimates, including the SAS programs used to compute them, is available from Barbara Bergmann <bbergman@wam.umd.edu>.
3. The cost estimates we present here do not include the extra costs of such services.
4. Our simulations suggest that the proportion of eligible children *whose parents would want them in paid care* who are currently being served is considerably higher than the proportion being served as estimated by HHS, whose estimate may encompass all children in the relevant income groups rather than all children whose parents choose to have them in subsidized care.
5. In making this estimate, we used the CCDF program rules of a single state with approximately average benefits (Iowa) whose costs were taken to be representative of average costs in the entire country. Iowa's program rules, like those of all but eight states, limit benefits to families whose income is considerably below the 85 percent of the state's median income that the federal rules allow as the top income for receiving benefits. See Child Care Bureau, Administration for Children and Families, *Child Care and Development Block Grant: Report of State Plans for the period 10/01/97 to 9/30/99* (Washington, DC: U.S. Department of Health and Human Services, 1998). If it were desired to give benefits to all families eligible under the 85 percent standard, the cost would be considerably above the estimate for the interim plan that we quote here. The top income for families to whom benefits are allowed under Iowa rules is 52 percent.

6. Studies of the reaction of mothers' labor force participation to the cost of child care are reviewed in David M. Blau, " Means-Tested Child Care Subsidies" in *Means-Tested Transfer Programs in the U.S.* Robert Moffitt, ed. (Chicago: The University of Chicago Press, forthcoming).

7. This figure includes enrollees in the free federally-funded Head Start program, which serves the same age group. Anthony Raden, *Universal Prekindergarten in Georgia* (New York: Foundation for Child Development, 1999).

8. See Barbara R. Bergmann, *Saving Our Children From Poverty: What the United States Can Learn From France* (New York: Russell Sage Foundation, 1996).

9. If two-thirds of the eligible children currently outside the program were to move into the subsidy program, the total cost to the public would be around $31.5 billion per year.

10. This is usually interpreted as care that gets a numerical grade of 5 on the ECERS scale. See chapter 4.

11. In the cost simulation, quality bonuses were awarded at random to the proportion of caregivers shown in the CQO data achieving a score of 5. The bonus was set equal to the amount that would have to be added to a center's cost if the wages of employees were to be brought up to market wage rates for people of their education and age, a rise of 39 percent, which adds 27 percent to center costs on average.

12. This assumes that the funds currently expended on the CCDF program, the tax credit, Head Start, and the state prekindergarten programs could become part of its funding stream.

13. If two-thirds of the eligible children currently outside the program were to move into the subsidy program, the total cost to the government would be about $59 billion per year.

14. If the Georgia program, which runs only for the school day during the school year, were provided to 4-year-olds in the entire United States, that might cost $7.3 billion, assuming cost per child in the United States matched those of Georgia. Extending the program to a year-round, 9-hour day would raise the estimated cost to $16.4 billion, or $8.7 billion more than the $7.7 billion estimate for 4-year-olds in table 9.1. Higher average labor costs in the United States as opposed to Georgia would raise the cost still higher.

15. If two-thirds of the eligible children currently outside the program were to move into the subsidy program, the total cost to the government would be around $158 billion per year.

16. "A Farm Test for the Senate", *The Washington Post,* 24 July 2001, p. A20.

17. Sally S. Cohen, *Public Opinion, Child Care, and Policy Formation* (Yale University School of Nursing, 1999). See also Ethel Klein, "Funding Early Care and Education: An Assessment of Public Support" in *Stepping Up: Financing Early Care and Education in the 21st Century* (Kansas City, MO: Ewing Marion Kauffman Foundation, 1999).

INDEX

(italics indicates table)

sensationalism (in the press), 58

sex roles, 7, 75

Shinn, Marybeth, 235, 241, 243

single parents, 7, 8, 90, 212

    child care costs 4, 7-8, 24-27

social benefits of child care, *see* child care

solutions to child care problems, *see* child care

space requirements, 71-73, 127, 134

Spock, Dr., 57

staffing ratios, 10, 36, 55, 72-73, 105, 127

standard of living, 16, 25-26, 28-30, 50, 202

Stepping Stones to Using "Caring for Children," 144

Stoney, Louise, 38

subsidies, 6-10, 17-18, 28-32, 34, 42, 53, 90-91, 99, 140, 160, 163, 168-69, 202, 211-12, 223-24

    appropriation of, 9, 12, 18, 23, 37, 45-46, 114, 179, 197-98, 200, 210, 212, 218

    employer, 40-41, *see also* employer attitudes toward child care

    as interference with the market, 52-53

    public, 22-24, 29-32, 45-46, 50-52, 84, 91, 99, 122, 141-43, 155-56, 161

supply, *see* child care

    of care, 3, 36, 84

    gaps, 176-78, 224

TANF (Temporary Assistance to Needy Families), *see* legislation

tax benefits, 44-47, 142, 168, 172-73, 212

    dependent tax care credit, 22-24, 28, 142, 228

    Earned Income Tax Credit (EITC), 24, 45

    tax breaks vs. appropriated payments, 23, 44-46

T.E.A.C.H., 182, 197, 200-1

Title XX, 8, 143, 228

training, 1, 8, 36-37, 43, 60, 71, 73-74, 83, 99, 127, 195-97

    adult education, 193, 196

    apprenticeships, 196-97, 205

    current level of, 102, 114, 119, 134, 141, 190, 193, 196

    degree programs, 55

    effect on quality, 56, 73-74, 114, 139

    importance of, 76, 127-28

    inservice (or on-going), 127, 128, 134, 139-141, 193, 225

    legal requirements, 114, 139, 140, 144, 157, 192-201

    preservice, 36, 127-28, 193, 225

recommended levels, 74, 146, 223

turnover, *see* child care workers

unions, 12, 39, 47, 189, 197, 203-7

    American Federation of State, County, and Municipal Employees (AFSCME), 204, 206

    Confederation of National Trade Unions (Canada), 207

    District 925, Service Employees International Union (SEIU), 204-5

    United Auto Workers, 177, 204

    United Child Care Union (UCCU), 205

universal child care program, 13, 34-35, 117, 207

vacancy rate, 18, 161

Vandell, Deborah L., 235

Vast, Teresa, 233

volunteers, 113, 145, 151, 156

vouchers, 17, 46-50, 98

    advantages and disadvantages, 10, 47, 48, 122, 175, 198

    for grades K-12, 10, 47

    recommendations, 34, 140-41, 157, 184, 207, 216-17, 223

    vs. contracts, 47-48

wages of child care workers, 11, 21, 44, 74, 100, 112, 150, 157, 188-91, 193-95, 197-208, 211-12, 226

Waite, Linda J., 248

weekend care, 94, 176-78, 211-12

Weisbrod, Burton A., 249

welfare, 7, 23, 24, 78, 168, 173, 206, 218

    program, 8, 38, 85

    reform, 8, 9, 23, 36, 38, 87-88, 91, 112, 142, 167, 210

Wheelock College Institute for Leadership and Career Initiatives, 196-97, 199

Whitebook, Marcy, 235, 240, 243, 247, 251, 252, 254

Willer, Barbara, 252

Witte, Ann D., 231, 250

Wolfe, Barbara, 235

working women, 2, 6-7, 51-53, 101-2, 109, 190

Worthy Wage Campaign, 188

Wrigley, Julia, 108-10

Zaslow, Martha, 234, 247, 250

Zigler, Edward F., 43, 233, 246, 248

Zinsser, Caroline, 101-2